Better Gardening

Better Gardening

Robin Lane Fox

David R. Godine
Publisher · Boston

First U.S. edition published in 1986 by
David R. Godine, Publisher, Inc.
306 Dartmouth Street
Boston, Massachusetts 02116

Originally published in the U.K. in 1982 by R. and L., Beckley, Oxfordshire
Copyright © 1982 by Robin Lane Fox

LC 85-81017
ISBN 0-87923-611-6

First printing
Printed in the U.K.

Contents

Preface

The title of this book is a reproach to myself. My own garden could be so much better, but I know what I want and sometimes I have it. From trees to alpines, this book dwells on many of my favourite plants which can be placed in a coherent style. Better gardening is a relative concept and I expect to end up writing fondly of almost every plant because it is better than golden-spotted laurel.

I notice that gardeners tend to become better gardeners at one of two times in life: before adolescence or after their thirties when they own a garden and have staked out a position, negative or positive, in the labyrinth of family life. I began gardening at the age of nine and was fortunate in having parents who gave me room to experiment. I began by rooting the cuttings which my father discarded from his geraniums and I moved on to alpines and small hardy plants; here, the seasons of my school-holidays and the Greek and Latin of a classical education were very helpful allies. Since then, I have expanded on all fronts and I look back now on a period of gardening which, for others, is all that they will enjoy in a lifetime. It has taken me to work in a great botanical garden in Germany; it has made some of my years difficult, others enchanting. It has also been the strongest of bonds with friends. For fifteen years, I have written one of the two weekly gardening columns on that great source of practical wisdom, the Financial Times. The many letters from readers remind me constantly of the undergrowth of gardening knowledge in all walks of British life. Those who know most about particular plants are too busy growing them to stop and write about them.

This book is about plants and planting, but it is not a list, unlike many English gardening books, nor an inscrutable catalogue, printed after a slim section of personal advice. It is about the plants which I love and some which I do not; I have assisted in growing them all, and perhaps killing some of them, in my own gardens, in those I have helped to plan and in the large gardens of New College Oxford where I have the help of three gardeners and the valued connivance of a committee who agree, on the whole, that our changes should not be put to the vote which custom allows. Not many big public gardens, I dare say, are run by voting; the votes which do take place are enough to make proponents of better gardening think twice.

In England, I published this book myself after the ferociously cold winter of 1981/2. The response exceeded any I had dared to expect and for a while, it threatened to make me a publisher, not a propagator. I am honoured by the chance of extending it to an American audience and I have thought it best not to try to remove the English details and allusions in much of the book. However, I have adjusted the section on flowering trees to suit most zones of your climate and your nurseries. Elsewhere, I stand before you as an English gardener, trying to help you choose and think, look and design while you plan a new planting and wonder, as I always do, how to goad your ideas into life. When I read American books and catalogues, I, in turn, make allowances for their American touches and problems of climate. A love of gardening is not the selfish love of one's own garden; some gardeners are really only decorators, interested in an ideal home. Gardening is a love which grows by exchange and contact, by seeing and hearing what others like and adapting it to what we already know. I hope this book may interest, perhaps even help, gardeners on the West Coast as well as the East, just as their ideas and journals interest and help me. They will best judge which plants they can try for themselves, but this book is also a tribute to the odd ways and connections which run between plants and people. Throughout history these features have travelled beyond the differences of soil and late spring frosts. It will be evident that I relish them.

It would, however, be less than helpful to heap suggestions on you and not explain where they can be found. I have retained my mentions of English nurseries because they will export to the USA and their lists themselves are so often an education. I have arranged with Graham Trevor, manager of Sandwich Nurseries, Dover Road, Sandwich, Kent, England that he will track down varieties you may wish to import. He will arrange despatch for orders over $70 value and his knowledge of the stock available in Britain and north Europe is at your service. Please check with your local Department of Agriculture, or relevant State authority, for details of any necessary import permit for plants in a UK order. Plants cannot leave the UK without this paperwork. It is not expensive, but copies should be sent with the order to any UK supplier whom I mention. My list of US nurseries owes much to guidance from your Botanic Gardens and also to the experience and researches of Linda Brownrigg, a West Coast gardener herself. The recommendations are based on the judgements of major private buyers, East and West, who have kindly shared their knowledge, while preferring to remain anonymous.

List of Suppliers for the USA

Trees and Shrubs

Wayside Gardens, Hodges, South Carolina, 29695.

Weston Nurseries, East Main Street, Route 135, Hopkinton, Massachusetts 01748.

Woodlanders, 1128 Colleton Avenue, Aiken, SC 29801.

Roses of Yesterday and Today, 802 Brown's Valley Road, Watsonville, California 95076. Not recommended for gardeners in the north-east, as stock is grown in such a different climate and does not adapt easily.

Peter Beales, London Road, Attleborough, Norfolk, NR17 1AY, England. Magnificent list of 1000 old, scented roses: willing exporter, but orders must exceed £50 (about 12 shrubs at 1985 prices); 10% surcharge, to cover the necessary root-washing; please note the need for import permit, as above. Experienced exporter.

Living Tree Centre, P.O. Box 797, Bolinas, California 94924. Fruit trees, especially apples.

Henry Lewthardt Nurseries, Box 666, East Moriches, N.Y. 11940. Excellent espalier fruit trees of all sizes.

Gossler Farms Nursery, 1200 Weaver Road, Springfield, Oregon 97478. 60 varieties of magnolia and much else: excellent.

Roger Reynolds Nursery, 133 Encinal Av. Menlo Park, California 94025. Trees and shrubs: excellent, qualified advice.

Verba Buena Nursery, 19500 Skyline Blud., Woodside, California 94062. Trees, shrubs, good perennials; also specialist in Californian native plants.

For figs, try Kelly Brothers, Dansville, N.Y. 144437 or J.E. Miller, Canandaigua, N.Y. 14424.

Border Plants

Wayside, Weston, Woodlanders as above; Wayside stock Crocosmia Lucifer.

Blackthorne Gardens, 48 Quincy Street, Holbrook, Massachusetts 02343. Excellent hostas, hemerocallis, and clematis.

White Flower Farm, Litchfield, Connecticut 06759-0050.

Holbrook Farm, Route 2, Box 223B, 2004 Fletcher, N.C. 28732.

American Penstemon Soc., Orville M. Steward (Sec), P.O. Box 33, Plymouth VT 05056.

Bressingham Nurseries, Diss, Norfolk, England. Biggest UK list and major supplier to all UK nurseries. Will export larger orders: good catalogue.

Lamb Nurseries, E.101 Sharp Avenue, Spokane, WA 99202. Good range of hardy perennials and rock plants.

Logie's Greenhouses, 55 North Street, Danielson, Connecticut 06239. Exceptional source of half-hardy plants, but also geraniums and herbs.

Kartuz Greenhouses, 1408 Sunrise Drive, Vista, Ca. 92083.

Bulbs

Potterton and Martin, The Cottage Nursery, Moortown Road, Nettleton, Nr. Caistor, North Lincolnshire LN7 6HX, England. One of our prized specialists in alpines, almost all my rare bulbs and cyclamen. Very willing and experienced shippers to USA. Recommended strongly.

Breck's, 6523 North Glena Rd., Peoria, Illinois 61632. Excellent.

Rex Bulb Farms, P.O. Box 714, Port Townsend, Washington 98368. Superb lilies.

Blackthorne Gardens, as above for lilies and much else.

Van Bourgondian Bros., P.O. Box A 245 Farmingdale Road, Route 109, Babylon, Long Island, New York 11702. Good basic range of flower-bulbs.

Alpines

Siskiyou Rare Plants, Dept. 52, 2825 Cummings Road, Medford, Oregon 97501. Excellent range, and lewisias a speciality.

Stonecrop, Cold Spring, N.Y. 10516. Cash and carry only, but a superb range and worth a detour.

Potterton and Martin, export, as above.

Nature's Garden, Route 1, Box 488, Beaverton, OR 97007. Ramondas, lewisias, gentians, primulas.

Far North Gardens, 15621 A.R. Auburndale, Livonia, Michigan 48154. Famous for Barnhaven and Silver Dollar primroses, auriculas; good range of seeds.

American Rock Garden Society, Norman Singer (Sec), Norfolk Road, South Sandisfield, Mass. 01225. Excellent source of advice and nurseries.

Seeds

Thompson and Morgan, Inc., P.O. Box 100, Farmingdale, New Jersey 07727. Top UK list, though sadly reduced since 1970.

Alpina Research, 18544 26th NE, Seattle, WA 98155. Seed bank, vast range offered, $15 subscription, and well worthwhile.

Miscellaneous

Dutch Garden, P.O. Box 400, Montvale, New Jersey 07645.
Best for bulbs, Hostas, Hemerocallis, Alliums.

Bovees Nursery, 1737 S.W. Colonado, Portland, Oregon 97219. Exceptional range of Rhododendrons, Azaleas, hardy in the northeast. Ask for Lucie Sorenson.

Chapter One

Better Gardening

A ny gardening is better than none, but some ways of
gardening are better than others. Better gardeners seem to
sense which plant is best, how to find the best oak or
primrose and how to place it for the best impression. Their roses are
the white Pascali with shapely buds and their geraniums are
Johnson's Blue, a hardy form which lasts from year to year. Their
clematis is yellow-flowered, at its best in late summer; on walls, they
grow Clematis Minuet whose purple flowers have cream-white
centres and hang in profusion from long stems. They raise alpine
plants from seed and they sow no marigolds, except for the peculiar
Tagetes minuta whose seed can be bought from a few specialist
societies. Sown under glass, this marigold reaches six feet or more in
a season and helps better gardeners wherever they have dug out
couch grass, bindweed or ground elder. These weeds cannot bear the
secretions from the marigold's roots and their fragments shrivel and
turn brown in its company. Better gardeners have no space for
ground elder, except for a rare ground elder with cream markings on
its grey-green leaves.

I know these better gardeners, you may be thinking. They live in
Britain with all the advantages, old brick walls and a staff of two or
three. Their homes have been gardened for centuries, heavy with
holm oaks and bulging yew hedges which set the guide-books
cooing, like the resident flocks of white doves. "Nestling deep in the
complicated headwaters of the River Itchen, which rises at nearby
Cheriton, Tichbourne possesses a garden of considerable charm
from which the famed Tichbourne Dole is annually distributed ..."
But if this is better gardening, I belong at the further end of the
queue.

The less promising your site, the more you are in my thoughts. My
garden slopes north in three separate sections of a third of an acre,
one a rough bank, the other a walled and terraced enclosure, the

6

third, in theory, a vegetable garden and orchard. The first is beset by a neighbouring dentist, young and balding, with more pruning shears than taste, the second by bindweed which has lodged in all the boundaries' stone walls, the third by the deep and intractable roots of Mare's Tail, a primeval weed which resists almost every poison and roots beyond all human excavation. There is no good to be said of it, except that a reader once sent me a recipe for boiling its young shoots and straining them into a pungent thin soup. The soil is limey and heavy. I shaped the ground into its plan of banks and terraces with the help of a mechanical digger some seven years ago. When my back was turned, the driver buried most of the top soil and left me with a surface of clay, stones and cracked Victorian china which had never expected to see the light again. On this corner of the heap, I have learnt my lessons.

The most general lesson applies to any garden, large or small. Wherever you choose a plant, the choice can be made for better or worse. In one and the same family lie good plants and very good plants. By watching, reading and experimenting, you begin to learn those which are better than others. The smaller the garden, the more precious the space and the more urgent it is to choose the best. Hence, so many small gardens have an originality which the great set-pieces of an English valley sometimes lack. From trees to alpines' carpets, from sixty feet to a height of two inches, this book is a selection of better plants and suggestions for their placing.

Where, though, can you find my suggestions in order to assess them and disagree with them, let alone to grow them for yourself? Every one of the plants in my first paragraph is listed for sale by an American nursery: Blackthorne Gardens in Massachussetts will sell you the types of Clematis, including a new viticella variety called Betty Corning with hanging bell-shaped sky-blue flowers which I would dearly like for myself. Like its namesake, Mrs Erastus Corning III, this variety is not available to us poor Englanders; Blackthorne Gardens offer free delivery by air to West Coast, Dallas, Fort Worth and Houston areas. In my preface's list of suppliers, Weston and Wayside nurseries will offer you much of what I go on to mention: the rare ground elder is sold by Wayside. If you think that American plant nurseries are still living in the Dark Ages, you should try the French.

Between us there has always been a two-way exchange, as there are no two countries whose gardeners cannot learn from one another. Americans have given England some of her loveliest garden designs: it is you who sent us Lawrence Johnston, quiet master of Hidcote, Lanning Roper, the greatest planter of the past generation, and private patrons in exile, like Mrs. C.G. Lancaster (formerly Tree, née Field) whose great garden at Haseley Court in my own Oxfordshire was the acknowledged masterpiece of gardens which were made from nothing in the 1960s. Living in its garden cottage in the early 1970s, I learned from her example and discussions how an American eye could bring style to British gardening and how the gardens of Virginia could inter-marry with our own tradition. Of course, there are few great American gardeners, and much indifference, but in Britain too, keen gardeners who think of colour and placing are also a minority. Reading your catalogues and journals, I, too, have had moments of envy. Your hostas and flowering malus are much more varied than ours. You gave us modern lilies and the best show primroses are yours from Far North Gardens, Michigan who rescued our Barnhaven strain. Your magnolias and arboreta stir any Englishman's ambition. Whereas we have a miserable flora, you have a vast range of native plants which make wild-flower gardening a work of art. Your specialist societies and alpine nurseries are fertile colleagues for ours and your seed lists go far to fill the gaps in the mail-order lists of border plants and alpines. Two years ago, I advised on a plan for the American Museum in Bath where a benefactor had offered an arboretum of American native trees and shrubs. Perhaps none of us can compete with the Chinese flora, but the planting of this garden taught me how rich and varied your wild plants are. In my Tulip Trees and Magnolias, I have American forms in mind: the primroses, hostas and day-lilies which follow are among the groups in which your growers excel.

No garden, however historic, can shut itself off from others' developments. A visit, a discussion can bring two traditions to bear on each other, as I hope may be the consequence of this book. The scope for such meetings came home to me recently, on a visit in autumn to the gardens of Kashmir.

Round the sky-blue lakes of Kashmir, the great Mogul Emperors once laid out their terraced gardens as a retreat from the wearying heat of India's dusty plains. Shalimar is the best-known name, but it is not romantically restored and maintained. "We laid out gardens with order and symmetry, with proper parterres and borders in every corner and in every border, roses and narcissus in perfect arrangement ..." For the echoes of a garden as Babur, the first

8

Mogul Emperor, knew and planned one, there is more to be sensed in the nearby Nishat Bagh, laid out by a courtier of his successor Jahangir, probably in the 1620s.

Beneath its canopy of ageing plane trees a small roof-top iris grows wild on the terraced walls: I walked once in this garden's midday shade, looking out past its ranks of annual flowers to the serene middle distance of the Dal Lake and its distant fort. This magical garden struck a curious note of discord; trees from the past Mogul centuries were matched with cosmos daisies and violas sown from subsequent seed. Entering the sun, I met with a man who inquired, in well-phrased English, why his plants were of such interest to my eye; I had strayed from the terraces into the seedbeds of the chief gardener, employed at Nishat for the past forty years. We exchanged our views on jasmine and on the times when seedlings were best pricked out. He showed me his grafted, wild white roses and I asked for the names of his Lotus. A long white cloth had been spread like a carpet beneath the chenar trees and on it he invited me to share a gardening lunch. I crossed legs at the head of this tablecloth of honour and sat eating curry with a scoop of the hand while his twenty two junior gardeners watched with puzzlement on either side.

Down the length of the cloth, we swapped stories of annual flowers which my host then translated for his interested staff. Until 1947, he explained, the British ladies had assisted in the garden's planting. Here, then, lay the cause of that curious discord, for the style of post-war gardening in Surrey had been mixed with the natural prospect which the Mogul Emperors had enhanced. When independence took Kashmir by surprise, the British left in a hurry and took their seed-packets with them. Only the bedding plants of 1947 had survived the summer, and were now kept alive from year year by careful harvesting of their own seeds. By the Dal Lake, therefore, I had caught a distant echo of that mixed blessing, the Englishwoman's garden. The clock, here, had stopped before F1 hybrids, Glitter Petunias and Snapdragons with ruffled flowers. These losses, perhaps, were not so serious, but the news of other selections struck home like words of a long-lost paradise. Modern pansies, I called down the tablecloth, now come in blues and whites, while Zinnias bear lime-green flowers and Nasturtiums grow six inches high. The wonders of Suttons and Thompson & Morgan were translated for the younger gardeners' benefit. They murmured at 'pansies in separate colours' and applauded the mention of

9

Love-in-a-mist in shades pink and white. We arranged to send seeds, but feared the Kashmiri customs' control. Perhaps Nishat Bagh is alive now with night-scented stocks and selected strains of Dianthus. But I suspect these flowers may be blooming in some bureaucrat's backyard.

In that meeting, perhaps, the gospel of better gardening took firmer root in me. It had always been fed by my natural dogmatism and faith in 'superior' garden plants. Like Chantreyland violas to my Kashmiri hosts, my Lespedezas and pale Ramondas may come to some of you as news from a desirable world. I know how grateful I am to those who first broke their news to me.

What, though, about the barriers of climate? So many of your zones vary that I would not dare to speak for them all. My own experience has mostly been on alkaline soil, unsuited for azaleas, and it is a limit which I have observed in most of my choices. Of climate, I can only say three things, apart from the fourth, that it is always unkind to us. In Britain, too, I write for a wide range of climates and find that people still gain from reading and reacting to ideas whose potential they can assess for themselves. Secondly, gardening is not only an influence or an inspiration if it is a type of gardening which you can share at every turn. "I must have that" or "I do not want this" are narrow, selfish responses to viewing or reading about others' plants. Thirdly, dedication can overcome the harshest obstacles. Here, I would only mention the late Claude Barr who wrote to me from the Prairie Gem Ranch in South Dakota and told me more than I knew about pulsatillas, which he grew by the acre on the prairies. In letters, he told me of his successes in this harsh, challenging landscape. Admittedly, he, too, had had a degree in classical Greek, but he grew violets in the hottest sun and loved and exploited the natural flora of the plains. His book, the Jewels of the Plains, is an answer to those who believe the middle west of America is unfit for gardens. Claude Barr wanted to grow flowers, and so he did.

For American readers, I have acknowledged that flowering trees are ideas too large to transplant between our continents. I have shaped my selections round those which your nurseries offer and hope that my opening list of suppliers will help you find them. Thereafter, I lead you down a more English tunnel, ending in my favourite English garden of all. However, more of the plants on this route are available in your lists than you would believe. Those which are not may point you to a good, maybe better, alternative;

otherwise, you can turn to Graham Trevor, in the harsh seaside climate of Sandwich Nurseries, Dover Road, Sandwich, Kent, who undertakes to find and supply varieties which are exportable and which you cannot locate yourselves. If you know of a good local nursery or a source of a particular rarity, I would be glad to know through my publishers for future reference. Sometimes, you will certainly know better; always, you know your own micro-climate, but perhaps I can still convey a taste and share some fixed ideas against which you can rebel and sometimes, even, come to rest.

Chapter Two

Better Trees

What would be a good tree for a small garden? Answers depend on the smallness of the small garden and the length of time in which you expect to own it. After sixty years, the most sober trees have recorded some surprising heights. Some of my better trees may puzzle your heirs long after we are dead. Shaping and siting will help to keep them in proportion, but only you can judge your concern for posterity. I set myself a rough twenty-five year limit within which my choices must still be tolerable in gardens of two or three hundred square metres.

In Britain, too, trees have strong, regional constituencies: when I write fondly of grey-leaved willows, people in flat fen counties write back to say that they have grown up with them and do not want to grow trees which they take for granted. If I then write about the ribbons of flower on the rose-purple Judas Tree, gardeners north of London say they never see them bloom. Their summers are colder and shorter. We all have to live with each other's local oddities, but in America the contrasts are greater: I cannot hope to please all gardeners all of the time. On the West Coast, you are bored with junipers and eucalyptus; in Washington your magnolias are finer than any of ours; maples are not exactly news to most of my Eastern readers, and it would be foolish of me to tell you how to grow and choose flowering Dogwoods, when most British gardeners envy the size and range of your plants. The plans for our American Arboretum in Bath reminded me how many of my favourite trees are your natives: the Catalpa, the Tulip Tree and also the lovely Halesia, or Carolina Silverbell, which will flourish in damp, acid soil in your zones four to nine. You sent this tree to us in 1756, but we have been slow to do it justice. Wayside Gardens will sell it to customers who want a broad-leaved tree which branches horizontally from low on its trunk. It flowers when young and grows to cover itself in thousands of hanging white bells in April and May, a perfect match for pale azaleas and the magnolias of great nobility. At Kew we are proud of a Silverbell which is almost 3 metres high and wide: in the right zones, you can have it twice this height and enjoy it as a rounded tree in isolation on a lawn.

Love of your Silverbell helps me shape my better trees. I will begin with flowering trees, move across the bridge between flowers and fruit and then cross from fruit to the trees with fine leaves. Here, I have not excluded some English touches, in the hope that good words for Whitebeams, Golden Acacias and Upright Tulip Trees may spur on American customers. Hilliers of Winchester, Hampshire, England are still our major suppliers, who will export whenever possible; in America, Weston Nurseries, Hopkinton, Massachusetts 01748 sell most of my suggested ·Acers, the Dawyck Beech, the Cut-leaf Beech which is almost as good as the Fern-Leaf, the Tulip Tree, the Amelanchier and the Dawn Redwood. Wayside Gardens, Hodges, South Carolina 29695 list some of them too, and together they can supply all the flowering and fruiting forms I mention without warning. No doubt, Whitebeams and unusual Sorbuses are lurking in centres off highways I have not yet travelled. The upright Tulip Tree is, however, a problem, even in Britain: my trackers in Sandwich will do their best, and as it moves best when it is still in a pot, you will not miss out if you import a small one.

When gardeners choose a flowering tree, they are often guided by their neighbours' choices: suddenly, you come on an enclave of the native Yellowwood, or Cladrastis Lutea, because somebody showed the district that it could be a success: good Maluses spread through a town or street like measles. Every urban gardener seems to start by thinking of a heavy-flowering Prunus and I spend my time warding off gifts of pink-flowering cherries in memory of this or that for my Oxford College's gardens. Out of flower, most cherries have very boring leaves and in flower, the stronger pinks are overpowering; Kanzan, with its sugary-pink double flowers, is a by-word in Britain for bad taste. Japanese cherries and their hybrids were unknown in the West until the late nineteenth century. Nowadays, spring time and cherry-blossom are a natural pair in every town dweller's thoughts, but they are not to be found in the landscapes of Victorian novels or poems by Tennyson and Wordsworth on the theme of spring. Quotations which mention them tend to be late in time, a very useful point for crossword puzzlers. Suburbs and the hybrid cherry grew up together, changing our perception of April and May. If I had to choose one variety, I would avoid the pinks, the forms with upright branches or very flat heads. I would choose the spectacular white Tai Haku, a broad branching tree which was known in the Far East as the Great White Cherry. To judge from my catalogues, it is not known yet to American nurseries, and while you agitate on its behalf, I suggest you plant the Winter Cherry instead, the best tree for gardeners in the entire family.

The winter-flowering Prunus Subhirtella Autumnalis is a native of Japan and is offered by Wayside and Weston nurseries, among others. To me it is a miracle. Its leaves are not so heavy or coarse as those on the spring flowering hybrids. As a standard, it makes an upright tree with a light canopy of gently-drooping branches. They have no flowers in May, but by mid-November the pinkish white buds are beginning to open on the bare branches. Much depends on the absence of early frost, which will turn the young flowers a stained brown. However, they usually enjoy a month's grace and, if they escape bad weather, their first crop will last into January. Against the bare branches, the white flower stands out like a soft veil, more delicate than any other flower in the family. If the weather behaves normally and relents in January, the winter cherry replaces its first buds with a fresh second crop. This opens out like white snow and if it, too, is caught by the cold, the tree may surprise you with a third, amazing attempt. If the spring weather is mild, its branches sprout short stems and give you a final encore, showing a scatter of flowers among the young leaves in April. At each stage, the colour of the buds and the length of their stems repay close inspection. I am not sure to what complication in the winter cherry's sex-life this triple flowering responds. I am only surprised that no catalogue bothers to mention it. This is a tree which will often flower for six months, from November, no less, until April. Its branches are excellent for cutting and using indoors and the plant can be grown almost anywhere as a bush or tree. After twenty years or so, trees are 20 feet tall and up to 15 feet wide, but they can be clipped and shaped in late spring and will stand unusually well against a dark background of evergreens or shaded walls. They tolerate any soil, acid or not, and do not object to towns or light shade. The bushes are very pretty, but there is now a special American form of Winter Cherry which branches freely from the base and grows to twelve feet. Called Hally Jolivette, it has a pinker shade to its flowers, before fading to the same delicate white. I have, however, found that it does not begin to flower as early as the ordinary form, which I still prefer, but it has only reached us recently and in the U.S. it may develop a longer season.

Even the older autumnalis has only been known in the West for ninety years and our great-grandchildren may yet be in for a pleasant shock. At maturity, the true winter cherry is awesomely old and far taller than the nurserymen now hint. It is the oldest variety of cherry for which we have any records. It turns up in Eastern records two years before the fall of ancient Rome, and in one Japanese temple-garden it is said that there is a specimen nearly 100 ft high, which the Japanese tree-experts reckon to be over 1, 800 years old, making it a contemporary of Marcus Aurelius. However, we tend to graft it onto our own wild white cherry, which may cramp its height. There is no particular need to do this, as subhirtella roots freely from cuttings and would grow to its full stature if you pinched a sucker from a friend. There is only one warning worth adding. You should be sure to buy only the subhirtella autumnalis variety and accept no substitutes. The double form (flore pleno) sounds robust, but only flowers in April. So does a weeping form (subhirtella pendula) which is available in pink and is overpowering when in full flower. I was placated with two trees of subhirtella ascendens when my nurseryman sold out of plain autumnalis. They are a fearful disappointment, stiff, severely pink and sparse with their flowers which only show up briefly in late March. Learn your better gardening from my own worse example. You must insist on the two names together, subhirtella and autumnalis, because all manner of dull rubbish will flower in spring from subhirtella's other forms.

On a larger scale, I would choose another Far Eastern native, the Chinese Scholar Tree, or Sophora. We have a superb old Sophora looking ample, furrowed and scholarly in Oxford's fine Botanic Gardens, but the bother, for British gardeners, is that this academic tree is very slow to flower. Moving house is a national pastime, and who will wait fifteen years to see their main tree flower? American tree-watchers have solved the problem by introducing Sophora Japonica Regent. This variety flowers after six to eight years and grows with heart-warming speed in dry soils, polluted air or poor positions. It is a straight, upright tree, eventually reaching forty feet or more, and its light feathery leaves are a very pleasant glossy green. The bark is green too, and the whole plant will flourish in zones four to eight and put up with hot gardens. We are scrambling to plant it in England: Wayside and Weston both sell it in the U.S.A., and the former print a beguiling picture of its pale cream-yellow clusters of flower, visible in July and August. All Sophoras have a most unscholarly toughness and resistance to bugs and disease: Regent is said to be the toughest of all.

Our Oxford Botanic garden also houses a noble Golden Rain Tree, brighter and later in flower but a lovely choice which should not scare you by its name, Koelreuteria Paniculata. I have high hopes of this Golden Rain in your dry and difficult sites, growing from zones four to nine. In Oxford I have given it a very responsible task, the rescue of a small College area of garden from that frequent academic distress, architecture by default and committee. The College happened to own a sturdy brick building in which Mr. Morris first made motor-cars: the front was protected by law, so we spoiled the back instead with a glowering facade of rusty brick and black decoration. People then tried to complement it with a monstrous Japanese maple, but the Koelreuteria won on a narrow vote and is now busy hiding as much of the building as a tree decently can. It stands in the building trade's idea of a hole for a forest tree, about three feet wide and three feet deep above brickbats and buried rubbish. In gardening, some things, at least, are international. Nonetheless, the Koelreuteria flowered charmingly in its very first August, showing long wisps of golden yellow flowers above leaves like an elegant ash tree's. It is growing busily, as it does wherever I plant it in sun, and I am certain that it prefers to be hot and dry if it is to flower freely. Eventually, it reaches forty feet, though it does not often live for a whole human lifetime. I hear from satisfied owners that it makes a fine, flowering tree in dry Californian gardens. In Britain, we have to admit that it is happier in sunny France, but it would suit you handsomely too. The young leaves open to a pinkish bronze shade and in autumn, they turn a pleasant yellow-brown before falling.

With yellow leaves in mind, I will interpose a British note. The False Acacias, or Robinias, are already familiar in America: in dry sites, they make pretty flowering trees wherever they are not exposed to severe wind, as their branches are brittle and will break very easily. Plain Robinia hispida will grow apace in zones five to nine and can be clipped into a neat shape along the boundary of a garden or as a small avenue on either side of a path. The pink-flowered form is offered by Wayside Nurseries and its combination of hanging flowers and green pinnate leaves is very beguiling.

It is not only of the green-leaved form that I wish to write. In the 1930s, a Dutch nurseryman introduced the golden-leaved form, Frisia, which has swept through British front gardens in the past two decades. We were slow to see its point and I cannot find it yet in American lists. It is worth importing, but when it reaches you, its outline ought to be respected. It is not at its best among other trees in a protective screen. Nor is it a tree for casting shade under which you can relax at teatime in summer. I think that it ought to stand in isolation on a small lawn so that you can appreciate the ruffling of its leaves by the slightest wind and the drooping and flexible form of the branches, on which the leaves hang like small green and yellow coins. It will not always grow a straight trunk and its branches ought to be allowed to sweep sideways. My favourite example was planted by that great American gardener in exile, Mrs. C.G. Lancaster, in the garden where I had my first Oxfordshire home. Already in her seventies, she sold most of her former garden to new owners, who ruined it, but she kept a small enclosure to herself. At her age, I would have given up, but she started again in a small space and combined two brilliant ideas: a circular garden sofa, made of clipped dark green yews, with a golden Robinia just beside it. As the yews matured they were clipped into seats and high compartments. Seven years later, she was sitting on concealed wooden benches in those banks of yew and looking up at the movement of the Robinia and its yearly changes from yellow to lime green. Nobody yet knows how tall this recent tree will eventually become. Like its green-leaved relations, it ought to start flowering, showing clusters of creamy white blossom among the leaves in June. I suspect it will top out at about thirty feet, but like others in its family it can be clipped and pruned, so you need not fear for posterity. Any soil seems to suit it, but it colours best in sunlight and in open loam, with or without lime.

In America, the nearest approach to this fine new tree is the tougher and sparser Gleditsia, or Honey Locust. Again, it is a brittle tree in a strong wind, but it will tolerate drought and in arid zones in California it is considered a common native. The plain green-leaved form called elegantissima has a delicate shape and airy, finely-cut leaves, but my favourite is the yellow-leaved Sunburst which was patented in America barely thirty years ago. Plants will have been grafted, so you must check that the buds are alive on the upper stems before you buy your bush, let alone your standard tree: Sunburst is not a plant to be ordered blind from a mailing list. I find that it looks very fine as a specimen shrub, pruned hard to keep it at eight to ten feet so that its cloud of bright yellow leaves can dignify the back of a long mixed border. It will flower modestly, and in autumn, its hanging seed pods are quite amusing: late in the year, they rattle like a dying man's cough, an arid intimation of winter when the wind is blowing through them. I am very fond of your Sunburst in a dry place away from the wind, and value its light leaves as a match for modern architecture and its blank, reflecting surfaces of glass.

Thorny though your Locust Tree is, you can be consoled that an Iranian form is even thornier. Up near the Caspian Sea in Iran, the seed-pods of Gleditsia Caspica started one of history's oddest industries. If squeezed, the pulp round the seed becomes sweet and sugary, like honey. We forget how slowly the pleasures of sugar arrived in history. Before the cane was ever transplanted to the East, this old Gleditsia filled the bill. Its branches were said to drip honey when first seen by soldiers on the march with Alexander the Great. Nobody believed them until the site was visited and the Caspian honey locust was found to support a local confectionery trade whose sweet syrups were sent to the courts of Persian nobles. For centuries Persian kings had enjoyed it at dinner. When the Ayatollahs ban sugar along with all other corruptions, this Caspian Gleditsia may come into its own.

Enough, then, of yellow-leaved trees: I have left a gap in the seasons between the last of the Winter Cherry and the best of the Chinese Scholar Tree. The family to fill it is the Malus, or Flowering Crab, another group in which the best varieties are mostly American, not British, and you have improved our lives. As they flower and fruit and turn brilliant colours in autumn, they are excellent trees for small gardens. The name, I suspect, is their worst enemy. Crab apples sound a fraud, apples which are too sour to eat and too stumpy to be trees. Some are prone to a scab disease, and a crab with scab would attract nobody.

Nowadays the Malus is more American territory than British; your borders have produced a score of varieties which I have had to hunt out in collections and arboreta. The fullest list is Weston Nurseries' who group them by colour and praise them as trees ideally suited to New England conditions. To my surprise, they omit the fruiting variety which we prize most highly in Britain: the orange-scarlet John Downie, whose branches droop delicately and whose fruits are not too big. We are also fond of Profusion whose flowers are wine-red and slightly scented against a setting of crimson leaves: I have illustrated its close relation Eleyi from my garden in order to encourage you. However, you have the crimson flowers and purple leaves of Royalty, again in Weston's list, and I would be happy with it instead. I am not a fancier of brown or purple leaves on most plants, but on a crab early in the season, they are small and charming. These dark-flowered varieties show them off to the best

18

advantage. I have a mature tree of Eleyi against a clump of the cream-variegated leaves of the lovely Dogwood, or Cornus. In late May, they are joined by a thick mass of cream-white Cow Parsley from the fresh grass on their bank. For a fortnight, they are a memorable group, suggesting yet another use for the crab and its versatile relations: Weston will sell you a white-edged Cornus alba argenteo-maginata to go with the Malus Royalty.

Confronted by so many Crabs, how do you choose? They vary widely in important details, and I must warn you about shapes. When choosing free-standing trees, I would avoid the upright forms of any which are called 'vase-shaped'. The branches are too stiff and I long to tell the tree to relax. Leaves also vary, and some of them are very near to the coarse, rank leaf which spoils modern forms of flowering cherry. A favourite Malus called Tschonoskii is an offender on both counts. It flowers pleasantly and it has the most vivid colour to the leaves in autumn: British growers have renamed it Bonfire and town committees have started to plant it freely as a street tree. Brilliant though it is in autumn, I would avoid it as a specimen because of its upright shape and dreary summer foliage. Its fruits are miserable.

Unhesitatingly, I would choose Red Jade instead. It is never too tall, perhaps only fifteen feet at maturity, and its shape is graceful and far removed from an upright flower-vase. It droops and weeps without looking fussy. In May, the flowers are white and pink, the leaves are a good green; the fruits are as big as cherries and are borne all over the branches in the greatest abundance. They persist far into winter and light up the long border in which I have planted these Red Jades at intervals of thirty metres. It is the nearest match for our John Downie and I never find a trace of the scab which can ruin other varieties. Red Jade was bred in Brooklyn and is well able to take care of itself.

The forms with white flowers fade conspicuously and look to my eye like poor relations of the Great White Cherry. The Arnold Arboretum's Mary Potter variety is everything the breeders promised, but not, I think, what better gardeners want: it is a dead white and spreads too broadly to be at ease in isolation. I much prefer the yellow-fruited Golden Hornet which Weston offer: in British autumns, I am impressed by its huge crops of yellow fruits and wonder how its owners have managed to grow rare apricots. We have given it every award and although the white flowers are not special in spring, it is a superb fruiting variety which lasts into

19

December. Royalty gives you flowers and leaves; Red Jade, shape and fruit; Golden Hornet, fruit in a distinctive colour. They are as tough as thorns in zones four to eight, and I do not intend to bewilder you with more varieties.

I will, however, remind you of their versatility. Flowering Crabs can be clipped like neatly-planted limes, so that they make a short, formal walk or a boundary line to a garden on trunks of six or seven feet. Nurserymen will sell shorter semi-standard Malus if you want to edge a vegetable garden with a wall of flower, beginning at a height of four feet. The standard-sized trunk is better for boundaries. Behind the trunk you hide your netting or fencing; above it, you have a clipped wall of blossom in May. You have no fruits, admittedly, as you must clip the wall to shape after flowering, but you can enjoy a degree of autumn colour. I find that some of the plain forms are best suited to this use, especially the blush white floribunda which has charming red buds. Weston list it, and it came originally from the wild in Japan in 1862. We forget, even in Britain, that flowering trees can be clipped into formal hedges, like evergreen yew or the ever-present limes. Avenues and alleys sound very grand, but they can be scaled down to smaller hedges. The prettiest walk of clipped crabs in my district edges a path of fifteen metres between beds of vegetables. Allow two metres between each tree and a further metre and a half for their heads to bush forwards toward the edge of your path.

The Crab Apples' glories are flowers, fruit and leaf: not many trees can compete with this variety, but one of the best is a delicate American native. Chionanthus virginicus is your Fringe Tree, which we cherish in Britain for its elegant clouds of feathery white flowers. It is not a big tree and it likes to branch out on several stems to an eventual height of fifteen feet. Be warned that it is late to show its leaves in spring and thus it is a tree to plant in a setting or against a background. In mid-June, it gives you the white, scented flowers which are not unlike a good Prunus. In autumn, the pointed leaves turn a bright yellow and the female trees bear berries like small, dark grapes when they reach a fruit-bearing age. Fringe Trees segregate their sexes so you need to plant a harem, a male to a few females, to be sure of this fruit at maturity. Wayside Gardens sell them and they flourish in sun in zones four to nine. Fortunately, they look their best in the well-spaced groups which their sex-life prefers. They are close relations of the lilac and just as pretty.

For fruit, leaf and flowers, by contrast, I recommend the quince. This tough, romantic tree is a favourite of great gardeners in Virginia and was brought to many British gardeners' notice by Lanning Roper, one of our geatest gardening imports from your continent. Unlike this great landscape planter, the quince is not an American native.

The home of the quince is Central Asia, as harsh a climate as anything in American gardens. It soon reached the Aegean, because early Greek poets already use the quince as a simile for the silky skin of a girl. The fruits and their points are compared with her other attributes. At the other end of the globe, quinces were probably the famous Golden Peaches of Samarkand which travelled with traders north-east from the river Oxus through the intervening deserts of the Silk Road to the courts of seventh-century Tang China. There is a story, later, that the Chinese bred their own 'golden peaches' by grafting a peach and a persimmon, but I do not think this refers to the original 'Golden Peach'. I like to think of its first arrival from Central Asia in the exquisite circles of Tang China, where it would have accompanied the dances and new music, furs, jewellery and radical religions which burst on Chinese society from their source in the distant West. Away beyond the White Dragon Dunes and the Mountains of Heaven lay the home of Golden Peaches. The thought sustains one's interest in a quince-tree, even when it has lost its leaves.

In Europe, the quince is at its best in hot countries, in Yugoslavia where it grows in commercial quince orchards and in southern Spain where it has lent its name to a township and to a bus-line which runs through its trees. At dawn, one April, I travelled to Malaga by the quince bus-company through Spanish orchards of pink-white blossom from which came commuting farmers, waiting to climb aboard in their bright blue denim suits. The quince will sometimes curl its leaves in extreme heat, but a tree from southern Spain is well able to cope with American summers. Most varieties fruit most freely after hot summers and in the past ten years my two thinly-stemmed quinces have grown away happily into a loose thicket, rather than two separate trees. In their early season, the leaves sometimes look yellow, but their vigour does not suffer and new branches fly out in all directions. Left to themselves, they make a tangle of twigs which suits my position for them. If you buy proper standard trees with a firm trunk, you can easily shape them into something neater. Space them about five yards apart and trim their branches back to half their previous season's growth in the winter after planting them. Keep them to a tidy shape as standards by pruning any sideshoots which they throw out from their main stem. In New England quinces tend to flower very sparsely, often because they stand in a rich soil and are not pruned. Do not pamper them, except for a top-dressing of sulphate of potash in spring.

Even in Britain, the quince is completely hardy. I am fond of the rounded greyish-green leaves on an ageing semi-standard tree, about ten feet high and as much across. When it flowers, I am captivated. Single, pinkish white flowers show up like enlarged apple blossom all over its branches in early May. There is less certainty about the fruit which only forms and ripens in warm summers, but even if your quince only flowers and gives you leaves, it is a tree worth having. Its stems are flexible when young and can be encouraged over a hoop or pergola to make a short quince walk at the end of a garden path. Sometimes, people try them as shrubs against a south or west wall, but I find them too leafy and too pale when in flower for this to be their best use. One such quince grows against the wall of my Oxford College chapel and we have had to enliven it with climbing plants for late in the summer. The use of climbers on free-standing shrubs or wall-shrubs is a favourite trick among better gardeners. They think of their plantings layer by layer, and these climbers are the final curtain or the upper storey. In our quince we use the white-flowered climbing Potato Flower, Solanum jasminoides album. It likes the shelter and it flowers from July till November, but it is not easily found, although pot-grown young plants could be imported to mild winter regions. Instead, you could clothe your quince with a late-flowering Clematis, one of the tough viticella forms, perhaps, or the yellow-flowering tangutica which climbs slinkily through others' branches. Late flowering Clematis like to be pruned in spring, so they are not an obstacle to the quince's flowers.

Are some quinces better than others? Any variety is good, but in mild regions I can recommend the Portuguese Quince, Lusitanica, which bears especially silky fruit; a Yugoslavian form called Vranja has brilliant yellow leaves in autumn and downy fruits whose shape would qualify for Playboy magazine. In ancient Athens, the bride and bridegroom were required to eat a quince in the bed-chamber on their wedding night before they turned to serious business. Nobody quite knows why, and I doubt if the shape of the quince-fruit was relevant. Much depends if the fruit was cooked. The ancients themselves said that the quince made the bride's breath smell sweeter; I have wondered if the quince was eaten raw, teaching the couple that in marriage, the sharing of unpleasant experiences would often precede their better moments; however, I had a pupil who thought it was simply a touch of romance. "They dined on mince And slices of quince ..."; it would not have been so seductive, she wisely pointed out, if the dinner had only been mince.

If you are keen to find old and unusual forms of fruit trees, I recommend an amateur association in Illinois whose membership has even written to me in London: North American Fruit Exporters, c/o R. Kurle, 10 S.55 Madison Street, Hinsdale, Illinois 60521. They are crusaders against woolly standardized apples and if anyone knows the alternative to overblown strawberries, it will be somebody, somewhere in their ranks. Perhaps they will support you in the search for figs, to which I now turn as trees with uses for flower-gardens.

Figs like to be hot, dry and starving. They would suit your arid zones and in milder areas, they would be as lazy as they are in Britain. It is odd what the experts have seen in their fruits. "The most characteristic feature", writes that authority, Mr. Bean, "is the peculiar inflorescence which consists of a concave receptacle almost closed at the mouth and containing numerous unisexual flowers". Botanists will be botanists. Perhaps Mr. Bean never sank his teeth into those voluptuous centres of red-brown flesh and gritty seeds. I prefer the tastes of an old Roman emperor. The foam on the jaws of a dying wild boar, the splitting seams of over-ripe figs; these, in a vivid perception, were the favoured sights of Marcus Aurelius, paying the world's first prose tribute to the autumn fig.

Converts to fig culture must confine their trees at the roots so that they cannot feed themselves too well and run densely to leaf. I had two old ones between my former house's windows where they were soon a menace. By late autumn their branches were thickly-leafed and spread all over the glass because the trees had not been properly confined at the base. A former owner had manured them when she found that fruit was seldom set and thereafter, it was scarcer still. In nature, figs' woody stems and rough leaves hold the moisture on bare rock faces in Greece and the near East. The best British fig colony is itself connected with a Greek adventurer.

On our south coast, in Worthing, the British fig industry has long been at home. It is a most unlikely fig-base, but nearly two centuries of history run behind the Tarring Fig Gardens outside Worthing, an extraordinary oasis of half an acre of well-spaced fig trees, thick with fig leaves and up to 25,000 fruits a year. In the favoured village of Sompting, during the 1870s, one of literary history's most tireless liars lived out his later years, looking out across these local orchards and still giving not a fig for the truth. Edward Trelawny had known both Byron and Shelley and his literary memoirs have made him known to their biographers ever since. After some grand adventures in Greece during the 1820s, he gravitated home to settle in England and live by the stories of his early life. The tales grew with the passage of time, but his small house at Sompting still stands with a view across fig-trees, reminders of the figs which he had once known during his years in Greece.

The fig likes to grow in the bare heat of a Greek summer; like you and I, the trees are unproductive if they run to fat. There is a well-known view that fig trees fruit more freely if their roots are confined and prevented from running too deeply. It sounds savage, but I am confident, after experiment, that it is worth the effort on any fertile soil. Line the flowerbed beneath your figs with concrete in order to stop the roots thrusting even further and letting the trees become too leafy. I leave two or three holes in this concrete base, small, but sufficient for drainage. Imprisoned figs fruit better, but you must also feed them when the young figs begin to form.

In 1981/2, British figs were ravaged by a very cold winter and in many old gardens, they seemed to have died altogether. Not until July did they put out new leaves, but two such trees in my Oxford College then fruited heartily in 1982/3; against a sunny wall, the fig is hardy enough. Growers, however, forget that it bears its ripe fruit only on last year's matured growth. From this fact, one point follows which I have often seen violated on old trees. When the leaves have fallen or the fruits have been gathered in autumn, you must not lay into your fig and tell yourself that you are cutting back ruthlessly into the old wood. You would remove the very shoots which are most likely to crop ripe fruit next year. Yet figs have to be contained, for their branches will soon smother most south walls. You have two courses open to you. You can thin the growth very cautiously whenever you remember. Better, you can stop the thrusting end, or 'extension', growths in mid-summer, leaving them the length on which to fruit while stopping them soaring over the gutter. This is a worthwhile job in early July. The fig's habit of fruiting on last year's wood goes far to explain those heavy crops of unripe little figs which worry their owners, even if mature fruit has formed below them. They are not a sign of weakness. In their first year, many young branches like to put out these figlets before their proper crop in the following season. They are not indicating their

1. Robinia pseudoacacia Frisia

2. Malus Eleyi: a flowering Crab

3. Liriodendron tulipifera Fastigiatum: upright Tulip tree.

4. Gleditsia Triacanthos Sunburst: Honey Locust tree

5. Acer saccharinum: Silver Maple

6. Philadelphus Belle Etoile with Artemisia Lambrook Silver and Senecio: Mr and Mrs Michael Hornby's Garden at Pusey House, Faringdon

7. Buddleia Lochinch

8. Euonymus sacchalinensis (planipes)

demand for more fertiliser and better soil.

It is important to choose the right variety. Two are usually offered, but be warned that Brunswick is very big and only fit for high walls. Brown Turkey is far smaller, almost so modest a tree that you need not worry about limiting its roots. Brown Turkey, then, is the gardener's best friend. Connoisseurs, however, will keep an open eye for the old Black Ischia of Edwardian walls. This has the driest flesh and most distinctive flavour. Its fruits turn from green to black and its shoots go up to a height of ten feet eventually. I cannot name a certain supplier for you, but it turns up from time to time. When I picture Cleopatra's last hours, it is from a basket of Black Ischias, dark and slender-necked, that I imagine the asps coiling their matching heads.

Two tips, finally, and a suggestion about placing a fig tree in a small space. Small unripened figs appear in October, but these should be picked off the trees as they allow rot to creep into the branches if they hang on too long. Those which start to ripen should not be picked unripe in the hope that they will mature indoors. Figs must split and ripen on the tree. While they hang, you are advised to protect them in their final week on the branch. Use gauze or nylon cut into a square and tied round each fruit. Polythene bags are a mistake. They heat up the fruit and cause it to rot within two days.

How can the owners of sunny but small gardens make any use of these delicious fruits? Plant a Brown Turkey in a large pot and be patient with it. Otherwise, acquire a larger tub and put a Brunswick at the foot of a sunny wall on a paved terrace. You have to be sure of a top-size tub and pay close attention to its water-supply in summer. Figs will fruit very well in pots, but they are not an idea for casual gardeners or for those of you who dislike watering with hoses in summer after work.

Back now to trees which have every virtue for the eye, if not the stomach. I would be surprised if you have not already found what you want, but perhaps you dislike winter-flowering trees and find the choice of Malus bewildering. If so, there must, surely, be a Sorbus for you somewhere. This family is a large and invaluable one, to which I will return for ideas of greater height and width. But the Mountain Ash and its relations are trees, nowadays, which no small garden should ignore. Even in the plain, suburban forms they were lovely enough, though I preferred to see their bunches of bright red berries among clumps of native trees. I once encouraged a reader to mix red-berried Mountain Ash with a big planting of the white-flowered Rubus called tridel Benenden. In May, the Rubus stole the show, one of the finest white shrubs for any garden. It remained elegant in leaf and red-brown stem, a good foil for the Mountain Ashes when they burst into berry in early autumn. The two plants happened to suit each other and his site round a weekend cottage. That, I assure you, is meant to be a compliment.

The varieties, though, have multiplied way beyond the days when you could complain that Sorbus was ordinary and that its fruits were stripped by birds. The pinkish white fruits on the hupehensis variety are almost bird-proofed, while the grey-green leaves live up to the tree's distant home in China. Its shape is rather upright, but the leaves turn a clear red in autumn and are not as hackneyed as those of the plain old mountain ash. Some of these Far Eastern Sorbus are not easy to grow well, but hupehensis will not let you down. I am pleased with two which I recently tucked into the angles of a high brick wall at either end of a new Oxford border. The border's colour is planned to be dusky pink, pale blue and silver from suitable leaves. The finely-cut leaf of this grey-green Sorbus has matched it excellently. If you buy standard trees at a price from Hilliers of Winchester, you will plant them more or less at their likely height after ten years' further expansion. For this Sorbus does not make greater progress upwards in its early years. It is one of those useful trees which you can plant in a border without storing up future embarrassment or killing everything beneath it.

Among the other unfamiliar Sorbuses, I can vouch for the orange-red berries on the essertauiana form, a most unusual tree whose late crop is ignored by birds and whose bold little leaves open sparsely in spring and pass from copper-brown through green to bronze before they fall. You seldom see this one, but you could pair it with Notcutts' selected pink form of the hupehensis variety and be sure of two attractive trees at either end of a long border, neither of which would seem too artificial. There are many named forms of Rowan, some easier than others, none brighter than the ten-foot high scopulina variety which is a fine sight when in full scarlet berry among a mixed border. If it escapes the birds, it is a spectacular contrast for the year's last Michaelmas daisies. But the pick of the family for gardeners who want value and no trouble is surely the admirable Joseph Rock. This is a small tree, well suited to life in a flower border or one of those circular sweeps which people seem to like in their garden's design. Its leaves are more delicate than the common Mountain Ash's and remind me of a well-made fern's. It will branch out at a height of about eight feet and delight you with its leaves all summer. The flowers are not exciting, but in autumn its berries pass from a shade of pale primrose yellow to a bright orange. At the same time, the leaves turn an orange-brown which stands out boldly in any strip of autumn colour. The changing shade of the fruit seems to warn off the birds who leave the crop alone in every area where I know it. Long after the normal Sorbus's crop has been shed or stripped, Joseph Rock will still show its bright berries, breaking you gently into the bleakness of winter. It will grow slowly in any soil in almost any site, urban or rural. It does not cast shade or dominate a lawn or boundary, but among smaller garden trees there is none which I would rank above it.

Is that unfair on the popular Amelanchier? Connoisseurs like this tree and good nursery stock seems to sell at some curious prices. At £1.50 each, six years ago, I planted a line of standard Amelanchiers along my low boundary wall. They are transparent, but excellent if you do not mind seeing through their branches to whatever lies beyond. They give you no privacy, but a glorious burst of harsh white flower all over the branches in mid-April. If the weather is kind, this blossom will last for nine or ten days, lighting up the whole hillside on which my garden runs. Beneath it, I grow the crimson-scarlet Anemone fulgens and the scarlet Tulip Dover whose huge heads happen to match the anemone's season and colour exactly. I am pleased with this chance discovery and find that it dominates the garden. The trees' young leaves are opening at the same time to a soft, downy surface of bronze and the pairing of flower and leaf deserves a close look. Suddenly, after a week, the leaf gets the better of the blossom and the Amelanchier looks like a firework burning itself out. Plumes of white flower still run along its branches, but they are already fading. The leaf takes over and although the fruits are interesting if you look for them in summer, you have to wait until October for the next excitement.

In autumn, the Amelanchier's leaves turn a flaming red, as bright as any tree's, though the leaves are slight and the branches not overcrowded. For several weeks, it is a brilliant companion before closing down for the winter. No frost, wind, snow or soil can upset it, though it prefers lime. I have toyed with other varieties, but the best is the plain canadensis. In early April, it is a mass of pink-flushed buds, held all over the stems like the flowers on a Flowering Currant. It is a remarkably generous plant. My only anxiety is that you might expect more of it than it can offer. It is not a tree for isolation as your only specimen. It is a slender thing for much of its life and will not make a good boundary at any speed. In a pretty clipped avenue or along the edge of walls or vegetable plots, it is as good as anything in the book. It will probably throw up thin suckers and these root and transplant easily. Amelanchier is sold most cheaply as a bush, and I think that I prefer it massed on a bank or in a shrubbery where its slender form is no loss. Otherwise, I would use it in a town instead of yet more pleached limes or hornbeam. Its alternative name is Snowy Mespilus, and I dare you to call it that when anyone asks. In Canada, perhaps, it sounds less idiotic.

If you ignore my digression on Figs, every flowering tree on which I have lingered has so far belonged to the same botanical family. If your head is spinning with names, you may think I am teasing, but I have not strayed beyond that botanical hold-all, the genus Rosaceae. Unconsciously then, my taste must be consistent. All my first choices are lumped with roses as their close relations. As I like roses above all other flowers, there is logic in my bossiness. Rosaceae give you a coloured leaf, flower and fruit in one and the same plant, so they are a natural haunt of those who want good value. None, I promise, is difficult to grow.

I would like, however, to break out briefly before breaking upwards and going for greater height. Within the Rosaceae I will remind you first of the Weeping Silver Pear, sold as Pyrus salicifolia pendula. This is the queen of small grey-leaved trees, weeping down in a curtain of narrow silver leaves and slender branches which hardly exceed twelve feet at their mature height. In the wild, the Willow-leaved Pear weeps, but I prefer the one we have forgotten, the upright form with more solid branches. The weeper often turns up among clumps of gold, purple and bright green leaves, like some prize poodle in an exhibit. Be sure that you want a weeping tree before you choose this one for its silver-grey form. In its youth, it is much improved by a thinning of its branches so that it does not look like, a dumpy grey haystack, left in the middle of the lawn. Against a wall, it is altogether subtler, if you place its grey curtain correctly. On the whole, I am wary of weeping trees because they tend to lack height. Pubs have picked this one up, so it keeps strident company nowadays. In Holland Park Gardens, I was glad to find the selected upright Silver Pear and thought it an improvement on weeping nature. But in any form, this is a wonderfully elegant tree.

The Weeping Pear droops outwards, not upwards. Out of its family altogether, I would like to point you to the Maples in case you are still looking for your dream. Somewhere in the family you ought to find it, though I have never pleased the varieties which I admire most. Under the general name of Acer you will find more familiar trees than under any other in a catalogue. If in doubt, you will always find what you want in this family through the long list of a good nursery like Hilliers of Hampshire who stock tens of varieties. The Acers include Japanese maple, sycamore, box elder, Norway maple, and the lovely Snakebarks. You can still choose the best by a careful visit to a good garden of trees such as Wakehurst, Westonbirt or the RHS garden at Wisley. There is an acer for almost every site. The most spectacular are, to my eye, the least easily placed. In Japan you can still see whole woods of Japanese maples on the few small patches of upland which are not just a backdrop to factory chimneys or an adventure-playground for the crocodiles of heedless school-children. Massed by the hundred, these maples are an astonishing sight, far removed from the company of the dwarf conifer or rhododendron which they keep in English gardens. The past 20 years or so have seen new Japanese varieties which put the old red-brown sorts out of date. They are not cheap and cannot be left to their own devices. But if you can shelter them from cold winds and spring frosts, and if you can give them a damp, lime-free soil, they are able to light up anybody's autumn. Gardeners who grow azaleas should consider them closely. They are very strongly coloured in autumn, so I think you would prefer them as a focal point to a view at the end of a lawn or mown grass walk. They look their best beside a pond or stream. One shrub will go a long way beside a house where it is sheltered, say, by the walls of your front courtyard. There is an art in placing these brilliant shrubs, so I will first give you my views on it.

Avoid the gross mistake of the borders which many catalogues suggest for you on their back pages. They pile on the bright colours by proposing the best of each variety. A bright crimson maple keeps company with gold and blue-grey conifers and glowing pink berberis, perhaps with some carpet of heather under the ill-assorted mass. I have never seen a shrub-border which can take more than one dominant group of these bright leaves. Remember that you have to live with them throughout the year and when maples change, they are as bold as any bed of marigolds. They cannot survive another bright contrast beside them. Variegated dogwoods are about as far as you can go and indeed their mixture of white and grey-green is a very happy match. For the Japanese maples also have a fine shape to their leaves, seven-lobed and delicately-cut. Their Latin name reflects it: Acer palmatum heptalobum, after which comes any one of a host of Japanese names. None is an easy shrub to grow well.

Unless you have a damp, lime-free soil, do not waste money on them. I have one correspondent who assures me that he has the most desirable of all small Maples, the coral-barked Senkaki, growing happily in his lime soil at the end of a vista in full sun. I have to believe him, but although Senkaki might enjoy life among grass on a lime soil, it is much too expensive for me to take the risk. If you have room beyond the azaleas, the small Maples relish the same acid soil. I remember a fine planting in front of the wide-spreading Viburnum Lanarth where a half-acre garden ran out from its formal lawn to the rough grass and bulbs which a busy owner mowed four times a year. Yet even here, I would not leave these delicate shrubs to compete with encroaching grass in their early years. They have to be looked after and need at least a yard's diameter of clear earth in their home. The brightest, I think, is the green-leafed one called Osakazuki which turns a flaming red in autumn. A height and width of five feet are its usual limits in this country. I prefer the coral-barked Senkaki and in the conditions which azaleas like, it will grow up to eight feet or so. It is an unforgettable sight. Plain aureum is a good pale yellow in spring, deepening to yellow as the year goes by. Among the bronze-greens, Chitoseyama is the best of Hilliers' list, though seldom seen outside their arboretums.

These small maples are the shrubs in the family and are for connoisseurs only. I begin with them because they are the most delicate, not because they make trees in British gardens. As a tree, the acer divides into two groups; those which have beautiful bark and those which are taller and fitted for larger sites. The maples with pretty bark include one fancy variety which has suddenly obliged its admirers. For years, gardeners have envied the shape and cinnamon-red bark of Acer griseum, a tree which would fit perfectly into any small garden, growing steadily to a height of twelve feet. The bark peels away in tatters, giving the tree an artless appearance which appeals to me. Rows of griseum against red brick houses would strain my tolerance, but in a rural setting or a planting of mixed green leaves the bark makes a quiet point. Griseum, however, refused to set seed, so trees were extremely rare and expensive. Then, one griseum in Wales and another at Spetchley

Park in Gloucestershire broke the family's barren spell and set seed in abundance. At Spetchley, only the seed from the north side of the tree germinated, whereas the south came to nothing. Stock passed to the Pictons at Colwall, near Malvern who have sold most of it. Others are flowering again on their nursery and if they are equally fertile, the peeling bark of this maple may prove familiar in the 1990s. Opinions vary, but I like its light leaf and shape and cannot wait to acquire one as it is my pick of all maples for better small gardens.

More conventional bark is found on the Snakebark Maples, trees from Japan and America which grow at varying speeds. The classic style of the Snakebark is a thin greenish-grey trunk marked with white lines down its surface. The leaves often hang off pretty red stems. Perhaps the commonest nowadays is capillipes, a tree with both these virtues and the readiness to spread eventually into quite a wide canopy. My own favourites are Acers pennsylvanicum and rufinerve, a very similar pair of which the latter has the prettier leaves, reddish on their undersides and often red in autumn. On the mild and acid soils of Surrey, these trees can make rapid progress to twenty feet or more. Even for the rest of us, they are good garden companions, growing in elegance and interest until the trunk thickens at the base and spoils their markings. Try to trim off the side-shoots until the main stem has snaked its skin to a decent length and shows it without interruption. After twelve years in dry gardens, these Maples may only be slender, open plants, midway between saplings and serious trunks. Even if they take to your site they are tall, but not obstructive. At either level, you must not allow big side-branches to develop too low on the trunk, as you miss the snakebark's point. When well grown, trimmed and staked, these are distinguished trees for any lawn, my equal choice beside a Winter Cherry if you happen to want trees which do not flower. Their progress depends on your soil, but when suitably damp they can grow very swiftly.

Other maples are far more familiar, but they grow to quite a different scale. After twenty years they are big forest and hedgerow trees, fit for broad lawns and boundaries but not for the smaller front patch. 'Coldly, sadly descends the autumn evening . . . And the elms fade into dimness apace, Silent . . .'. If your elms have joined the fifteen million dead skeletons in our hedgerows, you might like to take the chill out of them with the stronger Acers, verging on sycamores, field maples and the like.

The Norway maple, sold as Acer platanoides, is a favourite choice at garden-centres. Crimson King is the most popular and is certainly worth a place if you are more fond of heavy purple-red leaves than I am. I find it hard to prefer any such colours to those in the lighter lines of the plain copper beech. The similar Acer Goldsworth Purple is equally good and holds its purple-red colour well throughout the year. I prefer the briefer show of this strong colour on a fine one called Schwedleri from which you can enjoy the best of both worlds. Its young leaves and shoots are an exotic purple-crimson but they change over to green as the year goes on. They spare you the sight of too dark a head in the tired stages of its life. If your garden is screened from strong winds, you should also consider the elegant silver maple, or Acer saccharinum. This grows apace, reaching a great height where winds allow. Its pale green leaves are finely cut on brittle branches and turn to a charming yellow. It is a tree for larger gardens where it will one day dominate a sheltered planting. In a bewilderingly large family, it strikes me as the best for modern gardeners in a hurry. I encouraged my father-in-law to try one on a damp clay soil in front of a huge old screen of well-furnished holly. A silver maple gratified him and rescued me by racing away to a height of fifteen feet in only six years. Its fluttering branches of pale green leaves had obviously sprung up in a hurry, but they contrasted very well with the staid and solid holly behind. I had no idea until then, how rapidly this tree could grow. Eventually, it tops sixty feet.

Smaller gardens are now way beneath us, but I intend to plant three bold exclamation marks near the end of this chapter before rounding off with three of my larger favourites, a class which is growing with the pace of silver maples. I will find my exclamation marks in the upright shapes of three good trees. Growing upwards, not outwards, they are listed as 'fastigiate'. I need hardly say that I dislike fastigiate flowering cherries in almost any site. But their coarse example should not deter you from a style of tree which is needlessly forgotten in gardens of all sizes. Place it carefully against a background and be patient while it is young. Keep it away from anything so vile as a Columnar Spruce.

'There is but one species of the Tulip Tree', wrote William Cobbett, who had a way of being wrong about trees, 'but that one, as the lioness said of her cub, is a tree indeed'. Fifty years later, a second species turned up in the Lushan Mountains in China, where its clumps must look spectacular. Hardly anybody bothers with the smaller Chinese form of Tulip Tree and I do not think that a nursery will sell it to you. If you happen to visit the great garden of Mount Usher, in Wicklow, Ireland, you can see a very big one which caught my notice because it was in flower. Otherwise, go along with Cobbett and be content with the American form, bigger, better and generally on sale. We have known this Tulip Tree, or Liriodendron, for a long while. It must have reached our gardens in the mid-seventeenth century and in some of them it is now a hundred feet high. There are avenues of Tulip Trees, single-trunked and thickly flowering, towering above the sycamores in Hampshire and Sussex gardens. But you can expect to enjoy one long before the end of this century, as the Tulip Tree grows quickly when you plant it from its pot. It must, however, be bought in a pot from a serious nurseryman, as its roots dislike the disturbance of a new home and will sulk for several years if they are broken. So you begin with a young plant, hardly taller than a tulip and no more resistant to wind. Its stem will bend or snap in two. Its large pointed leaves will look promising but nobody could mistake it as yet for a tree.

What happens next depends on facts of which I and others are not altogether sure. If your young Tulip Tree is pushed out into rough grass and left to fend for itself against a collar of thick old turf, I doubt whether it will stay the course. If you plant it in any exposed site where the wind smacks into it, it will almost certainly give up the struggle. A shallow soil, a few inches of loam above sandstone, brick or the foundations of an old shed, are most definitely not to its taste. Weekend gardeners wage one of their less recognised battles against sites which used to be pigsties, old farmyards or the area of a collapsed barn. It is not wise to plant a Tulip Tree where you cannot dig out at least a spit and a half of reasonably rich loam. A spit, by the way, is the depth reached by the full blade of your spade. Do Tulip Trees also dislike clay? I am not sure. There are some fine ones to be seen around Henley and I am watching one shoot away on a particularly sticky soil nearby. I am fairly certain that they like it and that clay may be one of the best soils for them. Like Snakebarks, they grow at two speeds, very fast or very slow. They grow fastest on a soil which is deep, rich, moist, fertile and all those other terms of praise, like friable, which gardeners lavish on earth as it crumbles in the hand. Clay soils, of course, are very fertile and can be penetrated by the Tulip Tree's young roots. They do not dry out too quickly, another point which pleases the Liriodendron.

Books dismiss the Tulip Tree's flowers, describing them as deflexed sepals and pointed pistils. These perhaps would not attract your fancy. They show up after eight to ten years but not before, and are greenish white with orange middles, so you have to be sure to notice them. They do not resemble most gardener's idea of a tulip and you must not hope for long candles of flower, as if some bed of Darwins was running vertically into the air. But if you pick them and study them, they are extraordinarily fine, as the colours are combined in no other shrub. The shape is intriguing and stands out well if you float the flowers in a flat dish of water. Some of the most famous botanical paintings have centred on the Tulip Tree's flowers. They are worth ten years' wait if you are willing to study them. You can console yourself meanwhile with the beauty of the lime-green leaves. They are big leaves, five-pointed and quite smooth to the touch. They crown their lives with a brilliant change to butter-yellow in most autumns, making the Tulip Tree one of the finest colourers in Britain. A maturing tree, happy on its sweep of lawn, is unforgettable in October.

By now, you must be longing to try one. But an ageing Tulip Tree is a very big tree indeed and few of you will have room for a giant over fifty feet tall. Here, the lesser-known upright form called Liriodendron tulipifera fastigiatum comes into its own. Admittedly, these too are known at heights of sixty feet, but they take very little width and could be placed in many lawns where uninformed taste chooses a beastly Lawson's Cypress. One day, your columnar Tulip Tree may touch the lower clouds, but your heirs will thank you for your audacity. Meanwhile, you have a rare and manageable variation on that 'lion's cub' among the world's wild forests.

On certain soils, a natural pair to its shape and manner would be the Liquidambar. This is not the easiest tree to grow well, and it is best bought in a pot as a young, brittle plant. The roots on older stock resent disturbance. The family is classed with witch hazels, but closely resembles the maples in the lobed form of its leaf and its full autumn colour. As these relations suggest, the Liquidambar likes to be damp, while standing on light soil, preferably without lime. On chalk, it is almost always useless. Although it is thoroughly hardy, it dislikes a strong wind and should be staked when young. This all sounds a bother, and when I add that plants vary widely in their willingness to colour, you might be deterred. The best known variety is the so-called Sweet Gum, or styraciflua, but I would hesitate before buying one blindly and risking a poor autumn colour. Instead I would agitate Hilliers for a named form, either the old Worplesdon which usually turns a deep maroon red or the more recent Lane Roberts. This, too, turns a sombre shade of deep red, but its shape and tone contrast with brighter yellows and flame-reds in autumn. When happy, these special Liquidambars are marvellous plants with which to frame the receding view across a lawn or a garden's boundary.

My final punctuation is the easiest and probably the best. You all know the Beech and perhaps you are keener on a beech hedge in winter than I am. But the upright, or fastigiate, Beech is very rare in gardens, although I doubt if its width ever exceeds ten feet. Eventually, it should make a tall tree, but after twenty years, it will be about fifteen feet on most soils, resembling a solid Lombardy Poplar without any of its fragility or widely-running roots. The upright Beech is generally called the Dawyck Beech, pronounced to rhyme with 'oik', if oiks are still current, or 'hoike', if they are not. It turned up by chance in Peebleshire and was moved to a nearby private garden where it lingered, unexploited, until the Edwardian era. In Oxford's St Catherine's College, it has been grouped to one side of a long rectangular lawn, breaking up its pattern with a sudden vertical emphasis. The placing is a touch of genius which deserves imitation.

Dawyck Beeches grow on all usual soils and have suddenly sprung back into the news by proving, like Acer griseum, that they have a fertile sex-life. In the private arboretum of a great Dutch grower, the Dawycks set seed. That was unexpected, but several of the seedlings turned out to be Copper and Golden Dawyck Beeches by a remarkable stroke of natural fortune. These variations were grafted onto the usual green form and two pioneer trees were planted recently by the Queen in a new arboretum at Wisley. They deserve the closest attention, for the golden Beech is only golden in spring and autumn while the copper is lovely anywhere. All owners of Dawycks purr with pleasure over their merits. If possible, use them to mark a view or a change of level or follow Oxford's example and leave them to break up the long line of your well-mown lawn.

It is not unfitting that these three exclamation marks should preface my three final ventures among trees. For the first is the Fern or Cut-leaved Beech and, in my view, it is the most beautiful tree which Britain offers you for a larger, open site. Nurseries call it Fagus asplenifolia, and you should buy it if you want a feature without flowers, a connoisseur's boundary or a specimen tree in roughly-mown grass. Its leaves are lighter than the usual Beech's. They are cut like a fern's and are airy and pale in a way that its parents' are not. In May, it opens to the palest shade of 'amorous green' and in autumn, it fades to a civilised shade of burnt sienna. After twenty years, in a field, it would stand about fifteen feet high and twelve feet wide on most soils, for like many variations, it lacks its parents' extra vigour. Buy it on sight or rumour even if this book serves you no other purpose.

You might, however, like to pair it with one or both of my final choices. They are not only trees for the landed and forested belt. Wherever you want a quick return from something other than the coarsest conifer, the whitebeam and the Dawn Redwood should fit your space. In late April, there is no mistaking the beauty of the whitebeam. This is a noble tree, to be found by the name of Sorbus in the family which includes those Mountain Ashes. It belongs above all on lime soils, although it will grow well enough on neutral ground which can take a few azaleas. It is native to Europe and Britain, and is almost indestructible if you plant it firmly in a well-dug soil. It would take a hurricane to break its branches. The snow never bothers it and the fumes from traffic will only coat it with a layer of dirt. Do not be deceived by the so-called Swedish whitebeam, or Sorbus intermedia, as its leaves are grey-green on their undersides and do not give you the white flush of a true whitebeam which is opening its new leaves. Look, instead, for the forms of Sorbus aria whose names are still a muddle. Chrysophylla is self-explanatory to gardeners who know Greek, a whitebeam which is really a yellow-beam as it has a golden yellow tone to the young leaves. I rate it with other yellow variations on familiar grey plants, the yellow-leaved Jerusalem Sage or the yellow form of that felted Helichrysum petiolatum. These yellow variations are not to my taste.

White, after a fashion, occurs on the two most common whitebeams, the plain aria and the special aria majestica whose leaves are far bigger, up to six inches in length. Just to confuse you, majestica also goes by the name of descaisnea. Of the big whitebeams this tree with a double identity is certainly the best. Its leaves are too big at maturity for any plants to survive beneath them, so they must be given their head in a park or field, a big lawn or along the edge of a drive. After ten years, you may wonder whether the figures for its eventual height are correct. Another decade will prove its power, and leave you with a tree over 25 feet high and 20 feet wide. Eventually it will top the 50-foot mark. Majestica, then, is not the best whitebeam for most of us. I used to think that the upright form of one called thuringiaca was a possible alternative. I saddled my limited garden with two good trees of it, but I now admit that they are poor substitutes, showing a dull grey-green for a week or two while they open their serrated leaves. Avoid this error. Instead, insist on the whitebeam called aria lutescens, because this variety is doubly white. It shows the same grey down and colouring on the upper and lower sides of its leaves. The first freshness fades by mid-May, but the ribbed leaves remain among the paler shades of green until they eventually turn a burnt brown-orange and fall off in autumn. After 20 years it will be 15 feet or so high, and about 10 feet in diameter. You could plant a whitebeam walk with a tree every six yards or so. Against the exceptional whiteness of lutescens, you notice the bunches of fluffy white flowers in early May, a prelude to the small red berries which appear like pellets in autumn. Neither the flower nor the berry is more than an added touch of interest.

Lutescens, then, is my first choice but I would like to see more interest in the weeping whitebeam called aria pendula. Last year, I met my first mature specimen of this in a big Sussex garden and thought it better value in most places than its only weeping silver rival, the weeping lime. It is tougher, less prone to disease and those sicknesses of the leaf which can make the lime a disappointment. At maturity, the weeping whitebeam is not so enormous. Like most weeping trees, it should be isolated where its form can be appreciated from all sides. It would be spectacular against a dark background and if you have such a site at the far end of your lawn, Hilliers of Winchester could sell you one.

For different soils and sites, I would remind impatient gardeners of my other recent planting, the Metasequoia. While placing one last week, I reflected how little impact this remarkable new conifer has made on British gardens. It is an upright tall tree, whose finely-cut green leaves are slightly similar to a yew's and even more similar to that glorious conifer, the Swamp Cypress. It is not a good tree for sandy or chalky soil. Although it will grow almost anywhere, it much prefers deep earth which stays damp. In its favourite conditions, it will race ahead and put on 40 feet in only twenty years. It is a thin feature which will take up less width than a well-grown Christmas tree. It retains the air of a conifer and it is incongruous in enclosed urban gardens. It belongs in a dell or shaded boundary among fresh green leaves, not fellow conifers.

The Metasequoia was new to our gardens in 1947, but its rediscovery was lost among those years of post-war austerity. It has not yet been given the mass welcome which it deserves. Its story is most peculiar. In 1941, the family was first described by a Japanese botanist who had no more proof of the tree's existence than the evidence of early fossils. Unknown to him, a Chinese gardener had also found it in the same year, growing wild in a small pocket of dry and rocky territory on the north-east borders of Szechwan. The evidence of fossils and forests coincided, proving the extreme antiquity of the garden's latest gain from nature. Metasequoias were as old on this earth as dinosaurs, adorning an age when the world's great trees were the Ginkgo and White Gean, a sight for which I would volunteer to become a cave-man. Three years later, the Metasequoia reached western botanical gardens where its light green leaf and bright brown autumn colour soon caught the nurserymen's attention.

Not many conifers are so civilised and few will average two feet of growth a year without looking top heavy. If you want to economise, you can grow one from a softwood cutting, taken off someone else's tree in July or August. These cuttings root with astonishing ease. Beside a whitebeam, this ancient tree would look very handsome, one of the few great discoveries for gardens during World War II. It ought to be in every garden centre, and while you congratulate yourself that it is not, you can round off your choice of better trees with a species as old as any on this earth.

Chapter Three

Better Shrubs

Swinging down from the branches to the level of better shrubs, I will not leave the days when the world was young and Dawn Redwoods dawned among the dinosaurs. Among mastodons and dimetrodons, what could be more natural than my own dying species, the Oxford ancient-history-don? Though long declared moribund, we are far from extinct.

Better shrubs begin, for my money, with the best of all, the Magnolia. There is no older shrub on the market, for Magnolias grew beside primitive moorlands some hundred million years ago. They are far superior to birds and bees. Beetles attend their cool scent and pollinate the flowers, groping blindly inside their white cups. In the days of the dinosaur, the world's other pollinators were not yet at large. The Magnolia, moreover, is much too venerable to bother with such recent inventions as petals. Having neither a petal nor a sepal, its flowers caused botanists to panic. In an erudite compromise, they ruled that they were made of tepals.

These tepals hang downwards or sideways, project upwards like stars or candles, come in all colours from pale pink to chocolate purple and breathe some memorable scents. Perhaps you can put a name to all these varieties already, but you may still wonder which is the best for your soil and surface area.

The Magnolias are at home in America and south-east Asia. It is unlikely that there are any good hardy varieties waiting to be found in unexplored areas of China and Japan. The tender varieties are less familiar, though they would loom large in any full family gathering. I have never seen a jungle Magnolia in a botanical garden's hothouse, and there may yet be surprises in the forms lost in West China. Meanwhile, we have hardy Magnolias in plenty, for the garden varieties are mostly resistant to our vilest winters. I have never seen Magnolias with thicker trunks than those Soulangeana forms down the boulevards of Washington where the winters excel anything we would tolerate here. The Magnolia's enemy is not so much the frost, in most garden forms, as their owners' forking and busybodying. After a hundred million years, they resent interference. Those big trees which run wild in forgotten gardens have made the most of the peace round their brittle, fleshy roots. 'Magnolias,' writes Neil Treseder, their British expert, 'will usually tolerate complete neglect.' That is most obliging.

When you plant a Magnolia, therefore, you must plan for permanency and look far ahead. Never waste money on the biggest stock, as it will transplant poorly. In April, buy plants which have rooted firmly into the soil in their polythene container. Try not to plant them where you will bother them by digging or by rooting up weeds and bedding plants around them. They deserve to be isolated in a lawn or against a wall. Dig out a wide hole, about two yards wide, and fork leaf-mould and rotted manure down to a depth of three feet. You will be repaid by quicker growth and flower. Magnolias have a healthy appetite and like a lime-free general fertiliser each autumn. They move more easily in spring.

When choosing your example, you must assess your soil's degree of lime and your preference for tulip-flowers over strap-shaped ones. I have to reserve the smaller strap-shaped varieties for large tubs because their most manageable form prefers a slightly acid soil. It is so good in a tub that I will begin with it. Magnolia stellata will seldom grow more than six feet high and as many feet across. It flowers generously from an early age when a foot or so high. It is the white magnolia which you often see in suburban front gardens against the low boundary wall or beside the front path. Buy it, but be aware of its slow growth and small scale. The home of this shrub is confined to one mountain area in north-east Japan which it left for our gardens about 100 years ago. The authority, Mr Bean, to whom I owe this point, goes on to remark that stellata should be underplanted with groups of a dark blue grape hyacinth whose flowering season coincides with its own. Stellata sets its buds profusely along the bare branches and flowers elegantly before the leaves appear. Hilliers of Winchester list and often sell a special form called Water Lily whose flowers are larger and more thickly 'tepalled'. It is worth the price, though others, pink and white, also claim this name. Plain stellata is good enough, and even if its open flowers and thin white tepals are sometimes spoilt by heavy rain or frost, it is quick to replace them with a second crop. When the flowers age, they open out and begin to bend their narrow tepals backwards, fading like the similar petals on the lily-flowered tulips with which I prefer to match them. Its roots revel in a spongy, acid bed of leafy soil, but move more slowly, I find, in lime. As pot-plants, they are seldom seen in Britain, but the Japanese have long used them in tubs, as I now do. They once gave the plant the name Magnolia of the Houses because they brought it indoors so often. As its flowers are scented, it is worth potting up some young plants.

Among the bigger, strap-shaped varieties there is some recent news, which still seems to pass many new gardens by. Thirteen years, for a Magnolia, are but the twinkling of an eye, but in 1969 a form called Leonard Messel took the RHS's highest award. It has a pale pink flush to its petals and boasts stellata as one of its parents. Born from the most valuable cross among recent magnolias. Leonard Messel is a variation on the desirable loebneri, the hybrid of a former director of Dresden Botanical Gardens. Loebneri tolerates all manner of soils, extending its tastes to lime and sometimes to chalk. It flowers, like its parent stellata, at a very early age, but it grows like its other parent, kobus, with unusual vigour and reaches ten or twelve feet quite rapidly. At thirty feet or so, it ought to stop. The branches are set with tepals like open stars before the leaves appear and in the Leonard Messel form, their pink blossom is best viewed in half shade against the darker background of your wild shrubs. Among Camellias, it looks appropriate, but it will dignify a lime soil too and will put up with quite sharp frost when in bud. The pink form is even tougher than the white one. Loebneri and its variations have yet to catch gardeners' imaginations. They are easily placed in the further distance of any planting and lack all the slight awkwardnesses of many of their relations.

Lovely as the starry forms are, I prefer the large tulip-flowered forms of soulangeana. These are the classic magnolia trees, flowering on lime or acid soil, though turning a yellow-green in their leaf when the lime is very strong. There is a splendid flourish, often quoted, from their breeder, M. Soulange-Bodin, a retired cavalry officer from Napoleon's army who saw sense and turned gardener after 1815:

"It is to this that I cheerfully devote the remainder of my life. I shall not retrace the sad picture of the past . . . The Germans have encamped in my garden, I have encamped in the gardens of the Germans; and it was with sword in hand that I visited the botanical collections of Vienna, Minden, Stuttgart and Moscow . . . It had doubtless been better for both parties to have stayed at home. We are returned there, and the rising taste for gardening becomes one of the most agreeable guarantees of the repose of the world."

Of his parents' children, I dislike most of the forms with dark purple flushes or exteriors to their flowers, as if their pure beauty had been dipped in chocolate sauce. That rules out Picture and the intriguing new crosses on sale from Washington with bouncy teenage names like Ricki. I ask only for a pure white, the exquisite form called alba, or for two fine forms with bold white flushes and varying degrees of purple, each of which is worth hunting down.

The finer of the two is called brozzonii. It is an Italian form which bears enormously long white petals, nearly a foot wide when fully open from their purple base to their white tips. This form flowers late, not until early May when the frosts are almost past. It grows just as readily as any other but is more spectacular.

The other, the older lennei, makes more concessions to deep purple. This large-flowered hybrid was born somewhere in Italy soon after 1848, though nobody knows where and one admirer is content to attribute it to the 'charming little bees of Lombardy'. Lennei's purple flowers have a white flush and a lovely white centre when they appear freely in late April. The tepals are fleshy to the touch and curve slightly inwards, giving you a strong sense of achievement when the huge flowers first appear in your garden.

Before me stands my vision of a better gardener, short of space, wary of large plants which may die in a hard winter, content with an alkaline soil and wanting a reward from this book within ten years. So I will pass over the marvellous evergreen grandiflora magnolia, fit only for British south walls and patient owners. I will urge connoisseurs with space and patience to pay for highdownensis (on lime or chalk) or the matchless wilsonii (best on acid soil). These are shrubs of an unbelievable beauty whose cup-shaped flowers are tilted downwards, like the covers on a soup-tureen. Their leaves, when happy, are grey-green and as fine as a Tulip Tree's. But rather than confuse or deter you, I will stand by stellata, Leonard Messel and a white soulangeana and move from this king of all shrubs to my own Top Ten among the others. Let your Magnolias rest in peace, feeding deeply after your careful transplanting. This job is best done in spring with an eye on their brittle roots and the droughts in your plant's first year. After five seasons, they should be the best sight in the garden.

If Magnolias are the best, what are the shrubs which are better than most others? Here, I must draw firm lines to help my dogmatism. I will exclude shrubs for acid soil, though the white azalea called Palestrina, any yellow-flowered Rhododendron and that reliable pink Camellia Donation would come near the top of my list. I will also exclude small shrubs because the best have their chance in the chapter on alpines. I will not mention too many shrubs from the families on which I intend to focus afterwards. I will aim for reliable choices, sound value for any beginner. There is a three-volume odyssey to be written about the good garden shrubs in my experience. This, then, is only an epitome for busy gardeners, and before you attack me for leaving out your favourite, be sure to read to the end of the chapter.

I cannot imagine I will be attacked for putting the Philadelphus first. I am not choosing plants which, ideally, we would all like to grow well. They must be easy, on my definition, and hardy in all but the worst of the recent winter. I have never killed a Philadelphus or Mock Orange Blossom, and I doubt if any sensible gardener could. I want it, of course, for its heavenly scent, as powerful as a tangerine's in late June and July, when the bushes are covered with their white flowers.

No variety is less than good, but perhaps I should name the single-flowered Belle Etoile as my favourite. The cupped flowers have a pink-purple stain in their centres and are less rounded than many. About six feet high and wide, it throws off mahogany stems in its youth. Beauclerc is its near rival, marked out by the golden anthers in the centre of the white flower. I would not bother with any other forms at this convenient height. If I wanted a more upright Orange Blossom where I could hide its bare lower parts, I would still choose the darker green leaf and scented double white flowers of old Virginal before any modern variety. Most of the small, single-flowered hybrids are marked with a purple blotch. Both should be more familiar. Plain old microphyllus is a neater and slower-growing plant, possibly the sweetest scent in the family. You must have room for it, a shrub up to four feet high. If you want to be different, I suggest you fasten on the cream variegated Orange Blossom, called Coronarius variegatus, which gives me such pleasure in a damp north facing bed. As so often, the variegated form is less vigorous than its green parent and stops at a height of about five feet. In June the white flowers are nearly lost against the white edged foliage, but their scent wafts everywhere and the leaves continue to bewitch me after their first freshness in April and May. This is a rare plant for no good reason, but Sherrards of Newbury sold me a young example and I consider it the prettiest shrub with white and cream markings. Cuttings, as usual, root easily off it in July. If you have room, then, go wild with Orange Blossom in sun or shade, in tamed or wild gardens. The scent has no equal and the profusion of white flower is one of the finest sights on a fading June evening. It lights up any hedge, wood or orchard like a pale twilight, touched by the moon.

I would turn next to one or other of my favourite Buddleias, named long ago after the egregious Mr Buddle. I hope the bad winter has not scared you off the most elegant garden form, the lavender-blue-flowered variety with grey leaves which sells as Buddleia Lochinch. With the slight shelter of a south or west aspect, the bushes I know all seem to be alive somewhere on their clutter of dead wood. This is not a coarse variety, like the usual davidii forms. I put it first among choices for the back row of a mixed border where its grey leaf, pale flower and honeyed scent would combine very prettily with rose Felicia, Day lilies and the pale mauve-pink and blue Lavenders. These two Lavenders, incidentally, make a very happy pairing of colours side by side. Above them, Lochinch roots freely from late summer cuttings, so you only need to buy a parent. Alternatively, I would take alternifolia, the variety with long, drooping wands of pale lavender flower in July. I much prefer this shrub with its back near a solid background so that it seems to cascade up and out in only one direction. As a standard tree, in isolation, I find it too wispy and unfocused. It is a back row shrub again, not a strict wall-shrub, but it buddles along in any sunny place.

I have much more to say about Viburnums, but for this list of favourites, scent and continuity tip me in favour of the winter-flowering form, called bodnantense Dawn. Its season is long and its vigour is beyond question, as it flowers during quite sharp frosts. About seven feet high and four or five feet wide, it is a hardy shrub and its white flowers, again, are touched in the bud with pink. The scent is slightly peppery, and nearly makes me want to sneeze. But it grows almost anywhere, and multiplies by young suckers.

Hydrangeas, too, will take a prolonged bow, but here I would choose the huge felted leaves and the big blue-white 'lace caps' of flower on the form called villosa. It thrives on chalk or lime. I grow it on an east wall, where it survived the winter, as did other young ones on open ground. It is a strong, rapid shrub of great quality, a first choice for any shaded wall. Sometimes the frost touches the leaves in spring, but the effect is only skin-deep, and soon disappears.

To atone for their slight tenderness, I would give fifth place to variegated Dogwood, or the form of Cornus alba with the longest name in the list. This marvellous shrub will mix with anything and even redeems the coarser sort of purple foliage. I like it best in half shade, competing with wild flowers, but it is a good foil to the old-fashioned roses in full sun. It appreciates a rich soil. Whenever you are at a loss for a background to bright flowers in a border-plan, this shrub and the grey-purple leaves of the slender, upright Rose called rubrifolia (up to six feet) will help you out of your problems. They look very well together, on lime or acid soil.

I hesitate here over hardiness. In a south-facing border in a south or sheltered garden, I would raise the rapid forms of shrub mallow, or Abutilon, to the top of my list. This group is one of the great discoveries since the 1950s, and reaches the heights in a Hampshire hybrid form called suntense whose open, violet blue flowers cover the light, tall standard bushes at a height of five or six feet. Cuttings, again, root for anyone, growing away like simple Fuchsias. My plant has survived the 1981/2 frost away from a wall, so I will indulge my taste for it here, a brilliant small tree of exotic flower which is fit for any novice and happy on chalk or dry soil. You can plant thickly around and beneath it.

I am tempted by the king of all Weigelas, the modest middendorffiana with yellow and orange flowers like small pouting foxgloves. About four feet high, this classy shrub would dignify sheltered gardens in a town, though they never try it. Elsewhere, I fear, it is too tender. Instead, I had better have an evergreen, and scent once more inclines me to the indestructible winter flowering Mahonia japonica, whose sprays of acid yellow flowers smell deliciously of lilies-of-the-valley. It grows anywhere, but if you treat it well, its leaves wear a finer bloom. I think it likes to be damp and shaded from the direct noon sun. I have just seem two good examples reaching for the light in tubs in a shaded London garden. Their leaf and outline are as bold as any palm tree's, especially in May when a small fan of feathery bronze growth appears in their top

45

crown of leaves. The winter sorted out all hybrids like Hope or Charity which had lomariifolia's tender blood in them. Anyway, they lack scent, so they belong with good, not better, shrubs.

In July, I would take almost any Deutzia for its elegant stars of white or pink flower. Monbeigii and setchuanensis tie among the whites, while Magicien is a superb French hybrid, up to four or five feet, whose striped pink flowers are edged with white. Although sun or shade suits them, they are too seldom found in the border. They flourish there if you prune them correctly. Immediately after flowering in July, Deutzias should be cut back on each flowered stem to a new young side-shoot about half way down its length. Older stems should be cut out like raspberry canes from the stool of old roots. All varieties are good, and my colour plate of one helps to catch their shared quality, a graceful elegance in flower and leaf.

For autumn colour, fruit and a quiet curiosity, I will stray to the unfamiliar shrubby form of Spindle Tree called Euonymus planipes, or sacchalinensis. Its hanging scarlet fruits are a joy in summer, while the dying leaves turn a brilliant red in autumn. Up to eight feet high, this is easy and containable, though it will strain, if left untrimmed, to the height of a small tree. I had to keep you on your toes with one surprise, so please explore this charming nomination.

If my final choice was allowed to be a variety which died last winter, it would have to be the lovely Cistus cyprius. Its greyish-green leaves grow rapidly into a mound at a height of five feet or more, which smothers itself in white flowers with a crimson blotch. It is the hardiest form with a blotch and the best value in this good family. It honours any south or west border, though it makes a broad bush. I have replanted my lost one at once, hoping that a younger one is still alive behind it. Having smuggled in a Cistus, I give my last place to a tied pair. One is the flowering 'quince', or so-called Japonica, in its long lasting blood-red form called simonii. This low shrub looks wonderful below a window on a sunny wall where the light reveals the depth of its red flowers in April. I do not grudge it an inch of my best south wall, because full sun brings out its richness. My top ten now turn into fourteen, a mark of my predicament among so many plants. For I make this red 'quince' (listed as Chaenomeles) dead-heat for my last place with a lilac. All lilacs are excellent, but I would pick the Canadian lilacs for their looser panicles and taller growth, preferring the rose-purple Bellicent from the Ottawa gardens of Mrs Preston. Up to ten feet, it lurches over walls, pergolas or old sheds and bears its flowers in plumes, not tight spikes. I would nudge the connoisseurs, however, to the ignored Chinese form called sweginzowii, the pride of a bed below my northerly french windows. If left unpruned, this bears sprays of light fresh flowers here and there in June after its young spring leaves of an exceptional charm. Twelve feet high, eventually, it grows coarser by late summer. But it wins space for the unacknowledged softness of those open plumes of pale pink blossom and exquisite scent, the finest in the family. Lilacs filtered east from China and Central Asia, passing quinces on the journey down that same Silk Road through the steppes. Reaching Iran, they multiplied and moved to the Bosphorus, coming finally to our notice through one man's diplomatic contacts in Istanbul. Ogier Ghiselin de Busbecq, no less, was ambassador from Vienna to the Emperor Suleiman the Magnificent. In 1562, he returned home with two shrubs in his diplomatic bag, a lilac from the Balkans (which the Turks had brought back with their armies) and a Philadelphus from Asia minor. Among many fine diplomatic plantsmen, Busbecq wafts to the head of my Top Ten, bringing Europe two scented shrubs whose names it has muddled ever since. In Persia, they say, men should give bunches of lilacs to their mistresses when the girls forsake them. Before you rush to strip your pale lilac Firmament, I would add that the plumes of a lilac turn my mind to summer evenings elsewhere, to those country estates in Tsarist Russia, lying deep among aspens, old willows and sensitive gentry, those self-styled 'superfluous persons', who looked back among the lilacs to their tales of youthful first love. From Magnolias at the dawn of time, I have come full circle to the Central Asian steppes again. Habits of thought die hard, so I urge you to try my top 'ten' before they drag on and become fifteen.

I turn now to a gardener's fundamental choice: evergreen shrubs or deciduous shrubs? Before you make it, remember that both groups shed leaves, but that most of the evergreens shed them discreetly over long periods. Firm and green in a good winter, several evergreens look less alluring in late spring or early summer. Among trees, the evergreen Holm Oak and among shrubs, the white-flowered Choisya are but two of the varieties which look wretched while they moult in the early growing season. Moulting, of course, is too mild a term for the conduct of most evergreens in the ruinous 1981/2 winter. As never before, they turned brown and died completely. For the record, I note one or two surprising losses, not peculiar to my own garden, although it faces north and sank to 26°

of frost. I had not imagined I would lose every one of the grey leaved Senecios, like almost everybody else in open territory, nor the scented little Sarcococca, a shrub for edgings, whose white flowers are vanilla-scented in late winter. Ceanothus of all sizes, ages and varieties, succumbed without exception. So did Choisya, the rapid blue-flowering autumn Caryopteris (not, strictly, an evergreen) and all Escallonias, including my prize specimen of the scented white iveyi some eight feet high by my front door. Deaths, however, varied with the site. For years, we hedged our mature Carpenterias with a polythene protection in their corner of my Oxford college garden. This past year, we forgot the polythene before the first December frosts, yet both Carpenterias came through the winter quite unmarked. A Ceanothus died ten yards away from them and a Camellia dropped most of its leaves. The white-flowered Carpenterias, resembling a scentless evergreen Mock Orange, is usually marked as dubiously hardy. Against a south wall, I begin to wonder.

Which evergreens, then, were left of those which are any good? The stronger types of white flowered Osmarea and Osmanthus survived with only the slightest browning, although their small tubular flowers were scarce in the following April. I consider that burkwoodii Osmarea is the best background, a fine buttress and evergreen shape for better gardeners on lime soils where they wish to run no risks. I admit that Osmanthus delavayi's leaf is glossier and finer, but it simply is not so hardy. The various types of Eleagnus survived, though I am not so keen on the yellow-marked forms which turn up freely in the garden centres. The best is the new one called Gilt-edged. Its name is regarded with suspicion by most of my F.T. readers for its past performance, but it is a reliable form with a bright yellow margin, not a broad yellow centre. My eye prefers variegated margins to variegated centres, on leaves of this size. But my favourite in this family is a mixture of silver and green, called macrophylla. The silver shows clearly in spring and persists on the leaves' undersides thereafter. This is a tough and undervalued background shrub whose branches sweep the ground to a width of ten feet, blocking out weeds. It bears tiny pale flowers, exquisitely scented in autumn and in its tough way I like it. It is far better value than the garden centres' usual ebbingei.

I would also run through the many good evergreen or near evergreen Cotoneasters, had the winter not played such unexpected havoc with so many of them. The red-berried old fishbone variety, called horizontal is, is a fine plant in its way, and its cream-

called horizontalis, is a fine plant in its way, and its cream-variegated form is a neglected beauty. But its commonness has brought other excellent shrubs in the family into a certain disrepute. I cannot say that the elegant grey-green rounded leaves of the one called franchettii will persist throughout the winter, but they are long-lasting and exceptionally pretty if trained on their loose stems as a hedge or screen round a compost heap, vegetable patch or the inner division of a garden. They are a very useful tip. So, too, are the yellow-berried Exbury hybrids, one named after Exbury, the other after the Rothschild family. These are tall arching shrubs to a height of twelve feet or more whose branches spread widely. They would look lovely behind the bigger shrub roses, Nevada and so forth. But I know old bushes which have died in the 1981/2 blizzards.

Perhaps the little-known Phillyrea should have crept into the last chapter, for it makes a tree if you let it and if you survive to see it after fifty years. I give it a turn here because its variety, decora, has glossy evergreen leaves which are so bright and civilised, leaves with a clear stamp of quality. They are shinier than an evergreen oak's and in my experience, far hardier. Their home is the Black Sea coast where they sport like their relation, the olive. Most of the leaves fell off in the fierce winter, but new shoots sprouted rapidly all up the stem. In the mid-twenty-first century I may be remembered for my Phillyrea, a dominating tree of olive-green leaf which glistens in the light. By then, its correct new name, Osmanthus decorus, may have reached the nursery catalogues, but the plant will be the same.

At a lower level, I would again explore the Hollies. Their prickly leaves are a menace, but if you are going to have prickles, you might share my liking for the very spiny Hedgehog Holly. Its forms are dark green or gold-variegated but never too tall for a border. The leaves are encrusted with spines, like a hedgehog gathered in a ball. There are no berries as these Hedgehogs are prickly, bristly males. Otherwise, I would direct you to a small, smooth green holly whose excellence jumped to my notice in the big border near the car park of Hilliers' Hampshire arboretum at Jermyns, near Ampfield. Called Cornuta burfordii, it is still sold at a fair price in their general list, but it is not a tall shrub, levelling off at only three feet or so. A fresh leathery evergreen, this is an ignored holly with only one spine at the very tip of its leaf. Hilliers' Manual of Shrubs remarks that it is much used as a hedging plant in the USA. Adventurous gardeners should note it in Britain as a slow green alternative to yet more miniature berberis. It is a splendid plant.

Other evergreens will emerge in the course of my comments on flowers, but I would alert you to the beauty of two of my flowering favourites, the Viburnums called henryi and burkwoodii. While they wait their turn, I intend to write as if that ruinous winter will not recur and frosts will be no sharper than those of the previous decade.

Surviving all previous cold weather, my pride was a well-placed drift of the shrub called Bupleurum fruticosum. I tempted fate in September 1981 by writing that I thought this shrub no longer deserved the suspicion of tenderness which the old books attached to it. My three biggest bushes, I rambled on, had pulled through some shocking winters, facing north without protection. Three months later, they were almost as dead as driftwood. This summer-flowering relation of the cow parsley seems to me to be a godsend to impatient gardeners placed, like myself, on lime. It has narrowish, soapy blue-green leaves, a reasonably upright habit and flat yellow-green heads of flower in August, an unusual season for a shrub. It verges on yellow more than green, but it is a pleasant colour, although flies seem to like the opening pin-points of its many small buds. There are other rarities in the family, but this one, sold by Sherrards of Newbury, is the winner for most gardens. The authoritative Mr Bean, I have just found, believes that in country places it is known as 'buplevers'. That, I fear, was before the spread of the suburb and the weekend cottage. Bupleurum is quite good anywhere and always easy and quick to a height of four feet. But in one place, it is superb. If you have a bank or a slope beside steps or a dry wall, it will spill out over the edge and fall loosely forwards in a dignified way. It is a fine evergreen shrub on a chalk soil. There was a time when I thought that the most handsome natural gardens of all were to be found spilling out of the chalk-faces of southern railway cuttings. In such a site, old buplevers would be in its element. This shrub is definitely worth another try.

Another such chalk-lover is the family called Rhamnus. This, I imagine, is a relation of the willow and the sea-buckthorn. The best is prettier than either, a pale cream-white variegated shrub with a bright leaf which is sold as R. alaternus variegatus. This, too, is a surprisingly rapid shrub and although it brings with it the darkness of its mature stems which makes Sea Buckthorn such a gloomy plant, it can look magnificent on a light, east-facing wall. I first fell for it in the ingenious garden of Keith Steadman at Wickwar near the chilly slopes of Wootton-under-Edge in Gloucestershire. He has always championed it and taught many gardeners to love its pale elegance against a wall of Cotswold stone. The past winter burnt the top half of my own plant badly but failed to kill two in Oxford. They will have to cover up their damage by some delicate concealment, but in normal years they are reliable and unrecognised shrubs.

I will gloss over the sad loss of my shiny green Escallonia called iveyi with its masses of grey-white flowers in July. The connoisseurs coo over this Chilean hybrid and sometimes applaud its scent. Winter after winter, I would wrap it in blankets when the wind veered northwards in the small hours. Twice, it disturbed my chances of sleep but on my best south wall it grew to reward me with a magnificent flourish of flower and evergreen leaf. It was a fine example, I must admit, but it is dead now, so I will also say that I thought it disappointing. The flowers were never a clear white and the fabled scent escaped me entirely. I liked the leaf, but I damn it here, for I feel I know it to be over-praised.

Not so the Ceanothus. Its forms have died by the hundred, but they must be replaced and allowed to advance at their usual headlong pace. They are a tough family, hailing from California where they thrive in dry homes and grow furiously. In all but the last winter, the evergreen burkwoodii form is hardy if you place it with a little forethought. That said, mine faced north-east on the edge of a cold hill and was quite unperturbed until 1981/2. The bulk of dark green leaf-mass was pleasantly emphatic in winter. I found that the main danger lay in heavy falls of snow which could split the brittle stems by their weight. I saved my plant several times by shaking off the first fall during an interlude, leaving the second drift to land on unencumbered growth. In snowy weather the Ceanothus is one of the first plants to need checking. When the main stem splits, sap will still course up to the branches if you bind the breach firmly with tape and wire. For once, I am at a loss to name my favourite in a family. I think I would put the rich powder-blue Cascade first for any tall wall because it flowers with a freedom I can never imagine until I see it. Its stems like to soar upwards, and a level of fifteen feet is not unlikely for their upper storey. Evergreen and early, it is a wall shrub only, where it matches a beautiful pair of rich blue sisters, the spring flowering Delight and the autumn-flowering Dignity. These are more hardy than other rich blues, in my experience. I prefer the deeper blues to the powdery ones because the flowers stand out more richly. So the tough veitchianus has always been popular in my plans, an evergreen which flowers generously in late spring and thrives against a wall. For the pale blues, I would rather use the deciduous varieties whose flowers are not lost in the dark leaves. Gloire de Versailles deserves its popularity here, though the deep indigo Topaz is gorgeous in a different way. They are marvellous plants for the middle and back rows of new borders where they soon shoot away and make a brilliant feature, adding weight to your border from an early age. This rapid maturity is a rare virtue and I cannot commend them too strongly in any sunny site. The pink Marie Simon is also charming, but not too hardy. I wish, however, we saw her more often in a border's back grouping beside the well-known blues.

I leave the most tantalising till the end, the hardy and low-growing thyrsiflorus repens. This is no creeping plant, but a widely-spreading mound of firm branches which grow to a height of three feet and a span of six or more. Nobody knows why it flowers brilliantly on some plants but scarcely sets a bud on others. My elder brother grows a magnificent clump of it whereas I have placed nothing but duds in others' borders. Sherrards of Newbury sold him his winner and if you enjoy the same luck, this is a tireless shrub for open, sunny ground. It smothers all weeds and knits neatly among the king of silver shrubs, that well-loved Senecio. A mass of creeping Ceanothus under tall Viburnums, silver-leaved Buddleia Lochinch and silver Senecio strikes me as a subtle way of shutting out weeds between your free weekends.

I ought, then, to say a word about Senecio. All but the smallest gardens have to include this harmonious shrub. The yellow daisy-flowers are harsh and ugly, so you can trim the bushes hard in May to stop them developing. There is only one form for most gardens, but nobody agrees on its name, greyi or laxifolius. Plants vary in the whiteness of their stems and the degree of green in their leaf. Much depends on the sunniness of their position and the age of the foliage. A well-clipped Senecio in a dry, poor place will look more silvery than a well-fed one with older leaves in semi-shade. Cuttings taken in July will root with ridiculous ease, so you need never buy more than one plant. Senecio dignifies any company, old or new roses, borders of bright daisies and slopes which include Bupleurum. I am not deterred by the ghastly losses of this shrub in the winter of 1981/2. In all other years, it sprouted freely after blizzards had cut it to the base, and I put down this one collapse to exceptional conditions. On a large plot, I would never garden without this godsend, two feet high and four feet wide, bright all year and a blanket against weeds. In the subtle garden of Bampton Manor, Oxon., well-placed bushes of Senecio alternated on either side of a small vista to lead the eye across to a concluding feature. Such was their silver outline that they guide your eye down their perspective before you could stop it wandering.

I will round off the evergreens with two families which I trust for any shaded bed. The Skimmias have fresh leaves and the ability to cover themselves with long-lasting red berries, when their sex-life is going smoothly. Their leaves are a light shade of green which is never oppressive. They are healthy in their growth and well shaped for any site where a firm block of leaves is in place. They keep good company in shaded beds with primulas, Solomon's Seal, an interplanting of white Lily regale and the excellent and easy tall orange Lily henryi. By now, their sex problems are an open secret. Most of their owners know that most females have to have one male to fertilise them and bring them into berry. Scotts of Merriott, Somerset, will supply separately sexed male and female stock. Like an ideal Muslim husband, one male can take on four females and make a respectable job of life. Plain Skimmia japonica is a fine form whose shoots and leaves are particularly fleshy. It does not insist on a lime-free soil, though it probably prefers it. My plants have yellowed leaves when the weather is dry beneath a wall which drops its lime on them. But they are still growing apace. In time, they will reach four or five feet and bear lovely scarlet berries, coloured like sealing-wax from an early age. You can place them with almost anything and enhance it. Some nurseries still sell the precious sort called foremanii, the one which has a self-sufficient sex-life and will grow on any soil. This solitary needs no companion, but is not easily found in most lists nowadays. Hilliers of Winchester can offer it and it is certainly the easiest though it is not the finest, to my eye.

Fewer gardeners, however, are aware that these glorious autumn shrubs are very easily rooted from cuttings. Perhaps you read gardening books only to tell yourself that you could never afford any of their ideas. Not so the skimmia. Find a friend with a good plant of it; break off a shoot about 6 inches long above any joint on the branch; put it in a pot of light compost and keep it damp but not sodden, preferably indoors. By next summer you will have a well-rooted shrub of your own, true to its parent's sex. Most skimmias are not plants for acid soils only, and I find that their one weakness is an over-abundance of flower and berry which can exhaust a young

plant. Too muich sex never did anyone's stamina much good. If you
ration the skimmia's female flowers when young, you will help it to
grow up normally. To my eye, skimmias have the neatness of a
small laurel without the same darkness of leaf.

I have never quite reconciled myself to my final evergreen, a
spreading horizontal 'laurel' called Prunus Otto Luykens, though I
must sign off with it because of its possible use against weeds on
your banks and mixed borders. It has not gained the attention it
deserves, a new break whose branches fan out across a span of five
or six feet and never pile up to a height of more than two feet or so.
In half shade or exposed sites, it is a poor man's replacement for the
creeping Ceanothus. As it matures, it looks less drab and its
lengthening branches of dark leaves gain a brighter gloss as they
extend. I prefer Skimmias, but this shrub is a very obliging cover
among grey Senecios. I wish it would not bother with its spikes of
white flower on their brownish supports. They depress me.

Out of these evergreens, then, you have a possible backbone for
your garden. I have omitted some very desirable ones, especially
the forms of Pittosporum from Hilliers, because I cannot call them
hardy in slightly fierce weather outside a sheltered town. I have left
you to choose your Camellias because I do not garden on their acid
soil. It is an old rule that up to half of a planting of shrubs should be
evergreen, but the recent harsh weather makes me even less
inclined to agree with it. Why should we fill up space with second
rate shrubs so that they can look slightly less wretched than anything
else in mid-winter? I value their leaves in spring and summer when
their solid form sets off other flowers. Most of the forms I mention
will either flower for their keep or reflect the light from fresh or
shiny leaves. I would never damn other evergreens as 'suburban', as
if there were not many masterly gardens sited in suburbs. But they
tend to have dull leaves with dark, matt surfaces and these are the
forms which I detest. The Spotted Golden Laurel is in a separate
class of horror, marked with a double X.

Having sketched in a possible evergreen backbone, I would
advise you to repeat your particular choices at intervals down any
long border or spacious design. This repetition breaks your garden
into regular bays or blocks and helps the eye to sense a unity in the
profusion of other flowers. To two families of such profusion, I now
turn.

Most gardeners, I have to assume, do not agree with my tastes in
flowering shrubs. When laying our their gardens they look round to

see what other nearby gardeners are growing and then plant it for themselves. They like heathers and conifers, big cactus-flowered dahlias and bushes of yellow forsythia. They do not want to bother with old roses which flower until October because their new floribundas will last until November without any advice. Some of these plants, perhaps, give such good value that they have simply been seen too often. Others have a colour and shape which would never be to my taste. But as I read a list of the most popular shrubs, compiled from sales throughout Europe, I can go gladly along with the crowd's high favour for the flowering hydrangea. Its one fault is that nobody ever pronounces it properly. In Australia, the sound of it would scare you off gardening for life. In English it should be pronounced with a 'dran', not 'drain'. With yellow forsythia, it is one of the best-selling shrubs in Britain.

Hydrangeas, like most of us, like to eat well and be warm. If your plants have failed you they will probably have been disappointed in one or other need. However, the two needs tend to work against each other, for the warmest sites are seldom the richest and most damp. Hydrangeas should never be allowed to be dry during the summer. This is ruinous. If you wonder why the leaves on your plants are wrinkled and whether a hydrangea-bug is eating them, you should simply reach for the hoses and water heavily. You should also feed the plants lavishly with a top dressing of manure and a yearly dose of any general garden fertiliser in spring.

Food improves the flowers several times over, but I have made the mistake of feeding my young plants from early July onwards in the hope of encouraging them while their flower-buds are forming. Such a late feed is no help. It persuades them to send up soft young growth until late autumn and exposes them to their one weakness in Britain, a sharp frost. The most popular varieties are those with big 'mop-heads' of flower, but they have been bred for the florists' trade and include many varieties which are only safe when grown indoors as pot-plants. You have to be very wary of these ill-adapted plants, however attractive their first flush of flower may seem in a shop.

The past winter taught me the truth of this. We needed a well-branched group of white hydrangeas for a damp north-facing bed and needed them quickly. Impatiently we fed them far into the summer and pushed them on quickly: hydrangeas will move rapidly if they are well-treated. They entered the bad winter with too much soft top-growth and too little ripened wood. The frosts cut them right back to the ground and there is not a flower in sight this year.

They are back where they started. The moral here is to feed them in spring and early summer, but no later. A similar moral extends to pruning. Complaints against hydrangeas often come from owners who are too free with the cutters too late in the season. Hydrangeas are usually planted in too small a bed for their eventual spread, so something has to be done to contain them after five years. It is easier to do something in warm weather, so they are pruned back in July or October after flowering. Pruning, of course, encourages the young growth again, so they enter the winter with a soft wall of young greenery. The frost cuts them back, taking next season's flowers with it. It is wiser to prune your plants in early April, and then very lightly. Do not shorten all the shoots on principle. Look only for a few weak old shoots which have died back and cut them right out at ground level, like raspberry canes. They keep out the light and cramp younger blood.

The next difficulty is the colour of the flower. Why are my hydrangeas pink, whereas yours in London or Stuttgart are blue? Their colour depends on the acidity of the soil, which governs their absorption of trace elements. The exception to this general rule is the white-flowered group. These will stay white anywhere, though in sunlight they age to a rusty pink. But the shades of blue and pink can be pushed around. It is more difficult to influence them if you live on a very limey soil. Your hydrangeas will have a rich pink flower and perhaps some yellow leaves. Although you can feed them on Sequestrene to counter the yellow in their leaf, you cannot change the flower from pink back to blue.

Neutral or slightly acid soil is more common, especially in towns. This soil leads to those mauve-pink and blue-purple heads which can look so bilious. Here, you have more power. If you dose the soil with iron and aluminium salts, you can tip the flowers over to a proper shade of blue. For years, intelligent gardeners believed that it was the iron which made the difference, but tests in America during the late 1930s showed beyond doubt that the aluminium, rather, tipped the balance. Iron stops a hydrangea's leaves from fading to a shade of yellow, but a dressing of aluminium sulphate shifts the flowers to a deeper blue. There are hydrangea dyes on the market, all of which use this basic compound. You can apply it quite cheaply yourself at two ounces to the square yard or 2½ pounds to each hundredweight of soil. Professionals reckon to dig up a wavering hydrangea every year and fork two pounds of aluminium sulphate into the surrounding soil before replacing it. If the weather

9. Bupleurum fruticosum

10. Deutzia longifolia.

11. Rosa Gallica Versicolor: in Mrs C.G. Lancaster's garden, Haseley Court, Oxon

12. Alchemilla mollis (Ladies' Mantle), a yellow-green match for Irises and shrub Roses at Sissinghurst Castle, Kent

13. Gillenia trifoliata above Pulmonaria saccharata in the Scotts' garden at Boughton House, Kettering

14. Crocosmia Lucifer at Bressingham Gardens, Diss, Norfolk where it was bred

15. Hosta sieboldiana Frances Williams at Bressingham

16. Milium effusum Aureum: Bowles's Golden Grass

is dry, this dressing ought to be watered gently into the ground. Otherwise, it can be released all at once by the first heavy shower and prove too much for the plant. The turn from mauve to pink is even easier. If you dose the soil with lime once or twice a year, the flowers will lose their aluminium and swing back to a bright rose pink. A blue, however, on strongly alkaline soil is less attainable. Heavy doses of aluminium sulphate will help, but you should also give your blue the soil it prefers. The plants are best in a large tub of special peaty soil or in a bed of peat which is lined with a double layer of polythene in order to keep out the surrounding soil. Tap water, rubble from a wall, leaf mould from trees grown on lime: all these intruders must be isolated, as they will start off the move to pink once again. On extreme soils, I would rather leave a hydrangea's colour to nature.

The usual varieties fall into two groups, of which I much prefer one. The so-called lacecaps are hydrangeas with flat heads whose middles, technically, are small fertile flowers, while the ornamental outer ring of coloured 'petals' are only borne by sterile 'florets'. The openness and contrast of these lovely 'flowers' is the group's claim to fame. Florists have taken less interest in them, so the varieties tend to be hardier. I have never seen them better than in the National Trust gardens at Hidcote Manor, Chipping Camden, Gloucestershire, where great bushes of lacecaps foam with blue and white flower in August. I rate the bold heads of Lanarth White as the best variety for gardens, followed by the misleading Bluebird, a variety which hovers round the line between pale lilac and pink. Rosealba is the most tenacious red, ageing to a deep ruby which will never shift to a blue, not even in a peat bog. These varieties need three years or more to settle into a new home and they do prefer a damp site. By the paths of a woodland garden they are most appropriate.

On chalky soils or less favoured sites, you can enjoy the lacecap's effect for little trouble by choosing the hydrangea called villosa which I named in my Top Ten. I am no longer scared by this plant's tender appearance, having found it easy and persistent against the wall which suits it so admirably. Its velvety leaves are magnificent and spread happily, needing next to no attention. The cold spring winds may scorch them, but they do not destroy them.

Inferior to these lacecaps are the full and heavy Mopheads which we meet in hotels, French *concours* and seaside bedding. These are very good plants, but part of their trouble begins at home. In Japan, the hydrangea grows in the wild. The Lacecaps inhabit the tougher climate of the mountains, while parents of the Mophead cling to the lower, coastal areas where frost and hardship are less frequent. To my eye, their fulsome heads of flower are less natural then the open and contrasting shapes of the Lacecap. But they trace back to a fine French farce, one of the best in the history of eighteenth-century botany. I give you the tale of how Mopheads probably earned their other name, Hortensias.

Several French kings were quite keen patrons of plant-hunters, none more so than Louis XV who backed a M. de Bougainville on a journey round the world. On the way, of course, he discovered that magenta sheet of flowers which Europeans grow and love as Bougainvillea. But he also discovered a fact about the birds and bees. It concerned his young third-in-command. When Bougainville set out, he picked as a companion a grand old man of botany, called Commerson. The grand old man refused to leave without a far from grand young helper whom he passed off to the world as the teenage M. Baret. The king saw them off with the usual flourishes about the cause of pure science. But even among scientists the quest for facts is not always enough. While they were sizing up Tahiti, the truth came out.

The Bougainvillea had just been discovered and the botanical task-force was relaxing in its camp. While the grand old men congratulated themselves, the young M. Baret, was absent. He was believed to be visiting a native settlement. Time passed and instead of M. Baret, a runner returned with the compliments of the village chief, announcing that his master wanted M. Baret's hand in marriage. Inside the village, the chief had seized the botanist's companion and unveiled an unexpected truth. M. Baret was no teenage André. He was a well-endowed and well-concealed young miss called Jeanne, or Hortense. Miss Hortense had been working her passage discreetly, as essential to the grand old man of botany as his collecting-bottle and floral maps.

The chieftain, after argument, allowed his South Sea bubble of a dream to be pricked. Hortense was returned to her master with much tut-tutting and reflection on the ways of the great and good. Her elderly master was so put out that he did not ever dare to return to France. He left the boat at Mauritius and took Hortense on a lengthy holiday.

It was from Mauritius that Commerson sent to Paris a shrub which turned out to be a form of Hydrangea. After his death,

Hortense returned to France, the first woman to travel far round the world and probably the only one to have made a large part of the trip under pretence of being a boy. She married officially and settled down, but the new 'hydrangea' received the suggestive name of Hortensia. 'The matter has been argued over by learned men for many years', concludes the best monograph on Hydrangeas, 'and no finality has been reached'. French society knew several Hortenses, but only one, the daughter of the Prince of Nassau, can rival Commerson's mistress for the honour. The Prince was serving aboard the botanical mission, but I like to think that the namers of plants had an eye for the *double entendre*. Round the world, the Mophead hydrangeas are still known by their second name 'hortensias'. I suspect that the word kills two separate birds with one stone.

On Hortense's side of the family, there are some obvious choices among the Mopheads. Mme. E. Mouillière is the pick of the whites, but her flowers burn with a red tinge in full sun. Soeur Thérèse, then, runs her close in a shaded bed which is sheltered from late spring winds. Among the deep pinks, my prize goes to the reliable Hamburg, while the long stems and lax habit of the variety called Vibraye conceal the winner among the blues. I trust this one to flourish on any acid soil where the flowers turn a pure blue and last very well. If the frost hits the buds at their tips, others branch out beside them, assuring a summer of flowers. Its full name, however, is General Vicomtesse de Vibraye. Sexual ambiguities, it seems, have flourished in the family of the Hydrangea.

None of these varieties measures up to the size of flower on the half-hardy forms which thrive near our sea-fronts. Here, Joseph Banks is the best known, a generous shrub with huge flowers for those who like washy expanses of lavender mauve. I far prefer the neglected Ayesha, a form which better gardens will cherish. Its leaves are shiny and its flowers are cupped, appearing in the usual 'mop'. The colour varies from pink to pale violet, but usually rests with a lilac-pink shade which appeals to my taste. It is slightly scented of lilac, but I think I would not trust it in an exposed site or garden.

When your shrub flowers, how should you treat the flower-heads while they age to a dead brown? I like their sad appearance, but even if you do not, you should leave them on the plant until spring as a slight protection for the vulnerable tips of their stems. All this advice may make the Hydrangea seem awkward, but I am only suggesting how to grow this easy plant at its best. One final tip, then, dredged up from your tea-cups: if you cannot find aluminium and you do not want to pay for chemicals, you can coax your hydrangea towards a blue on a suitable soil by mulching it with tea-leaves. I know gardeners who put tea-leaves on the garden because they do not want them anywhere else: they block the sink and look exceptionally decadent in dust-bins. But a Clematis likes them as a cooling defence for its roots. As good tea-leaves are rich in tannic acid, they will begin to give your General Vibraye a touch of the tea-time blues.

Gardens of hydrangeas are weighted towards the end of the summer, so I would balance them out by the range and variety of that marvellous group, the Viburnums. This family has a top-class plant for almost any position. The commonest two are tinus, or laurestinus, and that low evergreen davidii which will mate and bear blue berries among its dark evergreen leaves. Neither, I think, is anywhere near the best of the family. Although Viburnums oblige me by growing robustly on the lime which almost all prefer, I would use them anywhere for their scent, long season, leaf, berries and the shade of white in their flowers. If in doubt on a lime soil, call a puzzling shrub 'Viburnum' and you are quite likely to be right. Forgive the pun, but in April good vibes come from scarlet Ribes: I know a gardening 'expert' who dares to pronounce this shrub so that the words rhyme. But the best vibes come from scented Viburnum.

Several good varieties have been inter-married to the point where beginners must now be puzzled. A usual parent is the lovely carlesii, a compact shrub from Korea whose rounded clusters of white flowers are divinely scented in April and May. Carlesii is not the quickest grower, but I know no Viburnum with a stronger scent. It is a shrub which tucks into a border or any corner where its rather rounded outline can spread without colliding with a neighbour. It took all the prizes in its day and at Hilliers' Hampshire arboretum I was won over to the selected form Diana, whose scent, vigour and deeper pink tone struck me as the best news for alkaline gardens during mid-April. Diana is not cheap, but better gardeners will want it for its vigour, greyish young leaf, and freedom of flower. The experts are almost unanimous that old carlesii is inferior to its child, juddii. After following them, I consider they are wrong. Juddii is bigger and more willing to flower but it is not nearly so sweetly scented. Now that Diana is truer to its parent's virtues, I am happy to give this one a miss.

Burkwoodii is quite another matter. It would be my ideal shrub if it is was not quite so dull after flowering or so willing to begin to look its best in late February when the gardening season is hardly open. It is evergreen, however, in a burnished, glossy way and its leaves have a brown fluff on their undersides. Catalogues claim that it grows about six feet high, but I know taller bushes and I think you should be wary. With patience, you can raise it by the hundred from your own cuttings which root like bindweed. The flowers are strongly scented, like lightly packed snowballs dressed with a rose-scented powder. This is an essential shrub wherever something bright takes over after May. In a New York public garden, I saw a huge flowered hybrid called Mohawk which was the best thing on view. The competition, I grant, was not strong, but this is a form with a bright British future. For value, then, you must include burkwoodii and tuck in Diana for her scent. Their relation, bodnantense Dawn, is equally essential. From November onwards, this upright shrub bears those white clusters of flower from pink buds on bare branches. It grows in any open soil and multiplies freely by its own suckers. I made it one of my top ten shrubs and need only repeat that it carries the virtues of the April Viburnums into November and December, paying almost no heed to the weather. It contains the best of two good parents with whom, therefore, you need no longer bother.

As a match for its flowers, you could well use an evergreen relation. I am astonished how many bushes of the proven old laurestinus collapsed in the hard winter, casting a doubt over this white-flowered Victorian favourite. I had never much liked it and now it is stone dead. Instead, I put the tall variety called henryi among the best evergreens in any garden. Its leaf is a surprise, a thin and pointed tongue of glossy green which is like no other in the family. Found in China, this shrub has been grossly neglected since it won a First Class Certificate soon after its arrival in 1910. It is an upright, tall bush, some ten feet high, which dignifies any plantings of lower shrubs or old roses. Its flowers appear in loose, tapering bunches in June and are followed by berries if the birds are not watching. This is a shrub for quiet and perceptive taste, and I cannot imagine why we have all been so blind to it lately.

Perhaps the huge range of Viburnums is at fault. Once you have to pick one, henryi is lost among others with scent or a special shape. When I look at the modern forms of the Japanese snowball tree, or Viburnum plicatum, I can see why henryi is sometimes squeezed out. These are spectacular shrubs, robust and rapid on lime soil but just as good among rhododendrons. I have never seen such a huge hedge as in the Anglesey garden at Plas Newydd where these shrubs have careered to a height of twelve feet or more and a density of horizontal branches like a theatre's screen. Their noble owner thoughtfully ran tarmac paths through his garden and shrubberies in case his family and visitors felt too dreadfully tired to walk the few hundred yards to inspect their flowers. If the National Trust still permitted, you could cruise round Lord Anglesey's giant Viburnums without ever leaving your car.

In gardens, the Lanarth form is a first choice, a big shrub which is a weekend gardener's dream. After five years or so, its horizontal branches sweep sideways and screen all the weeds underneath. The flowers stand flatly on short stems and resemble a pure white lace cap hydrangea's. The outer florets are sterile, while the inner little pinheads are fertile. If you have too much space, try a mass of this May-flowering shrub in company with rampant wild geraniums. Between them, they will cover almost anything. In smaller spaces, you should choose mariesii instead. Its branches are more horizontal and the sheets of white flower are unforgettable. I first saw these plants in the garden of an octogenarian mathematician who had used them in a natural garden of azaleas, maples and pieris. I was still a schoolboy, but the memory has lasted far longer than my mathematics. I have learnt to prune these horizontal shrubs in early autumn in order to improve their shape. I like to clip out their leading branch and keep them flat, like a poor man's flowering Cornus. Be warned that they have recently changed their name from tomentosum, so either title conceals them in lists.

Lastly, I would put in a word for forms with berries. If the birds oblige, the best is certainly betulifolium, a large and bleak shrub until it weighs down its branches with berries like bright red currants. This, I think, is a worthwhile gamble for wild corners, on the edge of rough grass or compost heaps or in that no man's land beside a curving drive. It is a shrub which you only want to notice when it is at its best, but then it beats all other berries in the family. For value, I would prefer to give space to the neat form of our Guelder Rose. What, indeed, is a Guelder? A corruption, I think, of elder, this shrub is a water-elder which I discovered by chance to be twice as attractive on a very wet soil. Near a pond, stream or septic tank, the form called compactum is worth its keep. About five feet high and wide, it bears heads of white lacecap flowers at the time of the Lords' Test Match but takes on a brighter colour in autumn when the leaves turn brilliantly and the bush sets masses of shining red berries, as clear as currants. This compact form fits easily into mixed borders and ranks as my most reliable and useful shrub for autumn colours at that level. It is almost thrilling and always reliable. There are many other good Viburnums, but for me these are the best.

It is now time to pick and choose among roses. Among the modern 'floribunda' and hybrid tea bushes, I admire the stamina of white Iceberg and the shape of white Pascali and the peach and buff colouring of Chanelle. Among climbers, David Austin of Albrighton, Wolverhampton, will sell you the forgotten white Sombreuil, whose flowers are flat and quartered, a cream white shading to a flesh-pink centre and exuding a charming scent. Peter Beales, Intwood Nurseries, Swardeston, Norwich, will also quote prices for stock if your local sources fail.

Among the usual climbers, I put New Dawn first for its late season and delicate blush-white colouring. If you only want one climber, I think you should choose this proven favourite. If you want to experiment, you should read on. For how many gardens now bother with Rose Blairi No. 2? I marvel at this flat and exquisitely scented silver-pink bourbon rose, which can be staked or pinned to a height of six feet or so. Was it an afterthought, all that Mr Blair had left when he lost every plant, perhaps, of some long-forgotten No. 1? Is that why he never named it, but let it loose to the public as some ignored second-best? If so, Blairi No. 1 must have been a rose fit for paradise, too good for human enjoyment. Perhaps you like the sound of its runner-up, but mistrust it and fear disease. You can assess it next year at Sissinghurst Castle, Kent, where it is superbly shown. You must not allow Blairi No. 2 to become leggy and you must be willing to prune it and pin it. You will have to spray the fat buds against white fly and reckon that its leaves are indeed likely to catch black spot eventually. But in its single June season of flower, it is so sweet and so prettily-shaped that any keen rose-grower ought to have it. The wide heads of petals are so tightly packed that the scent, too, is doubled, like the fruit of a sweet white German wine. Among the big pink climbers, rambling Albertine and her coppery-buds rival the thornless Mme Gregoire Staechlin as the pick of the bunch. They will soar over high walls, while Albertine sprays sideways into a huge thicket if simply left to go wild on a sloping bank or wild garden. But Blairi No. 2 is a 'climber' too, if only for a tall square of wooden stakes and wire, into which it is hoisted upwards. It joins three other neglected ladies, all old but excellent climbers if you want roses with a difference.

For a warm wall or a house in the holiday sun, remember to think of taking Rose Lady Hillingdon with you. When warm, she would make a superb companion, a lady of no fuss, no pests, no nasty smells, healthy for a lifetime and free with her charms. Bred in 1910, she started climbing in 1917. It took her far. She is not so fashionable nowadays, despite the title and her good track-record. But her qualities are still not surpassed in any one rose. Her flowers have two seasons and a bud or two in the interval. They are shapely, as all the lady roses of her time once were. Their scent is exquisite, a heavy scent of freshly-opened tea which explains the name 'tea' roses. The leaves are grey-green. The young stems are a thrusting plum-red and the flowers are an apricot without any trace of flame or salmon-pink. In England, she finds the frosts at times too much for her. She likes to go south for the winter. In a Mediterranean bolt-hole, she would be at her best, some ten feet high if well-watered and fed. I would join her with two other ladies from those days when Edwardian women went south with protective creams on their faces and skulked in tweed plus-fours on the Riviera away from the seaside's burning sun. They are fine roses, much better than my accompanying puns.

Madame Seltzer, one feels, was a person whom Lady Hillingdon only met when she had to. No, this rose does not have a fizzing white sister called Alka. In fact, she is a rambler, but her flowers are prolific, still seen in old gardens where they were planted in the 1920s, proof of their vigour. They vary from cream to lemon-white, but stop at around ten feet and have the great advantage of being almost thornless. The shell-pink Alida Lovett shades into yellow at the base of the large flowers, but makes a fine companion, unjustly ignored since her birth in 1905. It was Lovett first sight when I saw her last summer on an old wall, not least because of her vigour and sweet scent. It is a commonplace that modern bush roses are never so good as the old ones. The same truth, however, is seldom seen in the climbers. But a rare subtlety of flower and leaf can still be tracked down in these forgotten forms of proven distinction and scent.

Among bush roses, I intend to state categorically that the best garden value is to be found in the group called Hybrid Musks and the single-flowered white hybrid Nevada. The Musks resist disease and grow into a manageable hedge or thicket wherever you want them. After shortening their growths by a half in their first year, you need not prune them unless you want. Some can be cut hard as bedding roses. Others, especially tall pink Penelope, will reach the height of a fair hedge. All flower twice, with a strong second crop in early autumn. They are moderately scented of tea and fruit in a pleasant mixture. Moonlight is a wonderful white for a border and Buff Beauty is a self-explanatory colour. It is vigorous, profuse and a marvellous choice for a mixed border against pale Buddleia Lochinch. Of them all, the queen is the shapely silver pink Felicia, my unhesitating choice as the loveliest rose for any gardener. Felicia has no vices or diseases. She lives as long as most gardeners and can be pruned as a bedding rose at a height of three feet. She belongs with silver leaves and pale blue flowers, one of those breeders' miraculous breaks.

Nevada is taller and sometimes prone to black spot on dry, light soils. Even so, it smothers itself in big, white single flowers which reappear more sparsely in September. Its leaf is lighter and wilder and it likes to spray out to a width and height of eight feet. A hedge of Nevada never fails to dazzle gardeners. If you place it well forward of the wire or background, it arches out into a wonderful concealment for tennis-courts, pools and other athletic intrusions. It is an essential shrub rose which grows anywhere.

Among smaller bushes, David Austin of Albrighton, Wolverhampton has bred several good modern varieties with old-fashioned virtues, but only one winner, for my money, which beats all small bedding roses. Called Wife of Bath, it bears persistent heavy-petalled flowers of a rich pink-white on stems about two feet high. Flat and full, the flowers breathe the intense scent of their parent, Constance Spry, but excel her by appearing freely throughout the summer. Wife of Bath goes beautifully with hardy blue Geraniums, the pale blue and white Buxton's Blue for its second flowering and the taller and clearer Johnsons Blue for its first. You ignore this Wife at your peril.

Among the truly old varieties for smaller spaces, I would not hesitate to place the York and Lancaster rose first, although it does not live for very long at its best. It is not the same as the Rosa mundi with which the lists often muddle it. Rosa mundi's background colour is pink and its stripes are rose-red. The York and Lancaster is white with a red stripe, the 'third, nor red nor white, which stole of both' in Shakespeare's poem and which the poet had obviously failed to grow as well as we do nowadays. 'For this theft, in pride of all his growth, A vengeful canker eats him up to death': Anne hath-a-way with most things in my garden, in other words, but cannot out that damned Black Spot.

The York and Lancaster will naturally grow upright to a height of about three and a half feet. Its stems are not very strong, so the bush will lean over unless supported. It is fair game for mildew and 'vengeful canker', so I prefer to cut it right down to the ground after flowering so that the effects do not show. This makes it quite a new plant, the sort of thing which you can mass near the front of a border, like the big June poppies, and conceal later in the year with Sweet Peas, trailing Violas, Nasturtiums or Michaelmas Daisies. Fifty bushes do not go very far for this purpose, so if you can afford to mass them for their great fortnight in early July, do not hold back. They combine so prettily with silver leaves or with a good grey-leaved pink, preferably one of the white and purple-pink blotched varieties. As you are rid of this rose from mid-July till October, you can find a space for it in any garden. It is a better colour, I think, than Rosa mundi, so be sure that your old rose nursery, Morrells, say, of Shrewsbury, know that you want the white background.

Altogether bushier, and perhaps as lovely as any, are that easy old pair, Ferdinand Pichard and President de Seze. Both reach a height of some four feet and about as much across. Ferdinand has the longer season, repeating later in the year. His flowers are rounded and their basic colour is pink, prettily striped, however, with a deep red and a red-purple. He is excellently scented and the best, bushy buy among the roses related to Hybrid Perpetuals which tend, otherwise, to be rather straggly. Old Ferdinand is well suited to a silver-leaved background and Artemisia Silver Queen will run prettily between him at more or less the same height. He is too good, I think, for only two or three bushes, as his season is not short. Use him, then, like a big bedding rose.

President de Seze is a Gallica and thus, if anything, tougher. His freshly-opened flowers are held at a height of four feet or so, and seem miraculous. The centre is an intense deep crimson purple, opening out to those heavily rolled petals of the classic French gallica flower. The outside edge is white-lilac, quite a different colour and the most delicate contrast in such a rich flat flower. The leaves are fresh and solid, the bush very tough and well set. Scented, of course, and so old that it can merely be dated 'earlier than 1836'. It matches with big grey-blue leaved Hostas most handsomely.

The last few years have shown me another, Robert Le Diable, at its best. I was landed with this spreading Provence rose as a present from a connoisseur who made it his personal first choice. For two years it straggled and bore flowers which were beautifully petalled but poorly coloured. Then came the hot summer of 1976 and the colouring, as he promised, pulled itself together. Slate-purple, scarlet, rose-pink and pale grey ran through petals which stood upright in the centre and reflexed at their edges. It is a wide spreading bush, unlike the others, but a subtle mixture which no breeder nowadays, could repeat. You forfeit a good second season for scent, shape and romantic colouring. For my money, these are worth far greater sacrifices. Old-fashioned roses are a vast field nowadays, but these few should start anyone off on a proper course without yearly plagues of excessive black spot. Incidentally, there is no known cure for it and the cheapest therapy is to use Jeyes fluid on and around the bushes from March until August. That compound's cheap use in the garden is often overlooked.

Returning to shrubs, I am reminded by those crushed old roses and fading shades of lilac that there are two less familiar shrubs which match with them in any surroundings. One, called Indigofera, bears short spikes of rose-pink in the joints of its leaves during July. The frost shakes it, but kills it no more than a Fuchsia. Tall Potaninii is the form for mixed borders, a lovely pair for the excellent white Rugosa Rose called Blanc Double de Coubert. At a lower level, the more tender Heterantha is a heavenly find, a three foot high shrub with loose pinnate leaves and rosy flowers at the foot of south walls.

The Lespedeza, or Bush Clover, is even slower to show any growth. The one called thunbergii is high among my better shrubs. From August on, its stems arch and flutter with silky grey-green leaves, like a true relation of the garden pea. The flowers are rosy purple and add to the effect. I have seen this elegant late shrub down either side of a long garden path among green Alchemilla and white Campanulas in a great French garden. It was a choice of genius, arching far and wide and fluttering loosely in the August winds.

I will descend, lastly, to a few better shrubs at lower heights, a class in which gardeners like to be bold and risk the winter by choosing a few flamboyant evergreens of marginal hardiness. I cannot decide how warmly to praise the more fleeting shrubs, destroyed in 1981/2. Three of my favourites are silver Convolvulus cneorum, white Halimiocistus whose flowers have a brown central zone and the glorious variegated form of the yellow-flowered Coronilla, another shrub from the general family of Peas. All are strictly for beds below south walls with very gritty drainage. It took 1981/2 to kill them in my Oxfordshire garden. Instead, I will begin with a brilliant and proven hardy choice for late autumn which all new converts to gardening are advised to pick out as one of the best selections in this book. Others, I hope, will enjoy agreeing with me and sharing a story they may not know.

Commonly known as the Blue Plumbago, this wiry shrub with two to three foot stems and sheets of flower in September and October turns up in the lists as Ceratostigma willmottianum. It has a fine story to it and a claim to be the most beautiful addition to our gardens this century.

Along the banks of the Min River in western China, this brilliant blue flower was first found by G.F. Wilson in 1908. It had spread into thick clumps all over the sides and lower slopes of this dry and inhospitable gorge, lighting it up each autumn as if true blue speedwell had suddenly settled on the dry craters of the moon. No doubt it still grows there, blue and unseen since 1908, one of the most entrancing lost landscapes in the botanical world. Seeds were shaken off the bushes and brought home. Only two germinated, in the Essex garden of the formidable Miss Willmott after whom they were named. From these two plants, all our stock nowadays is almost certainly derived. Ceratostigma will multiply very easily from cuttings taken between late July and mid-September, so a branch or two would have been a better collection from the Min Valley. When you see those hard and clear cobalt-blue flowers, to which the late autumn butterflies, the Red Admirals and harmonious Painted Ladies, are drawn, you are sure to want it for yourself.

It is easily pleased. As in China, it likes to be dry. It must have a sunny place, enjoying the foot of a south or west wall, and mercifully, it is happy on lime. By late November it will look wretched. The wiry stems are browned by the frosts and you will wonder what to do with them. Do not cut them down. Tolerate them until mid-April, like the stems on a fuchsia, as they will help to protect the main plant if the frost is very sharp. If you cut them back too soon, you will hasten the young growth from the base in the first mild spell in early spring. A later frost can hit this too hard. Quite possibly, new young shoots will already be appearing all over the old stems by the time you come to cut them back. If they bother you, prune lightly and you will do no harm. But they will appear again from the base if you cut them hard.

In most gardens, two bushes of willmottianum will go far enough. You have to wait until September to see why you planted them, and you have to leave them a wide space. I like to interplant them with late tulips which flower before the bushes have spread widely. That does something for their earlier appearance. The pink nerines, of course, are a fine match later in the year and as bulbs they, too, will fit in well beside it. They enjoy the same dry place below a wall.

A small, carpeting variety called plumbaginoides is often sold in the shops, not least because anyone can propagate it. I have never had much joy from it. It ought to be so good, about a foot high, bright and clear blue above a mat of leaves which runs far and wide. When you plant it, it will often refuse to expand for a year or two. Then, suddenly, it is off and away. At this point I long to be rid of it. In most English gardens I suspect that it never finds enough warm sun during a long season and thus flowers sparsely. Its leaves turn a charming shade of red in October but are not enough by themselves. In France or America it is a splendid edging plant, under roses or along beds of shrubs. But I cannot recommend it here unless you are stuck with it already. So be warned.

A warning, too, about my next better shrub which is only hardy under a south wall in a winter which obeys the rules. You probably know the 'blue'-flowered shrubby Hebes and perhaps you are very fond of them. I put them in the second rank as a reliable filling between slower and better features. The exception is a beautiful one called hulkeana. I cannot bear to think that these words may be its funeral address, but I doubt if it will survive a very sharp spell on my high hill. Against a south wall, it bears long and loose spikes of lavender blue flower, to a height of four feet, at most. Beneath a house or in a large pot, it is a superb shrub, well worth the first class certificate which the RHS allotted to it some years ago. It is evergreen, but not in the drab and chunky style of commoner Hebes. I have seen it in full flower in Edinburgh, so it is not a hopeless long shot in this country. A south wall is essential, and gritty soil with lime is much to its taste. You would have to name it the incredible hulkeana once you had seen its elegant sprays of flower. Again, it is just the right sort of shrub against the wall of a town house's front garden where it can spill forwards over the paving or gravel. It roots easily from cuttings taken in late summer, so you can store it in a cool shed for the winter. I rank it with the tender orange-flowered Mimulus called glutinosus, brilliantly grown in the urns of Sissinghurst's red and yellow cottage garden. Together, they are connoisseurs' plants for decorative pots and urns. A smaller version of this Hebe, named fairfieldii, entranced me in the Edinburgh Botanic Gardens in 1974, where it grew freely in the open. If it is hardy there, it ought to be investigated. Only two feet high, it is not even in Hilliers' Manual of Shrubs, the bible for this chapter. It flowers profusely, bearing the same lavender blossom.

On a tougher note, I will end with my favourite garden Fuchsia. I leave you to take your pick of the many hybrid Fuchsias, perhaps with the help of K. Jennings and W. Miller's excellent guide, Growing Fuchsias. All the garden bedding sorts are good, but the proven Lena is particularly good and I owe my fondness for the old and neglected Brilliant, a scarlet-red and violet single form with an exceptionally long season, to the magisterial eye of my F.T. colleague, Arthur Hellyer. If you can find it, buy it at all costs. I only want to commend two better Fuchsias for their leaves. The form called Graf Witte spreads widely and throws up flower stems of the usual Fuchsia colours. It is almost hardy anywhere and will last a normal winter outdoors. Its merit is the yellow-green tone of its leaves, a cool accompaniment to borders of shrubs which have faded by late summer. The other is even better. Called magellanica versicolor, its name varies, but usually hangs onto its last part. The young leaves unfold to a mixture of ash-grey and rose-pink shading which I know in no other plant. They age to a pleasant cream-white and green, but as insects tend to eat the mature leaves, there is always younger growth showing on the stems. Perhaps, like me, you have reservations about Fuchsias when bedded out in a mass. This heavenly plant dispels them, as it combines so well with the other lowly shrubs I have named and with the blues and whites of the better border plants which follow. It is hardy in all winters except those which kill rose-bushes and ruin everything else.

Fuchsias root from cuttings with the utmost ease. Strip off a side shoot in late summer and leave its lower half in a glass of water. Without any soil, it will probably put out roots and be ready for potting up. Brilliant is not hardy outdoors, so you should cover yourself by taking these young replacements. You can reassure yourself with a charming tale of the Fuchsia's origins which many believe, perhaps rightly.

In the wild, most Fuchsias were natives of South America where their flowers are reported to have been found in the cave-drawings of a subject people of the Incas. They came to Europe's notice incidentally, when a medical team was sent to South America in the early 18th century to bring back supplies of quinine, that necessary cure for malaria. With the quinine-hunters went a Father Plumier who found and sketched a wild Fuchsia, naming it after the great German botanist and herbalist, Dr Fuchs. The truth of his drawings was questioned, at least until late in the century when a British sea-captain is known to have given a specimen Fuchsia to Kew on his return from a voyage to the southern hemisphere, proving its existence beyond doubt.

Around this same date, 1788, the Fuchsia was set on the path of big business. It is said, maybe incorrectly, that a shrewd London nurseryman called James Lee had heard of a strange new plant in a woman's window-box in Wapping. Visiting her, he found she had a Fuchsia, left with her by her husband when he returned from a South American voyage. For a few pounds, she parted with it, and before two years had passed Lee was able to offer rooted cuttings to his customers at £20 a time. New species arrived over the next 50 years to break his monopoly, but the Fuchsia was now recognised as easily propagated and well suited to British greenhouses and gardens. Following the legend of shrewd Mr Lee, you should not hesitate to ask for a cutting of any Fuchsia which attracts your notice. They root very quickly, often within a fortnight. That lovely versicolor is at home in southern Argentina. Who knows what may not turn up in the window-box of widows, supplied from the recent British task-force?

Chapter Four

Better Border Plants

Beneath the better trees and among the better shrubs, I come now to better herbaceous and border plants. Here, if anywhere, I have to be selective. They have so many different uses, as a filling against weeds, a comparison to shrub roses and as a planned group of shapes and colours in their own right. The alert eye can see so much in them. I do not intend to write yet more on the virtues of aquilegias, bearded irises or show delphiniums. Many others have said it all already. I have nothing to add on border poppies, except my favour for the white flowered varieties and for a flight of fancy by Ruskin, among his rhetoric on flowers.

> "Gather a green poppy bud, break it open and unpack the poppy. The whole flower is there complete in size and colour, all packed so closely that the fine silk of the petals is crushed into a million shapeless wrinkles. When the flower opens, it seems a deliverance from torture; the two imprisoning green leaves are shaken to the ground, the aggrieved corolla smooths itself in the sun and comforts itself as it can, but it remains visibly crushed and hurt to the end of its days."

Those days, as gardeners know, end all too soon. By July, the poppies disappear, unless you grow the good double-flowered annual from seed. Otherwise, the poppy forces you to plan, both to hide its gaps and set off its fiery colours. Here, you are free, wondering how best to begin.

If you want to lay a better plan for your borders I suggest you set about it at the end of August. The trees are still in leaf, so their shape will not mislead you. There are enough flowers around to help you match colours and heights and you can sit outside while you ponder the problems on site. When you have finally made up

SYRINGA VULGARIS: *LILAC.*

ROSA CENTIFOLIA: *OLD CABBAGE ROSE.*

HOSTA VENTRICOSA: *PLANTAIN LILY.*

SPARAXIS TRICOLOR: *IXIA*.

your mind, the nurseries will not have sold out of the key plants in your scheme. There is much advice worth giving: the importance of shade and broken light, the need for a firm ground plan, the merit in deciding what you like and growing plenty of it. Try to work to a colour scheme, blue and silver, crimson and white, coral pink and fresh yellow-green, gold and yellow in a mass. Gardening is not just an art of growing the plants which you want. It is also a chance to match their colours, contrast their shapes and seasons and to use two different varieties to add up to something much more impressive than their sum. The larger the garden, the more you notice the use of colour in its plantings. Small gardens can span all the colours of the rainbow, running them into one another in such a profusion that no earth shows. In a small space it is easier, too, to keep a continuity from week to week. One or two features will dominate it, while the rest are past their best. But placing and planning are endless subjects, and in a larger garden they are crucial.

How do you know which flowers will combine calmly? Colours, in season, can be tested quite simply in combination. Pick a flower off something which you are considering for a new group and match it beside a clump of the neighbour which you have in mind. If that sounds too obvious to be worth suggesting, I would add that few gardeners ever think of trying this old tip. It saves a conjectural move, and another a year later, when the colours are found to clash.

Before you become an artist, there is a much more basic matter to discuss. You must learn how to use thugs. If you do not wish to be a prisoner to your garden, use the plants' own *force majeure* to overpower it. Trump one weed with a stronger one, but make sure that yours is easier on the eye. I will begin, therefore, with a bouquet of good words for the plain old catmint. It is not often that one hears anything good about this plant, but I cannot see why it is not top of every nursery's list in these days of limited time and labour. I would not contemplate a weekend or cottage garden without it. It puts paid to all those banks and blank patches which would otherwise go down to awkward grass and discontented Berberis. For beginners, I would only say that common catmint spreads forwards for a yard or so and that it can be trimmed back hard after flowering. It is thus the perfect plant for use with a modern weedkiller. Before the big spread begins, you can spray the earth between the plants with Weedex in early April. No weed will then germinate for two months or more, by which time the wide mats of the catmint have locked together and excluded them. A few plants can be spaced widely and divided into many more. I like the lavender-mauve flowers as much as the sharp scent in the ash-grey leaves. In July, catmint is the better for a thorough dead-heading, which encourages a second autumn season. For a dry bank, it is a godsend, at its best when used as the foundation-planting in a scheme which has room for one or two large shrubs among it at wide intervals. I have used it well with the strong Rubus tridel Benenden, that lovely May-flowering shrub with round white flowers and fresh stems and leaves. In the pretty garden at Kings Chantry, Binsted, Hants, a sea of catmint edges the hedging and double border, allowing a busy two acres to be kept by one man. Be sure that there are no perennial weeds before you put the catmint in. After one year, plants a yard or more apart will be touching each other in the weeds' season and nothing will come between them.

On a smaller scale, I turn now to the Godfather of all garden thugs, a plant for problems anywhere. Most of you know the green-yellow flowered Ladies Mantle, or Alchemilla, but there are still many gardens which are too much for their owners and contain not an example of this rampant beauty. I am overrun with it, so that early July is a season for yellow-green rivers of flower, falling down the slopes from the doorsteps where the first seedlings now begin. I well recall a fine photograph in the book by Graham Thomas which put ground-cover plants on the map. It showed a garden and a lily-pond under a caption of 'Alchemilla in complete control'. To my innocent eye twelve years ago it looked rather unlikely. But ten plants or so of this handsome menace have grown to take me over too. Eighteen inches high, and absolutely weed-proof, the Ladies Mantle is best in a slightly damp site. The clumps of fresh green leaves are at their finest if you cut them back hard after flowering, when the flowers are turned to a stale yellow, the seeds are preparing to catapult into your best rose-bed and the stems are falling flat from their central crown. An August trimming reminds the plant of its manners and returns it to a neat clump of velvety young leaves before autumn. The job is good, too, for your morale as you cut out armfuls of unwanted stems at very little effort. As a controller of excess space, the Ladies Mantle is still without equal. But if you do not know about this August cut, you will find that Ladies Mantle seeds itself by the hundred wherever you want it least. Its central stock of roots is tough and woody and the young seedlings develop stubborn roots very rapidly. No thug grows without any bother on your part, but the bother with Alchemilla mollis is usually concentrated into a day's pleasant cutting. The Ladies Mantle must be trimmed in order to look its best.

So, too, must another fine menace which desperate gardeners tend to forget. On a lime or chalk soil, the plain ruby-red Valerian of our escarpments and downland is a dry soil's equal for the Ladies Mantle. Again, it has loose stems which spill prettily forwards and throw their seed everywhere. You see it in stone walls all over the Cotswolds, but it is just as good as an informal edging beside a path or down a bank. The white form is far the prettiest, though you will have to grow your own from cuttings, as no nurseryman sells a true white. Valerian is not such a thug as some, because its roots do not run so widely. But on clean ground, its mass of stems give weeds no chance.

These thugs, so far, have been plants for bigger gardens or loose, informal groups, for rivers of flower and cascades of impenetrable stems. Your smaller plot, you are telling yourself, would be better off without them. If so, you need the harassed gardener's secret weapon, the family of Cranesbills, or true perennial Geraniums.

These are one of the best tricks for better gardening. If you crumple their leaves, they are often pleasantly aromatic. Their flowers last for weeks in pretty shades of pink, blush-white and rich violet-blue. Their clumps exclude all future weeds and divide into hundreds. They are a quiet, well-shaped background or under-planting in the few months when they are not in flower. They persist for years without needing any division for their health, rather than your convenience. Anyone can grow them and there are two varieties, especially, which will flourish in dry shade. So many plants are said to do this, but turn out to be useless, that I ought to have printed this virtue in huge capital letters. Of the two most useful varieties, the low-growing pink Geranium endressii has won me round, because it can be trained in any direction, up, out, down or sideways, without ever letting a weed through it. It is the small-flowered one, which goes on producing pink flowers in the unusual shade of a strawberry ice cream. It will grow anywhere, dry shade included. It is not a tidy plant but it saves hours of time under shrubs and in front of shrub-borders. It goes well with the smaller blue Campanulas which form huge mats if left alone.

There are two better varieties on the general market and I am pressed to tell the difference between them. Wargrave Variety commemorates a fine Home Counties' garden, A.T. Johnson a fine gardening columnist. Either is excellent, because its flowers should be a brighter shade of salmon pink without any tinge of mauve or rose. Begin with one plant and multiply it by the hundred from cuttings or divisions. Endressii trails prettily between and beneath tall shrubs and allows its open pink flowers to show naturally through the mass of leaves.

I cannot decide whether I rate another Cranesbill, called macrorrhizum, above this one. It is equally tough at a height of a foot, but it stays as a clump, not a trailing carpet. The flowers have one main season in June and are a delicate shade of pinkish-lilac, standing like open drops of water on the top of their stems. This is the plant which I use among my Ladies Mantle and trust to grow wherever growth is possible. It will put up a show in the dry gaps between a tall tree's roots. There are several good forms, a white one which I recommend strongly, a variegated one which is not worthwhile and the robust Ingwersen's variety whose rose-pink flowers are better than the type's. This is a well-behaved but essential plant. So, too, is the classic Geranium called grandiflorum whose showers of flower appear in June and light up those cheerful Edwardian paintings of pergolas and herbaceous borders, immortalised in high summer. Its stems cover the ground, for the leaves come on long supports. The colour is a brilliant violet-blue for a fortnight, a sight I would never want to miss. The clumps, again, are impenetrable and will grow thickly between better shrubs while they are deciding to establish themselves. If you cannot be bothered to cut off this Geranium's vast yearly growth, the next season's shoots will swamp the dead stems by early May. My father has had masses of it for twenty years and never divided it, except to give me ever more lumps of it. It is as good as the day it was planted.

If you want something smaller and are willing to risk a serious menace, you should entertain a small spurge for dry shade. Visitors seem to like it when they see it between my flight of garden steps. Euphorbia cyparissias runs with its roots and gives nothing else a chance. It is nine inches high, feathery-leaved with acid-yellow flowers in May and turns to brilliant yellow colours when it dies in late autumn. The colour varies, so buy a plant in flower, if possible. One will give you a hundred within two years. It will also fill any corners under tall climbing roses or between shrubs which are otherwise open to weeds. It is emphatically not a plant for a civilised border, but it will grow under a tree. So will the toughest spurge which is fit for a garden, the useful Euphorbia robbiae. This flowers in the majority of months and is a handsome evergreen wherever you give it a chance. It is gracious enough to agree to grow in the darkest shade and most miserable London gloom. In happier sites, it is a finer plant, a very dark green in its narrow leaf and a contrasting lime-green in its characteristic heads of flower. These earn the popular name of frog's spawn, because they are born in a bunch of separate, rounded 'eyes'. Beneath a clean and airy north wall, this indestructible spurge looks charming in spring, better than a plant for places where nothing else will grow. It multiplies like a weed, so you only need to pay for one parent plant. About eighteen inches high and wide, it is far more distinguished than its usual home suggests.

Between the creeping Cranesbills and the spreading catmint, you ought to find the proper thug to be your partner. If you want something huge for beds in rough grass or corners where you first mow in early July, you should also consider the giant Kale, or Crambe cordifolia. I love this plant's tall stems of flower, set with several puffs of spread-out 'baby's breath' in a shade of pure white. They reach six feet or more above the huge clump of cabbage-leaves which turn yellow and start to decay after flowering. An irremovably thuggish tap root, like a parsnip's, supports the whole construction and as the Crambe has flowered by 7th July, you can cut off all its leaves with your motorised scythe when finally levelling the daffodils and cow parsley. If the tap root survives, the plant will appear none the worse for this hasty departure. By late June it is on the way out and the leaves like to rot after midsummer. In the back of a big bed or in clumps among your orchard, this monstrous kale is a very exciting plant. Every piece of the main root will sprout and grow away, giving nothing else much chance around it. One plant, in June, has a diameter of a square yard, so a few Kales soon block out the weeds. Its worst enemy is its English name, for its spire of white flowers is far removed from those fields of winter greens. No soil is too bad for it.

Once you have settled your thugs in position, you are ready for more elegant gangsters, of which the most fashionable, though not the fastest, are the many forms of Hosta. These are the plants with big succulent leaves, green, grey-green or variegated in many different styles. Americans call them Plantain Lilies and if you imagine a plantain with fleshy leaves, you are near to picturing a good Hosta. They are popular plants and in the right place and varieties, I think they are magnificent. But they are seldom seen at their best, so I have views on them. There is hardly a hosta which shows up well in sun and a dry soil. They will flower, but the leaves look wretched. They like to be heavily fed and manured. A starved hosta is more common than a satisfied one. The sight of its half-hearted leaves will make you wonder why I give it space. Before you plant new stock, dig some rotted manure round it and top-dress it in its first spring with yet more manure. Feed it thereafter with liquid manure whenever you can spare the time. The richer the soil, the more luxuriantly most of the best varieties will develop their lovely leaves. I have proved this by an extreme experiment. Last year, I built up a badly-drained bed to a height of two feet and raised it with the richest possible material. I used bag upon bag of finely shredded pig manure. It cost me very little from a nearby pig-farmer who shreds his slurry to the fineness of a John Innes Compost. Emboldened by its obvious strength, I packed it in by the hundredweight, three-fifths pig manure to two-fifths of my heavy old loam. You are not a gardener until you have untied a festering bag of this shredded manure and mixed it up as top-dressing. It goes green in a trice. It stinks like a score of Black Berkshires rummaging around your lawn. It gives my hands a temporary rash and my earthworms the excitement of a lifetime. Within weeks, shoals of long worms writhe in and out of its lumps, pink, fat and sleek like well-oiled Loch Ness monsters. For the first few days, keep the windows of your house firmly shut. The smell has that richness which lodges, like catarrh, half way down your throat.

Is this the better gardening you hoped to discover? For Hostas, indeed, it is. No doubt this mixture breaks all the rules and begins with a sky-high level of nitrogen until the rain starts to wash it down. But Hostas frolic in it like fat piglets. Their leaves glisten with a new depth of green or yellow variegation. They look cool, luscious and very, very smug. No proportion of manure, I conclude, is too high for these princely plants. In their early years the leaves of a Hosta are far less impressive than at maturity. They are at their peak now in public gardens of the National Trust where you can see them after the fashion for mass Hosta beds in the 1960s. Mature Hostas are the hardiest of plants, despite the tropical look to them. Be sure that you protect them against slugs by ringing them with slug pellets. Otherwise, the leaves will be chewed into needless holes, and after two slow years, you will have no idea of their mature possibilities. When established, Hostas, too, are no mean thugs. Not even groundelder can fight its way through their thick core of roots, like a matted lily-of-the-valley's. The leaves are not evergreen, but in the growing season, they block out all competitors and stand nobly among bigger drifts of pink cranesbill or blue catmint. Hostas and beds of old-fashioned roses are a famous combination. Familiar though they are, I think that they remain excellent company. The Hostas' young leaves brighten up the beds before the roses' main crop. They flower simultaneously. The Hostas' lilac white flowers are not conspicuous by themselves, but they are set off by the similar mauves and crushed purples of good Bourbon and Gallica roses. Afterwards, their big leaves and thick clumps of impenetrable roots block out the weeds. In autumn, many varieties turn a bright yellow before retiring below ground. This autumn colour is wrongly neglected.

The most spectacular, to my eye, is still the huge glaucous-leaved Sieboldiana elegans. Bought from a conscientious nursery, the name elegans carries weight. The leaves are larger and more deeply ribbed. On any scale, they are big and bold. But they are also a superb shade of blue-grey, a truly glaucous plant. The lilac white flowers are in harmony with this cool colour in the leaf. There is a brilliant use of it among white flowers and grey leaves in the white garden at Sissinghurst Castle, Kent. If you can find room for a big block of it in a half-shaded shrub border, you will be rewarded with a more lasting feature than any passing flower. No weed has a chance among its huge leaves. But you must plant it initially in clean ground.

American breeders have let loose many new crosses on the top end of the market, some of which are less interesting than their publicity implies. Personally, I cannot see the charm in the new American crosses called Honeybells and Royal Standard, raised in Connecticut. Each has green leaves which are a black mark in my book, as the value of a hosta, to my eye, is the lighter colour in the variegated and glaucous forms. The American pair will flower freely, however, and are both slightly scented. I would not bother with them. Instead, I would watch for the newest Frances Williams, whose broad blue-grey leaves are marked with cream-fawn. This variation on plain Sieboldiana caught my eye last year at an RHS summer show. Bressingham Nurseries, Diss, Norfolk, list it at £3 a plant, but it ought to be cheaper soon if you can wait. There are several other slow-growing rarities still on the margins of the market, though shown and decorated at the Wisley hosta trials as long ago as 1973. Halcyon sometimes turns up and is a very worthwhile buy. It was bred on The Plantsmen's Dorset nursery and is a selected form, I believe, of one tardiana which was itself a surprising cross between two varieties, one of which was the big glaucous elegans. The attractions of Halcyon are the pointed shape and the glaucous tone of the leaf, tapered like a heart. It is not too large, and when well fed it does not show any brown spotting late in the season. My plant of Halcyon is a lone specimen, but it is now nearing its best. Not a fast grower, it is one, nonetheless, I commend to you and to any nurseryman who wants to follow up the Award of Merit given it by the RHS, and the wholesale stock still offered by Jim Archibald at Buckshaw Gardens, Sherborne.

Among variegations, I consider three to be above all others. Fortunei picta, or albo-picta, ages to a respectable colour, but in late May, the season of Chelsea Show, its young yellow-green leaves are irresistibly fresh. For three consecutive years, the Financial Times won Gold Medals at Chelsea for its open-air gardens and every year, we cast far and wide for the biggest possible Hostas to give body to our instant borders. They would arrive trussed up in sacking, straining the nets by the weight of their huge clumps of roots. Albo-picta was always the star of the show, for Hostas move as willingly as foxgloves, even when in open leaf. This yellow and green form mixes superbly with the acid yellow of spurge or the clear blue of forget-me-nots and blue-eyed Mary. The cool lime-yellow runs through the centre of the leaf and gradually tones down to a fresh green edge. I cannot have too much of this obliging plant, a first choice for a damp or shaded place in a town garden. If I were starting again, I would group it among lily of the valley in a raised bed near to the eye and nose.

As a tougher and quicker plant, the variety still generally sold as Thomas Hogg is excellent. This is the narrowly white-edged hosta whose green leaf is clear but not special. After two or three years, however, I find that it thickens out into an impenetrable mat and puts paid to all surface weeds in narrow beds below a wall. It is not the most subtle hosta, but it is bright, reliable and easily divided. Thomas Hogg is one for the busy gardener, though its name still covers some varying forms. The king of hostas with yellow markings is the slow ventricosa variegata. Opinions divide on this one, but I think it worth every penny of the high price at which Hilliers of Winchester will sell you it in a true form. The wide margin of golden yellow turns in towards the centre of the leaf and stays fresh for a long while. The leaves are large and bold, as good as a spring flower in their own right. Among a bewildering mass of names, this big one is worth holding onto, neither green-leaved nor small and slow, but the boldest among those with a gold margin.

Feed your hostas then, and give them time. At first they seem unlikely plants to cover a square yard at a density of only three plants to the area. But the leaves improve with age and expand with the mat of roots. By 1986, your hostas would draw the eye of any visitor in months when the leaves are showing above ground.

Hostas and hardy Geraniums should take care of most open spaces, but you might like a less familiar gangster which has just come on to the market. Called Strobilanthes, it sounds suitably sinister. But in a quiet way, it has been making a mark among connoisseurs. It has gone beyond the point where its owners show it and assume that nobody else knows the name of the two-foot high bush of lavender-blue flowers, formed like a border Salvia's into a terminal lip. It is a rather dusky flower, persistent but not spectacular. The plant grows into a well formed clump from its dense surface roots and lasts in flower for two months. You can divide it easily and rely on it to block out weeds. I like to see it beside the palest and prettiest of the so-called Knotweeds, listed less rudely under their official name of Polygonum. The good variety here is called campanulatum, a two-foot high plant with pale rose-pink little flowers at the ends of its stems and ribbed leaves. This bell-flowered Knotweed will grow in the dry shade of a bed at the foot of a north wall. It takes a year or two to gather speed, but after a slow start it will spread conveniently. Neither it nor Strobilanthes is a bold plant, but they do their job solidly in any soil and go well together as a pair. Bressingham Nurseries will sell you a young plant of each.

Picturing these gangsters amongst the thugs, I feel that they need something bold and arching to set them off. It ought to have a good leaf and look tidy throughout the summer. Here and elsewhere I would consider the better forms of grass. Grass, after all, grows all summer and exhausts us where we least want it. It comes in all manner of varieties, many of which behave themselves and look handsome throughout the year. I will begin with a small variety and work up to the finest, six feet or more in height.

For a low golden grass, I know nothing half so good as E.A. Bowles's golden grass, or Milium aureum. In a damp half-shaded place this is so good that you need look no further. It is not evergreen, but the light texture of its leaf is charming throughout the year, a bright canary yellow which shades to butter-yellow according to season and position. It is only as high as its central tuft of bright leaves, but it flowers at a height of a foot. Its only rival is a new grass in the garden centres which I tried by mistake and now dislike. Carex Evergold is helped by its publicity more than its appearance. This relation of the sedge-grasses is a small plant for an edging where it keeps its leaves throughout the year. But it looks like some late Victorian house-plant taking a breather from life in a glass bottle. The dark green leaves are thin and have a wide canary yellow stripe down them. They are bright enough in winter, but texture and appearance are against them. I much prefer Bowles's golden form which you can verify in Bowles's corner in Wisley Gardens. Milium divides easily into many young pieces and I like it more as a clump than a straight edging. In nature it likes a damp and shaded site and in the garden, these conditions bring out the brightness in leaf and flower-stem. I remember a fearful advertisement in which a schoolboy stared at his cornflakes as they fell into his dish and kept repeating 'They're all golden'. Of course they were not. But Milium almost is, the grass which Kelloggs never used, a plant whose flowers resemble those of a wild oat, dyed a seductive shade of golden yellow.

Working back into the border, you can continue to plant wild oats and prosper. At a height of two or three feet when in flower, you can count on the metallic blue-grey stem, leaf and outline of Helicotrichon sempervirens. This is a plant which garden centres would want to call 'ever-blue', like some of my friends' jokes. Behind the greenhouses at Kew, you can study a recent border of garden grasses and in its high-brow company, you may agree with me that this Blue Oat-grass is among the best. It sends up arching stems with heads of pretty flowers in early summer, feathered like an oat's. You can fit it into almost any border, from whose front a group of these flower-stems will bend elegantly forwards. When they are gone, you still have the steel-blue leaves, rather better than the small tufted Festuca which is thrust on us by landscape architects. This plant is cheap, easy and original. If you place your wild oats carefully, in the garden too you will be pleased to live with the results.

These are modest grasses when set beside my favourite in the entire family. I first saw the beauty of the large Stipa gigantea on a raised bed in that lamented retail source of rare plants, the Plantsmen's nursery in Dorset. My brother then chose it for the centre of long raised beds in his adventuous garden near Newbury and within a year, it appreciated the well-drained soil and arched up to a height of five feet. Two years later, I saw it again, placed brilliantly at the top of a flight of steps in the Voorspuys' beautiful garden at Folkington Place, Polegate, Sussex. It is an emphatic plant, good in company, best in isolation where you can appreciate the line of its red-brown stems which arch over with pale buff flowers. As soon as your plants arrive, you should plant them in a light, open soil. I have learnt to plant these and other grasses in late spring for safety and I advise you to buy Stipa in containers from Sherrards of Newbury in April. I killed off my first bare-rooted batch by leaving them in a polythene bag for a week after unpacking them. They hate to begin to dry out. I can picture an elegant planting of wild geraniums and catmint broken up by four or five well-spaced clumps of this magnificent plant. It will also fill up the back and centre of a broad border, but its outline ought not to be lost among too many competitors. The flowers are elegant on their stems, but their colour is merely a shade of brown.

I come now, as you may have feared, to the giant Pampas grass and begin with the question which intrigues all tidy and over-destructive gardeners: when should your Pampas grass be set on fire? There are some who would say as soon as possible, as soon as you find that one comes with your new house. They see it as a curiosity, on a par with a monkey puzzle tree and no better suited to the small space into which it is usually cramped. I disagree. Their admirers burn them, it is true, but only in spring when the old clumps are better for the removal of their top growth and the dead stems of their plumes. A benevolent bonfire helps them into the new season. If you see a man put a match to a Pampas in March, he is not setting out to destroy it. Pampas grass, my nearest catalogue remarks, will tolerate full coastal exposure and survive on sand dunes and in brackish swamps. This odd mixture of tastes is true. By the sea, it looks rather too predictable, a stiff shape and dingy leaf which reminds you that the seaside is beset by cold winds. In a damp place, beside water, it can be spectacular, but you must be sure that it fits in with your surrounding shrubs and hardwoods. I can see no point in a small Pampas grass. There is one which is praised as a 'dwarf', but it bears thick plumes on short stems and is a dirty grey-white. It makes no impact. Pampas grass should stand in a big clump as thick and tall as possible. In the great natural gardens of Sheffield Park, it is well placed beside water in which its plumes are reflected in autumn while the trees begin to colour round them. Beside water, I have also admired the combination of a tall Pampas grass and the largest red hot poker, sold as Kniphofia Prince Igor. This poker is a strong red-orange and reaches a height of seven feet if it is in the damp soil which makes it happy. Red hot pokers are another subject on which I part company with fussy gardeners. I think they are splendid, though Prince Igor and a Pampas grass might make refined taste shudder. See them before you misjudge them: the Pampas grass should only be a form called Cortaderia Sunningdale Silver. Its plumes are a fine silvery white, not the grey of a dirty squirrel's tail which emerges from unnamed forms. When happy, it is a massive plant, as fine as a tree or shrub in your front lawn or down a clearing in your wilderness. I would only suggest if for the biggest and broadest borders, but a clump there can be dramatic.

For the rest of us, there is some scope lower down the family. I expect to live to see ever more plants coming our way from New Zealand and Australia whose floras have still hardly dawned on Europe's gardeners. Meanwhile, New Zealand breeders have given us a bright new Pampas called Gold Band. Its leaves are dense but thin, and arch out into a bright clump of gold and green. This is too bright and vulgar unless you plan how to use it. I think I would like to see clumps of Gold Band in those pretty and fashionable borders of lime-green and yellow flowers and leaves. It joins the cut-leaved golden elder and the golden orange blossom as a strong clump of gold-yellow which can be toned down with cool lime-green and whites. I expect we will see it among the golden heathers and blue-grey conifers in small front gardens where its size and strong colour are overpowering. It only looks tolerable with its own kind, a plant for bright gold borders where it can dominate the planting. Its plumes of flower shoot up to six feet. Small plants cost about £2.50 each from Bressingham Nurseries.

Between the Pampas and the Ladies Mantle, you have a solid grounding in the garden's necessary gangsters. This mafia is useful to everybody, if only as a filling between slow-growing shrubs. While it fights off the weeds, then, I will work backwards through my plans for a better border, starting in the front row and soaring up to a height of eighteen feet, according to others' records, for the back line. There is so much worth choosing, but some choices are better value than others. I will limit myself to a few of the best. We can then stand back and reflect on colours, useful accompaniments and ways of giving a border body during its early years or after a hard winter's damage.

Feline in my tastes, I will begin once again with a relation of the catmint. Late in the season, on a dry soil, a plant called Calamintha is a fine choice for the border's front row, for the gaps in a path or a stretch of paving. It is a small relation of catmint, but it flowers abundantly from August onwards in a pale shade of grey-lilac. It grows freely in half-shade and will flower on stems some nine inches high, borne in great profusion. Indeed, I can think of no plant except bindweed which flowers so freely from such a small root-stock. Bees go wild for its sharp scent, cattier than catmint and too strong for my family when it lingers on me after a morning's weeding in its bed. Calamintha is a fine companion for big groups of scarlet Penstemons, those saviours of a late summer border which otherwise collapses into nothing but yellow. It will last at its best for about five years, so you must grow on cuttings for young replacements. A wet winter will damage it on heavy soils, but otherwise, it is an astonishingly free-flowering plant which makes a bushy edge to a path, terrace, bank or border from its first year onwards.

So, too, does the deceptively vigorous Gypsophila, or Baby's Breath, in its lowest form, called repens Rosy Veil. This is one of my favourites, for it exhales a great cloud of the tiny pinkish white flowers of Baby's Breath at a height of about nine inches. The plant seems very small until early July, when its trailing stems seem to spread overnight into a light, fragile tangle. This covers up to a square yard of ground. It breathes out a great puff of flowers which last through late July and August in any sunny place. When flowering, they make a vast cushion, well suited to the end of a dry wall. They revel in chalk and lime.

If these flowers are too light and airy for interest throughout the season, you should consider the beauty of leaves to be found in the smaller forms of Iris. I have nothing new to say on the bigger border varieties, except that I love them, for all their brief season. The smaller sorts will crop up in my alpine chapter. But there are three easy forms with different tastes which, between them, would distinguish the front of any flower bed. The most elusive is the fine evergreen variegation on the native Gladwin iris, sold as Iris foetidissima. This Gladwin iris bears miserable flowers among its leaves and shows seeds with none of the Gladwin's glamour. It is a useful plant only because its leaves will last the winter in a shaded bed, just the place where you want the lighter line of ivory on its darker green leaf. It is well worth the hunt if you are as bored as I am with the bergenia, a standard choice in dank and shaded sites which need a indestructible plant with bold leaves. Beth Chatto, White Barn House, Elstead Market, Colchester, Essex can usually send stock of this Iris. You probably know the plain green form which is notorious for its red and yellow seeds in winter and the strong scent of roast beef when you crush its leaves. About two feet high, a clump of this divides quite easily, though the variegated form is less vigorous. Beth Chatto writes enthusiastically of her improved form of the plain old Gladwyn, which she has called Citrina. It sounds brighter in seed and flower, but it has yet to mature with me, so I suspend judgement.

There is no doubt about the toughness of our native flag iris, nor about the reliable charm of its yellow-striped form. This likes a damp place and in nature, it spreads beside ponds on that deceptive no man's land where the deep black soil spills over unwary boots. Some years ago, we showed a good group of this iris in the F.T.'s garden for the Chelsea show. It drew much comment and gained many new admirers, if only for an afternoon. Nurseries sell it as Iris pseudacorus variegatus. There are no difficulties to it, but you must not allow it to sit for too long in a dry place. There are various striped reeds and grasses on the market, which find their way into the edges of small garden ponds because nobody has bothered to think of anything better. This tall, striped flag iris is a better buy, especially as an emphatic plant for a small pond's outline. Keep an open eye for its first show of young leaves. Until early June, they are in their prime, the equal of any flowering iris in the family.

I reserve the best buy until last. The striped form of Iris pallida is often on sale nowadays and its grey-green leaves are striped up the middle with a line of cream-white. The Gladwyn grows in dry shade, the flag in damp places, but the small pallida, scarcely a foot high, is an Iris for the front of a sunny border. My visitors make straight for it, whether or not it is showing its subtle lavender blue flowers against the vivid leaves. Books claim that it is vulnerable to wet soils, but I feel I have refuted them by placing it among my luxuriant Hostas in that wet and heavy bed of shredded pig-dung. I believe now that it will grow anywhere. By September, the leaves turn brown on their upper half and ought to be removed. Until then, it is as bright as any flower and would go well with pinks, violas, gypsophila or calamintha. The bigger the clump, the bolder the effect. In 1977, I began with three plants, but by dividing them in mid-July, I had 50 within three years. The parents are too expensive nowadays for you to buy a clump in full.

Cheaper still are the best two border plants at this height which I have ever grown. They are the two blue forms of the common Flax, or Linum, perenne and narbonnense. The former changes colour in my garden as the day proceeds. When I go off to work, its small saucer shaped flowers are a deep blue. When I return, they have faded in the sunshine to sky blue, before shedding their petals and opening another round of their endless buds on the morrow. Narbonnense remains a darker blue throughout the day. Each form is excellent so long as it stands in full sun where the flowers open widely. Flax is a hopeless plant in shade as it never opens its buds. The shape of the plant is slender and upright, so it will fit into almost any grouping. I use it as an inter-planting among white roses where it seeds itself quite happily. It makes a long stream of pure blue flowers down the border at a height of scarcely two feet. The last time I called a plant fool-proof and gave it to a colleague, it promptly died on him and he felt his intelligence had been insulted. I think the blue Flax is nearly impossible to kill in any sunny and open soil. After flowering, it does not live long, but it seeds itself profusely and you can always grow on more young plants. The seeds germinate for anybody and need no heat. Sown in July, they will flower brilliantly in the following year. From May till late June, these flaxes are in their first flush above their thin stems and wiry, invisible leaves. When they falter, you should cut back their stems to half their length and in August they will flower for a second time. Seedsmen usually list perenne, but I wish they would bring back its companion as its deeper blue flowers are even more beautiful. The plants are sold by Broadwell Nurseries, Moreton-in-Marsh, Glos. Last year, I visited the huge gardens at Hatfield House, Hertfordshire, planted and richly re-planted over the past thirty years. Among many fine plants, the finest was a self-sown example of Linum perenne lodged in the brick of a flight of steps beside an old Tudor brick wall. Its silky petals shimmer in the breeze and when the wind blows, the plant seems to tremble with modest pleasure. Each one grows about a foot and a half high and as much wide. They come so easily from seed that you can plan for hundreds.

On this high note, I will leave the border's front row, dropping only a passing good word for all forms of the sprawling herbaceous Potentillas, especially old Glory of Nancy whose grey strawberry leaves match the semi-double flowers of scrambled orange and crimson and the full-double crimson Monsieur Rouillard. Their long stems trail over a wide area and are far more willing to flower in a poor, stony soil in full sun. Everybody now grows the shrubby yellow Potentilla, but these border forms are subtler, less tall and almost as willing to flower for three whole months. They are very valuable friends, but should never be allowed to frolic in pig-manure and dodge the business of flowering.

Spilling into the front of a sunny bed or straying back through the middle, the recent forms of hardy Agapanthus are my unhesitating first choice. I have lost none of those I mention in the 1981/2 winter, although I never covered them with straw. In August, they are spectacular, never better than in the Hampshire gardens round Winchester where the late Lewis Palmer chose the hardiest strain. You should no longer be nervous of them, as they have become as easy as a border iris after the efforts of post-war breeders. Above all, they spring up from seed, so you can all afford a long river of their blue and white flowers. These Agapanthus seeds are unmistakeable. They are firm, black and easily collected from the round flower-heads as they begin to droop and turn yellowish-white. You should save them in any dry airtight container and sow them next spring in a box of light, well-drained compost. They germinate freely, looking slightly like young onions if you are not wholly familiar with them. Prick them out as if they were bedding plants, moving them into boxes two inches or so apart, if you are growing a mass of them, or into pots if you are only growing one or two. In the autumn, when they die down to those odd clumps of fleshy roots, you should line them out in a corner where you do not mind their slow progress for another year. Move them into their permanent home in the following spring, the second after germination. They will flower that autumn, but they will be at their best in the next year. This is a routine process; I describe it only as a reminder of how easy it is. The hardiness of these South African flowers is now beyond question. They dislike wet in their crowns, which rot too easily, and this may collect more freely in any covering of straw and so forth which you put on them. Otherwise, they like an open, light soil, preferably not clay. They must face the sun, south or west, and are at their best, physically and aesthetically, below a south-facing wall. If you do happen to buy a few mature plants do not be puzzled by their trails of fleshy roots and the unobtrusive apex from which the growths will appear.

Spread the roots out neatly and plant so that the top is just visible at ground-level. Supermarkets have begun to sell stocks in polythene packets for spring planting. These are quite a sound buy, as most of them do not object to drying out before you plant them. But your own seedlings are cheaper and more fun. Older plants are infinitely divisible.

What is the choice? You must have some white ones among your blues. As long as you start with some named white stock you can be virtually certain that some of your seedlings will repeat the colour. The one to buy is the hardy Campanulatus albus, which is tough and never a trouble. For the rest, I am keen on various named forms of the blue campanulati, not least the dark and free-flowering weillighi, now sold by the brand name Isis to suggest an Oxford depth to its colouring. There are other selected sorts, particularly a softer blue called Profusion which lives up to its name. But as good a plan as any is to sow seed of all available varieties, especially the famous Headbourne hybrids, which were raised with patience in post-war Hampshire. These are the varieties which made the Agapanthus's name. They are thoroughly hardy and compact and span a good range of blues. I suspect they are selected seedlings, not true hybrids, as the Agapanthus seems to vary, not to intermarry. The older sort which used to grow in tubs is now known correctly as praecox. Orthodoxy has it that this is not strictly hardy, yet I still have divisions from plants in a tub now some 20 years old which stand the winters below a south wall without protection. Their flower-heads, to my eye, are a little bigger and better and thus worth preserving. But they may be a variation of the type, for variation is the greatest pleasure of seedling agapanthi. You are never quite sure that you may not have raised a winner yourself. From my last batch I had whites, sky-blues, dark blues, milk-blues which I chucked out, and a startling group of variations, the leaves of which were blotched in the centres with a cream-white splash which comes and goes with age. The latter are not unknown, but they have come to me quite by chance. You must watch, then, for the first flowers on your young plants, usually in the second year, and choose any you like from their range. Wistful gardeners sometimes remark how they wish that they, too, could discover some new variety and give their name to it. Seedling agapanthi seem to me the easiest way of raising your own home favourite, something you can then perpetuate by division. The more seeds you sow, the more selective you can be. The agapanthus's name must mean, I presume, the 'flower of love'. That does not seem to me too strong when its streams of true blue flower-heads are everywhere in a patient seed-collector's August garden.

You are beginning to realise that I have a weakness for blue-flowered plants. I like blue and primrose yellow, blue with white and silver leaves, or lilac, lavender and nurseryman's 'blue', that shade of violet or pale mauve, among flowers of a dusky shade of pink. So, obviously, I love Campanulas of any kind. But while I brace myself to write of this great family, I will speak up for two harmonious plants which sophisticated gardeners now tend to despise. They are not, I promise, a hotter and redder poker with which to stir the embers of your disgust, nor a Pampas grass from Brisbane with purple leaves. I have merely been enjoying very good and cheap Gypsophila and purple-mauve Thalictrum Hewitts Double from W. Harrington of 173 North Bank, Wisbech, Cambridgeshire, a wholesaler who sells in batches of ten or more. These are plants which the smart gardeners avoid. They think that they belong in florists' shops. But that is precisely their value. They send up clouds of small light flowers to a height of three feet in July and August and can be fitted into any summer border. They come from a manageable root-stock and do not lie in a nest of heavy stems and leaves too early in the year. Gypsophila is also sold in a lovely tall pale pink form which is well worth having. It will need to be propped up, for such is its billowing head of flower that the weight will sometimes tear the stems away from the central root-stock. Be warned of this, as you will lose the plant after only one year if it is left to pull itself to piees. Gypsophila is the family of the Rosy Veil which I praised for the front row, the well-known Baby's Breath. These are the taller forms of this family, whose botanical name means 'chalk-lover'. They will also grow in half shade, so you can tuck them in anywhere for a bright July and August. They belong in an artful planting because of their lightness of shape, so unusual in late summer flowers. You can use them among heavy petalled roses, thick-headed phloxes or the strong vertical lines and drum-heads of the splendid Agapanthus. The Thalictrum, too, looks most unpromising when you buy its little bunch of dry, hanging roots. But these will all thrive, even in a difficult summer. The leaves are most delicate, like a rounded grey-green Aquilegia's. The stems of flowers are set with small points of a distinctive mauve-purple, adding up to a charming colour, some three feet high. I have it, by chance, beside the plain white rose Iceberg and think that it sets off the strong white colouring most pleasantly.

I am now up to the task of praising the Campanula. To my eye, there is not a dull plant in this family, least of all the grey-blue forms, the forms with tubular white or spotted flowers or our silver-blue native Harebell. I must put in a word, first, for the Canterbury Bell. If you want good plants of this for next June, you should sow seed in May or June of the previous year. It is cheap and easy, but it is a biennial, lasting for only one year. You sow it in a box or in a cold frame. You can prick it out at the end of a month and move it onto a spare bit of ground, spacing it about six inches apart. In April next year, you would have some individual plants strong enough to take their place as early summer bedding. The pinks and whites are a pretty match for the ink-purple variety, so you can be content with a mixed packet. They spread out quite widely and go up to a height of three feet or so. If I was starting a new garden, they would be one of the first plants to which I would turn in order to tide myself over the first blank year. My family do not share my love of the double forms, especially in shades of ink-purple, but you may agreed with me in liking their gross vulgarity.

Among the perennials, my prize still goes to the plainest, the 'peach-leaved Bell flower' if you translate its Latin name. Like flax, it is one of my essential plants and grows like cress from its cheap seed. July is the best month for sowing it. From one packet, you should get 50 or so plants which can be tucked into any border the following year. The prettiest cottage garden in my area is thick with blue and white Campanula persicifolia in high summer. They all began as seedlings. These are plants of the thin-leaved variety whose slender stems are set with open cup-shaped flowers to a height of about two feet. Their roots will fit in anywhere, among irises, between stones, beside a path or on the edge of a slope. Plain alba is a lovely white and Telham Beauty is a pretty silver-blue. They last for ever once you have raised them. Grey-leaved hostas, striped old roses and a mass of these July flowers would suffice for any busy gardener. They can easily be split, divided or left to their own devices. The white is my particular favourite, especially among the roots of the big border irises where it does no harm and prolongs the season after the irises' blaze of flower.

These Campanulas tuck in or near the front row of your border, the home, too, for many other good ones. I will have more to say on alpine forms at this level, but I would single out the white-flowered trailing Campanulas as a charming edge to a path or paved front

91

garden. They are prettier and less rampant than the two mauve-blue creepers with impossible Latin names, which are sold in chain-stores as a first choice. At Cranborne Manor, Dorset, a carpet of the white forms runs across the terrace above a fine white garden. The best ones have ash-grey leaves to complement their sheets of flower – Mist Maiden, garganica alba, white arvatica, the harebells of pusilla alba, and lovely white hallii. Any of these are worth grouping beside a path, along a wall or in paving stones, though their strength varies. The plain white form of carpatica is one of the most vigorous, but its cups of white flower are also among the strongest whites around, so be sure that you can place them.

At a greater height of eighteen inches or so, refined readers would also like the tubular Bellflowers. Though seldom seen, they belong to a border's front row and are easily grown in any open soil. For a grey and white garden, one called burghaltii is fashionable and well worth finding. The flowers are a slate-blue which occurs nowhere else. They last well and are a fine match for stronger colour. But my pleasure comes more from an inky-mauve variety called van houttei. This is quite unjustly ignored. It is a bolder colour and flowers profusely. You can mass it in the front of a border where its heavy crop of tubular flowers will draw any eye. I consider this a very fine border-plant indeed which splits easily into 10s and 20s after a year.

For a long season and two foot high stems of white bells, you should hunt out alliariifolia Ivory Bells. This useful plant has still not made the name which it deserves. The rough and heart-shaped leaves will grow almost anywhere, even in dry shade. The stems arch prettily and although the flowers are not in the first class, they last from late June until September or later. Everybody knows the hosta, but nobody bothers with this equally obliging Campanula.

In the middle to back row, bolder colour and bigger flowers mark out a tough variety called latiloba. This, too, will grow in surprisingly dry shade, even at the foot of a hedge. It is about three feet tall, saucer-flowered and quite indispensable among shrubs, roses or out-of-season clutter. You can pull dozens of new pieces off any old plant. The variety called Percy Piper, after the hybridist at Bressingham Nurseries, is an especially deep blue violet. It goes well with white and the clumps end up by blocking out weeds. At Kiftsgate Court, Chipping Camden, Gloucestershire, the old Highcliffe variety of this Campanula runs happily in the dark shade between shrubs and the dry ground beneath the trees on the main escarpment. It is so robust that I cannot understand why nurseries now ignore it. Kiftsgate's owner wisely sells plants of it to the garden's many visitors.

I have left the most harmonious until the end. At a height of four or more feet, the pale sky-blue Campanula called lactiflora is a splendid tall July border-plant. Oddly, it sets ripe seed within a month of flowering and can be raised by the hundred if you sow it quickly in the same month. Last year, I put the admirably easy Lily Enchantment among and in front of it. Its fiery orange-red and the Campanula's milk-blue were all the better for each other. Pale blush-white hollyhocks rounded off this easy and happy accident, raising a long flowerbed quite out of the usual rut of Phlox and Alchemilla. This excellent plant needs a year or two to settle down and its responds to a damp soil by growing taller than ever. There are named and white forms around, but I prefer the plain milk-blue, variable in colour from its own seedlings but easy to select in its purest and most delicate forms. It is the answer to all those fiery reds or scarlets and is still a star turn in our gardens.

In the middle ranks, I like to match it with two of my best recent re-discoveries. Neither is a new plant but in their different ways, they reach two or three feet in a most unusual manner. The most graceful is the little-known Gillenia. The great garden at Sissinghurst Castle, Kent, makes excellent use of this June-flowering perennial whose neat fresh green leaves set off the simple white flowers and reddish stems. It looks like a slender wild flower from the woods but it does not lose all its petals and fall flat on its face as soon as the first summer storms break. Catalogues give an exaggerated view of its flowering season, as of almost everything else which they try to sell. Mid-June till mid-July is its moment, but at a height of three feet you should find room for this unpretentious white flower among the old roses and hostas. Anyone can grow it in half-shade, if they give it enough water. I know a distinguished couple who met and fell in love because of it. On seeing it in a nurseryman's frame, he remarked on its virtues while she was working in the potting-shed. Ah, she thought, he is a man who even knows about Gillenia and from that flowered a romance between two great gardeners.

Nobody, I think, could begin their romance with a bunch of the bold Morina longifolia. It is horribly prickly. But this thistle-like plant is one of my best, a deeply-rooted expanse of bright green leaves like a giant thistle's from which shoot three-foot high stems in

July, opening into hooded heads of flower, like a sage's, in shades of rose-pink and white. These flowers whiten as they age and fade altogether to green seed-heads. I cannot see why catalogues are wary of this memorable plant. I have it in a stony, damp stretch of ground which soon runs into the sub-soil of the garden, but Morina grows gloriously and seeds itself all over the surrounding irises. I have it in the front row, ready for the weeks when I cut off its long stems. As an admirer of all thistles, I am confident that this, when happy, is the best.

These are long-known plants, but the middle ranks can also profit from families in which breeding has not stood still. From, all the recent work on border plants, the best results have come, I think, in the Day lilies and the relations of the orange-flowered Montbretia, as gardeners call it. In the world of flowers, it is a short-sighted gardener nowadays who misses out on the new arrivals among Day lilies. I had my doubts at first, when the breeders strove to give us a flower which they could describe as red. They have settled down now to some flowers of exceptional beauty which make the old oranges and burned pinks quite out of date. Kelways of Langport, Somerset, stock a splendid range of newer crosses. I am delighted with a large flowered lemon-yellow called Nighthawk, a deep red Stafford with a yellow line to each petal, and any of the peach pinks, especially the vigorous Pink Prelude. I cannot stress too strongly the ease and value of these lovely plants. They will grow in sun or shade, in any good soil. Perhaps a westerly aspect sees them at their best, but their great clumps of roots will block out any weeds and do your job for you. My only complaint is that their length of time in flower is exaggerated. Two to three weeks sees the end of them, though the different varieties stretch the season from July to mid-August. Perhaps the name 'day' lily has caused nurserymen to over-compensate by assuring us they last for several months. One good crop is followed by a few late flowers, but these are quite enough. You can edge them with longer-lasting flowers, the violas, potentillas and so forth. Day lilies have style and body and stand out among those lighter flowers which come and go like gaily-coloured hay. Norton Hall Nurseries, 115 Kynaston Road, Panfield, Braintree, Essex, are another good supplier if Kelways have sold out. The Latin name is Hemerocallis.

The so-called Montbretia, that old orange-flowered corm, also wears a new look. Itself a garden hybrid, it was raised by the French genius, Lemoine, and has long been crossed with its taller and brighter relations. The best results are now listed under Crocosmia and there are changes, here, which no sunny border can afford to ignore. Some of the newer corms are completely hardy, others will survive anything except 1981/2, though growers were once told to grow Crocosmias as cautiously as a Dahlia. Their colours are clear and brilliant in the most appealing way. Their leaves, like a slender iris's, stand up without support to a height around three and a half feet. The flowers are a welcome shade of orange or scarlet in August and are often held so that they look up at you horizontally. I will never garden without the best of them and expect some winners from the breeders in the next decade.

To be fair, they face strong competition already. In the 1920s, a Mr Morris bred some lovely shades of pale yellow and burnt orange into the so-called 'montbretia' and named them the Earlham Hybrids after his own home. Nurseries still sell them, but they die out in a cold winter in my garden, having tantalised me by their beautiful flowers. A Mr Mason tried a better trick, crossing Crocosmias with a solid, tall relation from South Africa called Curtonus, or Antholyza. One child strikes me as his best in the confusing family, the Crocosmia called masonorum which came on sale in the late 1950s. It has the strong leaf and height of the curtonus and bears spikes of a flaming red which are twisted to a horizontal plane and held at about three feet. It likes the sunny, south-facing bed I give it beside my white Agapanthus and I must admit to thinking its August show of flower is exceptionally bright in my care. Perhaps I was sent a variation on the true form, but the Crocosmia glows at me from its sheath of fresh leaves. I think it a magnificent mid-border plant and in acknowledgement it seeds itself freely.

On different lines, I like an open-flowered improvement on Lemoine's 'montbretia', named Emily McKenzie. Her deep orange flowers are marked with a red-brown throat. At a lower height, the new Jackanapes mixes yellow and orange in the same flower, while Emberglow is another vigorous advance on the old Curtonus, tall, a dark burnt orange and a very free grower. But far the best of all is the new Lucifer, a brilliant scarlet which was bred at Bressingham Nurseries. It took the 1981/2 winter in its stride, and I think it the best new border plant in my lifetime. If you want a flaming red-orange, I can vouch for the cross called Spitfire, about three feet high and willing to multiply in a dry soil. Like Lucifer, it is close to Mr Mason's original cross.

These brilliant flowers spring up from small corms, like a crocus. They like sun, an open, sandy soil and a year or so in which to settle down. After that, they make a strong clump which can be split up as usual. You should plant them in early April and prepare for a bright surprise, one of the great improvements over our grandfathers' well-stocked borders.

Crocosmia, I feel, takes me back at last to the tallest row. Here, I confess to preferring many shrubs with handsome leaves, that elegant mixer, the purple-grey Rose rubrifolia, the grey-leaved Buddleia Lochinch, quick-growing bushes of upright deciduous Ceanothus which flower at four or five feet in their third year, shrubby pink Tree Mallow, or Lavatera, in a form more pink than mauve and even my inevitable Orange Blossom in an upright double form for the sake of its magical scent. Already you have that magnificent grass on the list, my Stipa gigantea. I like the tall and slender white Veronica called virginica alba, drawn up to six feet in August with its thin spires of white flower. I am less keen on double yellow daisies, tall white Spiraea or the leafy blue thistles and leguminous plants of a strictly herbaceous design. But if you fear for the width of a back row of shrubs, there are two old friends for which I can say nothing but good.

I have a miserable old book which dismisses one of them as a weed. The tall, single yellow Evening Primrose is nothing of the sort. It puts down a root like a parsnip and spreads into a rank and heavy set of branches in only one year. It seeds itself into your rarest alpines and cannot be stopped from spreading children all over your paths. But it is a marvellous plant and for years it was the best thing I had in a developing border. While others fretted in the drought, the huge Evening Primroses beamed at me with their ascending stems of bright yellow flowers, glowing through the half light of a July evening with an intensity particular to their colour. No nursery dares to sell it, but this strong Oenothera lamarckiana is a superb back-row plant, so long as you cope instantly with the potential seed heads and prepare for it to lead you a merry dance with its multitudinous children.

Finally, remember the Hollyhock. Many big borders ignore it, but a well-staked row of blush-white, primrose and crimson hollyhocks is as lovely a background as any for the border. They come in all colours from seed sown at midsummer and by the following season, they will delight you. Their failing, of course, is the dreaded rust which strips them entirely of their lower leaves.

However, it does not spread to other plants and if you wedge your bare-legged hollyhocks behind thrusting clumps of Crocosmia and pale blue Bellflower, the worst of the damage is hidden. I thought I would like the smaller annual hollyhocks, launched by the seedsmen five years ago, but they have served me poorly and I am no longer prepared to give names like Silver Puffs the benefit of any doubt. If you are taking up Hollyhocks, make sure of the Giant Sky-High Multi-flowered Double Mixture, otherwise known as the good old Hollyhock from cottage gardens. How tall, though, will these hollyhocks grow? It seems to depend on what you give them to drink. Beer and hollyhocks are a famous pair among country gardeners. Those codifiers of much old garden lore, the Boland sisters, claim to have met a man on a 'bus who forced his hollyhocks to a height of eighteen and a half feet by feeding them on beer. I wonder, but the yeast is probably nutritious. I have a border against a wall whose back row has to stand up to be seen, and I would not be unwilling to split a can of bitter with it. Lager beer, I dare say, is less stimulating, a liquid best kept for smoothing the creases on your top hat. Having reached the border's highest point, I feel we deserve a break, time for thought and a glass of the only fertiliser which is common to the tastes of plants and men.

By picking and choosing, I have now built up an appealing border for a west or south facing site on a sunny soil. Better shrubs could give it body and permanent bones. The better alpines which are to follow could enliven the front row. I have not given many clues about colour, a topic which you would prefer to settle for yourselves. Myself, I think that the many yellows and oranges of late summer have to be placed carefully. They are most tolerable when massed together, I feel, in one carefully graded bed. I am not alone in preferring a planned limitation of a border's colours. Blues and pinks, reds and whites, mauves and dusky pinks, fresh yellow and lime green: these are all happy pairs and they could each make the theme of a single border. Like most keen gardeners, I prefer the cool whites, greens and blue-grey shades of those hostas and other bold leaves as the main colour tone of the gardens. But I also like the warm, vibrant reds and clear primrose-yellows, the dark purple-violets and of course the pure blues. I view rosy-pink with more suspicion and the nearer the colour comes to orange or carmine, the more the flower has to justify itself by an elegant shape, season or scent. These, perhaps, are personal preferences, but they happen to be shared by the best British gardens. Of one point, I am certain. In all but the smallest gardens, you should not dot your different plants around in ones or twos, building up a border by confusing too many different varieties. Unless you are a defiant plantsman and want something of everything, whatever the general effect, you should help the eye by working with generous groups of your best plants. That is one reason why I am not bewildering you with long lists of possible choices. Better gardening begins when you decide what you like among plants which like your soil, and then you grow plenty of it. If you want your garden to be a picture, do not confuse it with touches of unrelated incident and muddled detail. Limit the colours, then, of each bed, nor necessarily to one main colour but, I feel, to not more than three at any one season. To liven them up, resort to the planner's best ally, those obliging plants with silver leaves.

If I wanted a quick return, I would use at least a quarter of the space in my border's sunlight for silver leaves. Silver-leaved plants are easily increased and can mostly be planted from pots throughout the summer. Some have elegant shapes to their leaves, the sort of shapes which bad handbooks describe as filigree or the work of nature's very own silversmiths. Do not be deterred. They are a fine background and when repeated, their clumps draw a garden together. I am always on the look-out for good new arrivals in the class of silver plants. Over the past three years I think that the new form of dead nettle, called Lamium Beacon Silver, has proved its excellence. For a start, it breaks the rules of the preceding paragraph. It is best in a rich, damp soil in shade. There, it spreads into a mass of pale grey-green leaves, silvered as if someone had showered them with paint. The mauve-pink flowers are quite in harmony and the whole plant is easily divided from small pieces begged off a friend. It makes a pretty carpet in front of a pink rose, like that fine, small-flowered variety, The Fairy. It will also match the older roses, the Hostas or my beloved Campanulas.

Among the taller silver plants, I am not alone in thinking Artemisia Lambrook Silver as good as any. Stocks of this sell out quickly every season. They are never abundant as the plant is oddly difficult to propagate: cuttings taken generously in mid-July have had the least bad results with me, a point confirmed by bigger growers. If you see it, buy it. The plant has two phases. Until late June, it is a lovely arching clump of grey-silver leaves, firmly cut like the enlarged top growth of a carrot. In July, it bolts into bud, showing the typical tall stems and drab grey little dots of flower which appear on other members of the Wormwood family. Cut these off, as they cannot support themselves and they flop far and wide in the first summer rains. You are back, then, with another fresh clump of finely cut leaves. A group of three suffices for a square yard. Well trimmed, it is a splendid companion for clumps of roses, especially the easy old hybrid Musks which catch no diseases and hardly need to be pruned. Perhaps Lambrook Silver ought always to be given plenty of gravel and stones wherever you plant it. Sharp drainage and poor soil are the demands of almost all silver plants, but this is one which I have never lost in wet weather or on clay soil.

The taller stems and finer leaves of Artemisia arborescens I have now abandoned. However lovely, they are just not hardy. If you want them, hunt for a named variety sold as Faith Raven, chosen because it is tougher. I know two gardens with it and in one, it is still thriving after a cold wet winter. Ramparts Nursery, Colchester, Essex, are specialists in silver plants and their catalogue grades the varieties usefully by their hardiness and likely survival on heavier soils. Arborescens, justly, scores a low mark. A better Artemisia in most gardens is the recently-named Valerie Finnis, one of the many crosses and discoveries which that fine plantswoman has given us from her garden of raised beds. About two feet high, it is a willing plant on all but the heaviest soil. It may not help you to know that correctly it is a form called borealis. But it is a front-line plant which is unusually bright when first in growth. Later in the summer, it has to be trimmed, but as a start to a border its young shoots are as vivid as a white star. It is sold by Beth Chatto at White Barn, Elmstead Market, Essex, along with an improved form of the felted grey Helichrysum plicatum whose two foot high bushes have white leaves and rather dingy yellow rounded flowers in summer. This selected cross, called White Barn, has caught my notice at the shows and in two south-eastern gardens. Its leaves are larger, whiter and more ample. A group of five could easily be contrived from cuttings and would stand prettily beside the glorious blues of hardy Agapanthus.

If you do not want to send off to a specialist, you could stay with plants of the low growing Artemisia splendens. This is a commoner plant whose thin leaves are like pale foam in late summer. Like most silver plants, it should be cut back fiercely to stop it showing its loathsome flowers. Dry soil, sun and hard clipping bring the best out of these silver varieties. Artemisias include the wormwoods and the source of absinthe. Absinthe makes the heart grow fonder, as they believed in nineteenth-century Paris, so I am keen on all the good garden forms which the Artemisia offers us.

From Ramparts Nursery, I like other felted grey features, their splendid furry grey foxglove, listed under Digitalis, the big biennial Verbascum Broussa whose large leaves must be guarded against slugs and, more awkwardly, the upright semi-shrub called Perovskia which is magnificent in late summer when properly staked on a dry or chalky soil. It grows into a four-foot spire of thin, vertical white stems which cover themselves with lavender flowers. You have to prop it up to see it at its finest, some four feet high where the drainage is good. The best buy here is the form called Blue Spire, if you order it from a reputable nursery. Mix grit and sand into a light loam and allow it to face west or south.

In the back row, there is nothing to beat the metallic silver sheen on well-grown silver thistles listed under Onopordon. These are easily raised as biennials from their firm, black seeds, sown in June from any good seedsman. By late autumn, you move them into their border's back row where they put down a long tap root and race up to six feet high. There are two varieties, of which I much prefer arabicum. Its leaves are lusher and less spiny than its brother's and look far less like a rank thistle's. If possible, you should sow the seeds where you want your plants. Their root is too long to enjoy being transplanted, though it will survive the shock. After the plant has flowered, it dies like all biennials. But it drops seed generously and keeps itself in your garden. So, too, does the well-named Miss Willmott's Ghost, a pale but somewhat spiky memorial to one of our most lavish and rebarbative Edwardian lady gardeners. Listed as Eryngium giganteum, it is a sea-green sort of thistle with heads of flower like a teasle's. It fits in anywhere and reaches about two feet, but improves any group into which it seeds itself.

Perhaps you suspect all thistles and feel happier with the ordinary woolly grey carpet of Lamb's Ear (Stachys) and the conventional grey of the shrubby Senecio. These are proven plants, though the 1981/2 winter upset most Senecios which I know. They would bring grey and permanent interest to your border's front ranks, but you might also like to consider the good old Flower of Jove. It races away from a seed packet, and its magenta-crimson flowers on branching two-foot stems are set off so prettily by the hairy grey leaves that I can always find a home for many of its endless seedlings. Once you have it, you never lose it. The white form, listed under Lychnis flos Jovis, is perhaps more easily placed. The pink Horts Variety is far more refined. But I still put the brilliant magenta form first when it is mixed with pale yellow or hangs from a wall or rough bank among a good drift of the smart white Valerian. It can be moved at any season. It seeds everywhere and lightens my July, before the Evening Primroses. Maybe you think it too plain, but it never lets a garden down. Not even last winter nor the least greenfingered owner can do it to death. If you garden under duress and want colour, then the leaf and flower-head of Flower of Jove are as sure a tip as you can be given. By planning these grey and silver interludes among your grounding of limited colours, you make a good border very much better. There are many other silver plants and a host of other border varieties whose excellence I have taken for granted. Blue Anchusas, all those paeonies and the tall white phloxes of late summer need no more praises here. I would like to round off a better border with one or two trimmings from seed, familiar trimmings, on the whole, but touches which do help to enliven it, especially in its early years.

Few gardeners do justice to the range of the modern nasturtium. I cannot see that these fool-proof flowers are common or boring in the way in which French park-bedding schemes or marigolds are both. They have so many unrealised uses. If you find yourself with a terrace, roof-garden, wall, window-box or space which the former owners called a patio, you should hunt out the many good new varieties on sale. Most of them are unusual in their ability to flower far more freely if they are treated roughly and given a poor soil. Not for nothing did the nasturtium spread with those old acres of pink on the far-eastern atlas. In a hot climate, they were one lone echo of the British home counties which actually preferred to follow those builders of empire into the desert and thrive in a hot, dry Indian soil. I do not recall them among the Cosmos in Kashmir, but I expect they stood there in 1946.

Nowadays, you have a wide and interesting choice of shapes and colours. I am pleased with the new Red Roulette, a small variety whose flowers are a good red-orange and semi-double in a pretty way. They stand well clear of the leaves and face upwards at you, without the edging of spurs to their petals. A more fiery shade of red can be found in the excellent Spitfire, a clear yellow in Primrose Gem. The double varieties have a scent which is noticeable if you bend down into them but they are not so long-stemmed nor trailing, if you want them to hang over the edge of a roof or a window-box. The absence of spurs on the flower may also strike you as a sad loss. Plain Magus mixed, sold often as 'tall climbing', is the type which spreads furthest and most widely. It can be used ingeniously in a border. You can grow it over a shrub or a paeony after its flowering season, up wire and walls to a height of several feet, through fading poppies and anchusas, or down the front of dry walls, perhaps the most spectacular site for a trailing nasturtium. The big, round seeds are easily placed wherever you want them, because you can press them like peas into the ground at wide intervals. Begin them in early May. Remember that no seed will thrive in a dry wall whose top is faced over-solidly with coping-stones or cement. The best walls for seedlings are open on top to the weather and free of concrete. You can fill in the gaps between their stones with some rich compost, water it, and press the nasturtium's seed firmly into its pocket. Water it again in dry weather. I have found it easier to start a dozen or so plants in pots, and then transplant them when their roots are well-formed into a ball of earth. My results have not yet been as fine as those on a West Country wall, which first gave me the idea. But reports from past readers encourage me to repeat this topical suggestion, which clearly worked very well for others.

Three centuries ago, in the well-documented gardens of Woburn, the nasturtium, known as Indian Cress, was being relished as seldom since: 'The flowers, tender leaves, and seeds are laudably mixed in the kitchen with the colder plants, while the buds, as also the young, green seeds, being pickled or candied, are likewise used in stewings all winter'. I find it hard to pass a healthy plant of the dark-leaved Empress of India and her deep crimson flowers without picking the leaves and chewing them for their hot flavour of mustard. But you do not meet the flowers in most restaurants nowadays. I doubt if many gardeners will find temptation too strong and eat the seed packet before planting it out in pots on the balcony.

Nobody would tangle at dinner with my favourite plant from seed for the border's middle to back row. Called Salvia turkestanica, it has clearly ignored the advice which its Best Friend gave it. It stems and leaves reek of an over-heated crowd who have not had a bath for two weeks. From time to time, it seems to be visiting my reading-room in Oxford's Bodleian Library. Perhaps it has blown in from the nearby college borders where it struggles against the tidiness of the head gardeners and survives by its copious seeds, dropped after flowering. If you forgive its scent, it is a superb garden plant, rising with a tall stem of purple-white flower to a height of three feet. Forms seem to vary, the best having large leaves and fat buds. These droop naughtily in the big leaves and suddenly straighten their suggestive tips and erect themselves into a tall spire of flower. Their colour matches almost anything, a mixture of mauve, white and pinkish-purple flowers set all up and off the central stem. When the flowers fade, the seed heads keep a good pale colour into September. Thompson and Morgan of Ipswich still sell it and I would hate to lose it. If sown in June, it germinates freely and can move into the border that autumn for the following year. It looks lovely with pink or apricot roses.

Lastly, in the back row, I need only remind you of the loveliness of Sweet Peas. Why do we banish these to vegetable beds or cut-flower borders? They will race up a tripod of tall bamboo canes or green Netlon and wave their exquisite stems of flower high above the Salvia and Day lilies. The Salvia, I assure you, only smells if you rub against it. The scent, however, of the Sweet Pea steals up on you, one of the sweetest in the garden.

Sweet peas, well grown, are a labour of love. If I had no other interests, I would gladly devote a summer to them. When computers have cost us all our jobs and when those gloomy voices start complaining that we will all become violent because, like the owner of the gloomy voice, we cannot think of anything to do with our spare time, I give a thought to the sweet pea. It mops up labour as quickly as a new council-office. It gives you just enough to do in a summer morning between the newspapers and the start of the Test Match.

Seedsmen have started to revive the varieties which they call 'antique'. I wonder if they know the sweet pea's long and far-flung history. The sweet pea was first recorded as a wild flower in Sicily. It was noted there by a priest, one of the Catholic Church's unremembered legacies. He put it in a book on botany and in 1699 sent seeds at once to the master of a grammar school in our own Enfield. Dr Uvedale of Enfield was already well known as the owner of six garden hot-houses. No doubt his school was also a forcing-house, but his fame in Europe rested on his adventures with exotic plants. The sweet pea, he found, was a drab arrival, short stemmed, twin flowered and a shade of maroon purple which can still be seen on Sicilian hillsides.

Meanwhile, dried flowers were being sent to a Dutch botanist from the Far East and among them was word of a new and brighter sweet pea. It appeared to have been found in Ceylon. The first masters of botany took this seriously and divided sweet peas into a Ceylonese group. This prompts intriguing thoughts: nobody has ever found such a plant in Ceylon again and experts are almost certainly right to deny its existence. But the owner of the dried flowers was not a stupid or fraudulent man. I suppose that he might have put a sweet pea into the bag by mistake, but it is still just possible to wonder whether a branch-line of the family might not have rambled in the Indian Ocean with good qualities which ought to have been saved.

Others rambled, certainly, in the South Seas. In 1744, a ship owned by Lord Anson put in at the Magellan Straits and while the other sailors rid themselves of sea-legs, the cook strayed on shore, perhaps to look for green vegetables. On the beach, he chanced on the Magellan sweet pea, pocketed it and brought it back for gardeners. It was no beauty, but it seemed to offer hope of a break into a blue colour. But the Sicilian and Magellan sweet peas were not very exciting. For two centuries, breeders tried to do their best for them and some of the results can still be seen in the old Painted Lady strain, offered recently by Thompson and Morgan of Ipswich. These white and rose-red peas are sweet, small flowered and a legacy from 18th century city gardens. I prefer to skip to the age after 1850 when breeders pushed things along more quickly. They were still private growers. The most enterprising remains the remarkable Henry Eckford who entered the game in 1870 and turned out more than 100 new varieties, contriving several new colours. Almost single-handed, he made men realise that the sweet pea would deserve a bicentenary show in 1900. It is one of my favourite flower shows, partly because of the speeches which survive, but also because within one year most of the exhibits were out of date. In 1900, many growers of sweet peas were still clergymen, and their horizons were missionary. As a background to our hymns Ancient and Modern, I cannot resist the bicentenary address to sweet pea enthusiasts which was given by a country parson. 'Gentlemen', he told them, 'the sweet pea has a keel that was meant to seek all shores. It has wings that were meant to fly across all continents. It has a standard which is friendly to all nations. It has a fragrance like the universal gospel'. Hardly had he sat down before the keel took a new and famous direction.

In 1901, the sweet pea enjoyed its first national show in London. The omens were memorably bad. 'Well do we remember the day', recalled one of the leading exhibitors, 'for the dirt which bespattered the table covering etc., owing to the heavy rain of a thunderstorm that raged all day, percolating through the roof to the

FRITILLARIA IMPERIALIS: *CROWN IMPERIAL.*

LATHYRUS LATIFOLIUS: *PERENNIAL SWEET PEA*.

CAMPANULA ROTUNDIFOLIA: *HAREBELL*.

VIOLAS: *GARDEN PANSIES.*

discomfort of everybody'. But the sweet pea made history, for in 1901 no fewer than three private growers produced varieties whose flowers had wavy edges. Nowadays, these fine British forms are remembered as the Spencer varieties. In fact, they were raised by the Earl of Spencer's gardener, a Mr Cole, whose first variety was shown under the name of Lady Spencer. Lady Spencer, says my breeding book, 'proved variable'. No doubt she did. But in 1902, she drew the crowds, and a note of sheer frustration sounds in the memoirs of fellow-exhibitors who had brought their straight-edged sweet peas to perfection, but found themselves beaten into second place.

Since 1901, the sweet pea has hardly stood still. There have been many recent mixtures, gloriana, floriana and multiflora. All of them are good, but in the 1970s the sweet pea suddenly decided to prophesy. Its older Cuthbertson varieties were crossed with others which had Spencer blood in them and produced a six-flowered strain of strength, scent and distinction which the breeders called Royal Family. By its own romance with a Spencer, the sweet pea had already run to royal blood. Nobody saw the omen, and instead, we had newer small forms to distract us. Among recent crosses, Patio Mixed and Bijou now fit into a window-box, while Knee-hi succeeds as a bedding plant. Scores of single colours have been developed from the Spencer type, pink and white Mrs Bolton, deep lilac Leamington and the rest. The sweet pea is a flower where the moderns, to my eye, are all better than the ancients. Antique mixtures claim a superior scent but it seems to me to be no stronger than the scent of the best big modern colours. You can sow the seeds either straight into rich ground during mid-April or singly into one and a half inch peat pots. Then you can bed them out in May without checking the roots, a lethal mistake. Armed with your own Sweet Peas, you can set sail for a border of scent and pure colour, spreading the gospel of better gardening, while I descend to lowlier themes, the flowering bulbs and smaller alpine plants.

Chapter Five

Better Bulbs

With pleasure, I come now to bulbs. Bulbs are the beginner's best friend. They arrive with next year's flower tucked safely inside them and so long as you plant them the right way up, they will probably give you a full flower and leaf in their first year. If you think that even you could not plant a bulb on its head, you should take a look at the dry corms of hardy cyclamen or a packet of wild anemones. They would puzzle anyone. So you will probably start with daffodils, Dutch crocus and as many tulips as you can afford. In a new garden or a bare flowerbed, they are a blessing. They brighten the place up in one year and give you something to look at while you are fretting over my better Magnolia, cursing my better Lespedeza and hunting for snails in the remains of my better Campanulas. If you have some rough grass, you will want to brighten it with naturalised bulbs and will start, quite rightly, by thinking of narcissi. Before I turn to my better bulbs for beds and frames, I have an idea or two for bulbs in a wilderness.

In closely-mown grass, my favourites are the blue, pink and white forms of the Mediterranean Anemone blanda. These are only three inches high, so they are lost among tussocks or rough meadows when they flower in early April. On a lawn or mown path or as the edging to a shrubbery, they are sensational. Plant the hard, nutty corms with their convex surface downwards at a depth of about two inches. If the convex surface is not detectable, do not worry too much, as the corm will probably sprout from either end. In isolation, the pale blue form is a glorious sight and in light sandy soil it will spread like ground-elder. There is only one point to remember. These anemones open their ray of petals in full sunshine, so they are not bulbs for a shaded place. I have had better returns from them over the years than from any other bulb in the book.

Better Bulbs

If you want something different for longer and rougher grass after planting your daffodils, there are few cheaper or easier choices than the Blue Bear Grass, Quamash or (correctly) Camassia. This is so seldom seen that I wonder every year why nurserymen continue to supply it. I am thankful that they do, for it is the most useful bulb for a wilderness and will flower in dark shade, drably maybe, but none the less visibly. In half-shade or among long grass it is tall, elegant and conspicuous. It flowers in May and throws up tall stems which are set with pale blue or dark violet star-shaped flowers, slender but very pleasing. It is often said to flourish on clay, but I have never had to plant it on such unfavourable soil. Maybe it would prefer it. Two varieties are usually offered and having enjoyed them both, I do prefer the more expensive. This is usually named cusickii and is the paler and taller of the two. Its bulbs are big and heavy and have to be planted with a spade. Its flowers are pale blue, like a Chionodoxa's, and its leaves are long and awkward but not so drab as the ordinary Blue Bear Grass. This is called esculenta, presumably because the Indians in its native America used to eat it. They must have been quick to serve it up as this is not a bulb to keep in a paper bag for very long. Unlike a crocus, it rots rather than sprouts. But it is pretty when planted punctually, about two inches deep in groups of 20 in rough grass. The flowers are a plain dark violet and are not as striking as its paler relation. Cusickii is harder to plant, as each big bulb should go down some four inches. 'They are not very showy', says that authority, P.M. Synge, 'and flowering in June when there are so many more striking flowers, they have never become very popular in English gardens'. Judged by a rose or bearded iris, they are indeed a poor second best. But there are not so many tall bulbs for long grass in June, let along for heavy and half-shaded soils. If Blue Bear Grass prolongs the season of your wilderness and stops you cutting the Cow Parsley and old daffodils too soon, so much the better for them all.

A month earlier, I would like to find Stars of Bethlehem in my orchard. True, they are made into tranquillisers, but if you think I only want them to mend a broken heart or stop me carving names onto my apple trees, you misjudge me and mistake a beautiful group of small spring flowers. Visitors to the Middle East will know how the hillsides of Syria and Israel are covered in carpets of grey-white flowers which grow in little soil and less water and are brought into blossom by the first weeks of spring. These flowers were once known locally as 'dove's dung' because of their prolific show of grey-white flowers. They will be equally obliging in rough grass in your garden. They spread everywhere and are not plants for a controlled flower-bed. Ornithogalum umbellatum is the name which conceals them in catalogues and you should not have to pay more than £2.50 for a hundred. They are short-stemmed and should be placed in the front of your taller naturalised narcissi. They last well when in flower and are at their best in late April. I defy you to kill them off.

There is, however, a more unusual variety which I would want in any patch of long grass. Ornithogalum nutans has attractive green stripes on the back of its hanging grey-white flowers. It is much taller and its stems exceed a foot. In a few British woods it has run wild, probably from nearby gardens. But it clearly likes our country. It tolerates semi-shade, multiplies from year to year and is enough of a flower for an arrangement indoors. I like striped flowers, and know no other bulb with such spinach-green markings on its petals. In moderately thick grass, you should enjoy this without any trouble.

Leaving the wilderness, my better gardening takes an ominous turn. It extends to bulbs which are not the most hardy or the most persistent, but which conceal some fool-proof varieties or respond to a few, easy tricks. There is no point in writing at length again that the species crocus are prettier than the big Dutch hybrids, or reminding you that any hardy cyclamen is lovely in a pot, if you buy it when in leaf from alpine nurseries. These and the many fritillaries I have covered elsewhere. I may seem now to choose bulbs which cannot be bought safely as dry stock in autumn, but I am concerned that your adventure with better bulbs should persist from year to year. Anyone can grow a bulbous iris for one season, but fewer keep it happy for a decade. Here, bulbs become a test of skill which you can enjoy in any garden, however small. Through bulbs, great plantsmen and gardeners have often been born. They need little space and their routine will fit round a busy life at work in town or country. You must start to think of them as plants for pots and clay pans which you can protect from the weather and bring indoors when in flower. To play their game properly, you ought to consider a plunge bed. This is not the latest concept from Playboy; it is simply a bed of sand which is laid to a foot's depth, at most, below ground level, into which you plunge the pots up to their necks while leaving their surfaces level with the surrounding soil. However you grow your bulbs, plunging is a good trick. You dig out a hole to match the width of the frames which you mean to set about it and then you fill it with sharp silver sand up to the soil's level. You poison the surrounding earth with Super Weedex and isolate the sand pit from all possible weeds. Ordinary builder's sand is less satisfactory, as it drains poorly and can sprout a green slime. After potting up your bulbs, you sink the pots up to their necks in the sand-pit. Once they are in, you will find that you have to water them far less often. If you choose spring flowering varieties, you can take your August holiday and not worry about watering them at all. The sand will also take the edge off the sharpest frosts and save the bulbs from being frozen into a compost like pieces of rock. Plunge beds are cheaper than the conventional frames which garden centres will bring to your notice, VAT and all. If you sink your pots up to their necks in sand, you need nothing more than the standard type of Dutch lights as a shelter above them. These are long wood-framed sheets of glass which you can make for yourself quite cheaply, if you remember that horticultural glass is far cheaper than other brands and just as good for this purpose. The carpentry is simple enough, even for me. The Dutch lights have to be propped horizontally over the sand-pit, a job for a few stout pegs banged into the ground. You then have the outlines of a frame, but you do not need to fill in the sides and the back and front with wood. Instead I would advise that you tack chicken-netting over the gaps between the roof of glass and the ground. This keeps off the cats. Against the prevailing wind, block in the back with the strongest type of plastic sheeting. If you choose a thick type, this takes the edge off a bad gale. There is absolutely no point in boxing the whole bed in at great expense. The better the ventilation between the glass roof and the ground, the happier the pots in the plunge bed beneath.

You see, I hope, how cheap and simple it is, and perhaps wonder when and why the Dutch lights are needed. They help to control the watering and will take the edge off the frost. For most of the growing season you will not even need to keep them in place. It is often best to leave pots exposed to the winter rain which will water them for you. Only in very wet or cold spells are the glass lights necessary, but remember that for a bulb all wet spells are relative. When your pans of small narcissi are in flower, any rain overhead will spoil their petals. Earlier, rain is helpful, so bulbs at different stages will prove tougher. The Dutch lights allow you to make the most of a wet English summer and are often the secret of growers who show us those enviable pots of small bulbs from hot native countries. Obviously you ought to think of two plunge beds, or at least two separate areas when you arrange the glass roofs above the sand pit. One should be for the summer-flowering bulbs which will want to be dry and dormant in autumn. The other should be for the spring varieties which begin to be watered when the others go to sleep.

Whenever you pot up your rare bulbs, there are two golden rules. Never overcrowd a pot, because you will lose most of the crowd after one or two years. Try to plant the small-sized bulbs beneath twice their own depth of soil, while putting larger bulbs, the big Muscari or Alliums, with their bulbs three-quarters of the way down a deep pot, not a pan. Remember that bulbs like to be built up after flowering. Out of season, remove the old soil from the pot down to the level of the bulbs and replace it with a fresh mixture. So long as the bulbs show any leaf, you should feed them freely with liquid Phostrogen. You must never ignore them after flowering, for the period between flowering and losing their leaves is the time when next year's flower is born. But in a sheltered plunge bed, you can ignore the other hazards, while ensuring a cheap and handsome source of pot-plants for spring and summer in your less-heated rooms. With the plunge bed in mind, I will survey the plants which could lead a double life, some in pots, some in beds outside.

If I could only save one spring bulb from the garden I think it would be a Dog's Tooth Violet. The fritillary could count as an early summer bulb, at least in a normal season; the prettiest crocuses flower before Christmas: the anemone grows in herbaceous and alpine forms which are not too remote from the brighter flowers of the wild corms. But there is no way round a Dog's Tooth Violet. There is nothing like it, and I am always surprised that it is not planted as often as the snowdrop. It is less temperamental than most of the special Snowdrop varieties. But it has its peculiar ways. Dog's Tooth Violets do not dislike lime. They object strongly to drought and will come to nothing in a dry place. They like an open, crumbling soil, darkened with leaf-mould or enriched peat. They are woodland plants, ill suited to full sun or the strains of life away from the forest floor. If you have a damp peat bed or a corner which smells of rotted bark and humus, the Dog's Tooth Violet would be happy there. Obviously these soils tend to be acid, but these beautiful flowers are not out of your reach in a garden which cannot grow azaleas. I have seen them flowering happily in the grass beneath tall apple trees on a heavy loam, bordering on clay.

There are two branches to the family, one from Europe, the

110

other from America's west coast. The common European form is still the most obliging. Erythronium dens canis is not expensive and will spread under the sort of tree which does not drain all the food from the earth and which feeds its own shade with rotting leaves. Dog's Tooth Violets are always best suited in this light shade. If you are apprehensive of their name, they are only so called because their bulbs look like some large and aged eye-tooth, an Alsatian's maybe but certainly no ordinary dog's. Their leaves are more sinister. They are blue-green, with purple spots and mottled blotches, a mixture which suggests some poisonous arum or weird woodland orchid, and which earns them the pleasant American name of Trout Lily. I first saw them in some bad illustrations for a fairy book and instead of taking the fairies seriously, I fell for the shelter of Trout Lilies and bought them instead. The flowers appear in late March on stems only six inches high. They hang downwards, reminding me of a cyclamen whose segmented petals have not been turned fully back. Like the cyclamen's, these petals are often marked with a darker colour. There are pink, lilac, rose and white forms, the white being the most lovely. At flower shows, named forms of this Dog's Tooth type still turn up, of which the best are Pink Perfection and Snowflake. This year, I cannot find either in a catalogue, but you may be luckier. A catalogue is your safest source because the best Erythroniums should never be bought as dry bulbs from a shop. Like Snowdrops, they hate to be kept waiting in polythene bags and if they dry out, they refuse to grow. Try to order them in April from an alpine nursery like Ingwersens of Gravetye, East Grinstead, Sussex. A few bulbs soon go a long way as they multiply into a clump when happy. Dog's Tooth Violets turn up in Siberia, so there are no worries about their hardiness.

The American branch of the family is more spectacular. It is at home in the damp woods of Oregon and California and the many possible varieties have still not been fathomed by British gardeners. For safety, you should probably keep the best forms in pots and use them to christen your new plunge bed. They, too, are totally hardy, but their flower-stems are taller and their hanging flowers are too good to be spoilt by rain and mud in a British spring. After flowering, the pots can be returned to the plunge-bed and kept shaded. The name Trout Lily covers some, but not all, of the American varieties. On damp slopes in California, the lavender-flowered variety called hendersonii is in its element. In British lists, it is now rare but it is a strong and free-flowering form for a damp

111

peaty soil which ought to be one of the features of better gardening. On one stem, I once saw ten separate flowers and others, I believe, have seen more. This is a fine bulb for a pot.

It is easier to track down a large-flowered pink variety called revolutum Pink Beauty. At home on the West Coast, this has the happiest match of flower and mottled leaf. The lavender-pink of the petals matches the odd markings on the leaves, making it a favourite at the shows. It is not so tall, but the flowers are unusually wide. Names vary for the best white variety, and it is probably safest to call it White Beauty and leave its parentage to the experts. Of all Trout Lilies, this is my favourite, a hanging flower whose pure white petals run back to a brown-orange base. I found it the most obliging of American varieties when planted outdoors. It would persist in a summer as dry as 1976 with help from the watering can, whereas Pink Beauty died out. Fortunately, it is readily available, at a price around 80p for a pot-grown example.

Even so, it is not the finest Erythronium. The family is capped by a Californian beauty called tuolumnense Pagoda which is listed by Broadleigh Gardens, specialists in these and other small bulbs at Barr House, Bishop's Hull, Taunton. Its stems are a foot or so high, topped by hanging flowers of a soft sulphur-yellow. As if the plant knew that yellow would clash with the others' trout-like camouflage, it throws up long glistening leaves of a pale lime green instead. Never lost for a word, its American neighbours call it Adder's Tongue, catching the shape of the leaves very well.

There are other West Americans to challenge your skill, but they turn up only in specialist seed-lists and will take five years before they flower after germination. If sown in damp leafy soil, they will come up quite evenly after a while, so they are not a venture for specialists only. Personally, I would keep these American sorts in a pot where I could guard them against the weather and control their watering. They are just the right sort of plant for your better bulb frame. With patience, however, you can naturalise the pink Dog's Tooth Violet, from seeds scattered straight onto top-dressed grass. In the lifetime of a Parliament, they will pass from seedlings to maturity, a worthwhile result to take with you between one bout of voting and the next.

Bulbous irises are more familiar and more widely marketed than these lovely Dog's Tooth Violets. They enjoy a good name, but they still puzzle me by their refusal to settle down in most gardens. Every year, we buy them quite cheaply from Holland's wholesalers who price them at a level which implies contempt. A hundred Iris reticulata cost about £5 but no sooner have they flowered and flourished for one year than they disappear. These bulbs, says a noted catalogue, should be grown as annuals, an open confession of defeat. I do not care for post-mortem examinations in the garden, but these disappearing irises are so curious that I have tried to analyse them over the years.

First, I must remind you of the irises to which I refer. I am not complaining about the perennial winter-flowering irises whose clumps of grassy leaves thrive in dry flower beds and poor soil. These flower freely wherever they are warm and starved. The bulbous ones are more delicate, some six inches high in shades of blue and purple before the long leaves outstrip the flowers in late February and stand untidily among the first primroses. A group of six or so makes an impact. The flowers stand out like elegant butterflies before anything else is in leaf. They show up so well that you do not need a mass of them. The varieties are rather bewildering, so I will sort out the best before turning to their problem.

Not many gardeners realise how sweetly these reticulata irises are scented. I have tried them all and think that two of them are exceptional, Jeannine and J.S. Dijt. The former is prettier, a violet blue with bold orange markings on the falls. The latter is distinctive, a maroon-purple which I like rather less. Their scents are especially sweet if the bulbs are grown in a pot, where they should be planted in September at a depth of two inches. When the buds form, you can bring them from the plunge bed into the house.

Among the less scented varieties, I recommend Harmony, a charming mid-blue whose falls are slightly rounded and marked with yellow. Harmony has the merit of short leaves which appear with the flowers and do not sprout high above them. Plain reticulata is let down by its lanky leaf if you choose it for pots indoors. Harmony is a better buy here. For colour alone, I like the reliable Joyce and the unfamiliar Pauline. Joyce is an even shade of sky blue marked with orange red on the falls. She flowers strongly and does not fail. Pauline is spectacular, showing flowers of a dusky purple-pink which are set off by the notable white spot. It is worth paying a little more for these named varieties. Their colours are more conspicuous, though the flowers are characteristically shaped, holding three central petals upright like dogs' ears among the outer pairs. These stretch out horizontally and are pursed like lips.

Broadleigh Gardens are an excellent source of supply. Ten bulbs each of the varieties I mention would have cost you a mere £4.20 this year. While you are writing the cheque, you might like to add an extra £5 for one single bulb of the finest reticulata iris in the book. Called Katherine Hodgkin, it commemorates a great bulb-grower's wife and has the supreme distinction of cream-white flowers, marked with pale primrose yellow and sky blue. The price must surely come down as the bulb increases in commerce. Meanwhile, it is the very stuff of better gardening, a flower which excels all others in its group and has not yet been staled by familiarity. 'Bilious, but beautiful', say P. & J. Christian of Minera, Wrexham in their latest list, offering stock at £4.15 a bulb. In a cold frame, it is proving keen to persist and multiply. Its yellow-flowered parent is still disputed, but its breeder kept the other partner in his fridge in order to preserve its flower for the happy marriage.

If you are paying £5, you will want to keep each bulb alive for a second year. The Dutch, clearly, find no difficulties, as they send us the bulk of our stock. In England, they suffer two fates. Sometimes the bulbs and their netted coats rot through and turn black and soft. They are suffering from a disease which is a hazard of the game. You can weed out the dead stock if you lift your bulbs and check them yearly, but there is no certain prevention, in my experience. Otherwise, you must reckon with bulbs which split and dwindle. They separate into five or six lesser bulbs, no bigger than pellets, after their first year's flowering. These little bulbs can be grown on slowly to flowering size after several years, whereupon they will split again into tiny parts. It is most frustrating, and nobody seems to know how to stop it. Katherine Hodgkin's close friend and fellow-gardener, the late E.B. Anderson, grew excellent bulbous irises and discovered the variety which now bears her name. 'The driest and sunniest position is essential', he wrote, 'and always make sure there is ample drainage and as much sun as possible'. Broadleigh Gardens, who depend on them for a living, take a different view. 'Frequently planted as annuals, these irises will grow on if planted deeply or in a fairly moist shady situation'. Both the experts succeed with them, so you must take your pick. My inclination is to favour the sun and sharp drainage, but my results are not impressive. Plain reticulata persists without attention in cottage gardens locally which seem to have nothing in common. Yet drainage, surely, is their critical need, whether in shade or sun. I suspect that the soil must be lightened with sand and leaf mould and that this, above all, determines their survival. While the experts disagree, I would keep the particular varieties for pots in a plunge bed, bringing the flowers indoors where I can observe them closely. Outdoors, I stand by the finest bulbous iris in the book, the best flower I know for any garden in early February.

At 20p a bulb, Irish histrioides major is an unexpected bargain. It resists the weather, my soil and the competition of neighbouring alpines. In late winter, its buds poke through the ground like pencils and open out to large flowers of brilliant sea-blue marked with white and yellow. They seem to like clay and do not object to a frost when in full flower. 'The whole effect', wrote one of their champions, 'is like a sturdy little blue oak'. It even sets a few acorns, seeds which will germinate from their odd little holders, half-hidden under the soil. Native to the borders of Iran and Turkey, this wonderful flower is willing to multiply in most British gardens where it reappears without bother. After a while, the clumps thicken into small oak-forests, six inches high and set with flowers before the leaves have developed. Plain old histrio is still very good, a royal blue marked with a line of white. But its finer cousin has overshadowed it, and while you ponder how best to place your other bulbous irises, take heart that there is still this reliable star in the family, a plant which ranks with the Winter Cherry in my scale of better gardening.

Like these irises, snowdrops have a fan club which surfaces from time to time in my life and astonishes me by its devotion to detail. There are fanciers for the single forms, the big and small petal, the autumn-flowering snowdrop and the shades from cream to ivory white. Names are made by the purity of green on the edge of a petal, while everybody wants to be the first to breed a double primrose-yellow. Public libraries can still come up with the classic study, F.C. Stern's *Snowdrops and Snowflakes* which is required reading before you start snowdropping names. Snowdrop stories come in all shapes and sizes, from recipes for boiling the bulbs to a sentimental 'duettino' in a mid-nineteenth-century French gardening column between a snowdrop, Springtime and the warm west wind. The wind kills the snowdrop and makes Springtime fall in love with him instead. To date, French taste has added nothing to garden forms of our snowdrop, or 'perce-neige'.

I have no difficulty in naming the finest snowdrops I have ever seen. In the early 1960s they grew in the Gloucestershire garden of the late E.B. Anderson who combined a career with United Dairies and a mastery of alpine gardening. He acquired his bulbs on the death of no less a plantsman, John Gray of Saxmundham, Suffolk. Snowdrop John Gray was a single early variety with outstandingly strong and large flowers. Its owner increased it and gave it away freely, so it ought to be lurking in private hands. Perhaps your demand could bring it back onto the market. It was easy to grow in the usual leafy soil in half shade, but it still haunts my image of the perfect single snowdrop.

If you fancy some good snowdrops, February is the correct moment to order them from a specialist nursery like Broadleigh Gardens which will sell them as pot-grown plants in green leaf. By moving them while they are still in leaf, you avoid the loss of one bulb in two and can place the plants where you want them. I would never bother to order dry snowdrops in autumn unless I wanted the ordinary single forms for mass planting. The named varieties are far too precious and should be moved before April. Two years ago, I bought a few bulbs of the named form Straffan and hoped they were worth their very high price. Specialists promised that they would flower late and would run to two flowers on each bulb by their second year. They have proved their worth and do indeed give you double value yearly. At £2 per bulb, they have to be special, but they have a charming origin which almost justifies the price. The two flowers on Straffan are slightly different in form and open in succession. They reveal a fact about the variety's origin. One of its parents first reached England from the front lines of the Crimean War. While most cavalry officers were forgetting to reason why or wherefore, an Irish peer, Lord Clarina, had taken time off to send parcels home to his sister in County Kildare, knowing that she liked all early-flowering bulbs. In 1856, a parent of Straffan came home in a packet with the compliments of the officers' mess. It settled in the sister's garden at Straffan and started to mate with its neighbours, showing the stamina and briskness of any Crimean young blood. From a chance liaison with a wild Irish snowdrop came the form first named Straffan. Of its two flowers, the earlier resembles the Crimean parent, the later its Irish miss. Nowadays, there are several so-called Straffans and collectors will measure the lengths of the petals before agreeing to the name. But I have the story from the kindness of Lord Clarina's sister's surviving great-niece, a living link with the snowdrop's origin and formerly, its keen attendant under the lime trees of her Irish home.

Lord Clarina was not the only snowdrop fancier in the ranks. Lesser men sent bundles of bulbs to their families, especially the pleated double forms which grew so profusely round their camps. The best of the double bunch is called Warham, another souvenir from the Crimea. In early spring, their home must be a botanist's paradise. The biggest variety is hard to resist, though its names keep changing and the third name is still in dispute. Snowdrop elwesii commemorates a great collector and bears almond-scented single flowers above its broad grey-green leaves. It derived from northern Turkey and is relatively cheap at £2.50 for 10. I would choose it first when starting a collection, for it will startle any visitor who thinks of the snowdrop as a small flower. Its various forms reach nearly one foot in height and tend to delay their flowers until mid-March. The white petals are tinted with a lovely green marking, so they are best placed at the top of a wall where you can see into their centres. Snowdrops like damp, leafy soil but they will also run riot on chalk or lime. F.C. Stern, their authority, was a merchant banker who gardened in a chalk pit; although he could pay more staff to spread good compost than most of us could countenance, his own Highdown snowdrop and many others were the glory of his chalk garden in February.

I would not trouble with named varieties if they were not more exciting than the ordinary form which grows wild beneath hazels and overgrown shrubberies. They are not bulbs for a carpet but for a special bed or a deep pot near the house. However, two of the finest forms of the ordinary snowdrop arose as natural crosses in private gardens and whenever I see big clumps of them, I feel sure there may be another winner lying in their midst. Atkinsii was one such coincidence, a big and early white which stands out in any collection. Sam Arnott was noticed by the mayor of Dumfries and deserves a place for its big flower and strong green markings. Myself, I look forward to an old age as Snowdrop Inspector, retained for the little greenery which will remain by then in the Home Counties. If our grandfathers could watch the snowdrops under canvas in the Crimea, we ought to be able to find some crosses for the future, growing safely under churchyard yews or in the abandoned walks of old Victorian gardens.

While we all know snowdrops, very few people bother with snowflakes. This is a shame, as the snowflake is a splendid flower, natural to Britain and as elegant as its name. Its varieties have a long season, spanning spring and autumn, and its flowers are exquisite. A clump in full flower can detain you for some time as you appreciate the combination of green and white, the shape of the flower like a small scalloped lampshade and the angle at which it is held. The botanical name is Leucojum, meaning 'white Violet' in Greek. The name is traditional, as old as Tudor botanists and their random borrowings from the classics. There is a problem, of course, about these classical plant names, for their first Greek users, so sensitive to other distinctions in nature, were liable to call very different plants by the same name. Their Ion, our violet, was also stretched, I think, to cover relations of the wallflower. The snowflake first received its name because the flowers of some varieties would resemble a violet, if you turned them upside down. They also resemble the taller varieties of snowdrop, and it is hard to draw a line between them. At first, snowdrops and snowflakes were classed together by naturalists who knew the snowflakes in Britain's woods and Europe's sub-alpine meadows. Then, the great Linnaeus split them, and we are now supposed to believe that snowflakes have petals of equal length, whereas snowdrops have three long ones in the outer layer of the flowers and three short ones in the inner tube round the sexual parts. There is at least one snowdrop which breaks the rule, but rules are allowed exceptions and the families are still distinct. It is worth observing the differences when you look at the flowers in a garden. They are yet another of those small variations of nature which we buy because of their impression on the eye.

There is no mistaking the so-called Summer Snowflake, so long as you do not take its name too literally. The Summer Snowflake, sold as Leucojum aestivum, flowers firmly in early April. Its height and vigour mark it out, while the long green leaves are as obvious as those on a big autumn-flowering colchicum. They show through the ground in December and early January and are one of the earliest reminders that spring will one day rescue us from the cold and rain. I know no other plant whose leaves appear so far in advance of the flower stems, nor any other native flower whose presence in England is so often overlooked. It also turns up in damp places at points between Ireland and the Caucasus, but in England, it is best known in Berkshire along the upper Thames and beside the River Loddon where it is worth a visit. Its siting there is a clue to its taste in the garden. A riverside plant, it likes a good, damp soil, something which these recent wet winters have brought within reach of us all. Shade or sun are less important than damp round its roots. It is well able to cope with competitors as it is surprisingly tall and tough. It grows up to two feet and sends out strong and bright green leaves. I have seen clumps of it in light Berkshire woodland and have often wished that I had a small patch of hazel trees or alders in a garden beneath which I could mass it with good forms of Christmas Rose. The bulbs are like the brown bulbs of a narcissus and increase quickly when happy. Twenty would become a hundred over five years. The white flowers hang in twos and threes above the long leaves on stems which arch prettily.

Obviously, this is no plant for a small rock garden or a shaded plunge-bed. The leaves take up too much space and the flower is as robust as a hailstone, not a late spring snowflake. It belongs in damp shrubberies, beside a front drive or a stream. In the name of better gardening, I suggest you order a form called Gravetye Giant which has bigger white flowers. It was noticed by William Robinson among the bulbs which he scattered in thousands through the woods of his Sussex manor-house, when trying to prove his theories about wild gardening on a grand scale. Not all the theories survived practice, but Gravetye Giant was one good result and is still sold near its home by Ingwersens of East Grinstead at £2.75 for ten bulbs.

In spring, the so-called 'summer' snowflake is matched by the smaller form called vernum. There are a very few woods where it could perhaps be argued that this, too, is a wild flower, but it is probably best seen as an escape from gardens. I am very fond of its distinctive six-petalled flowers. They are usually spotted with green at the tips of petals which hang like a café lampshade. They are big and well placed on eight-inch stems above leaves which have a glossy green lustre, setting off the flower to perfection. The flowers are slightly scented and sometimes show yellow spots, or none, instead of the usual green. If I only had room for one, I would grow this because it is bold and not tall. Frost is no danger, but it must not be in a dry soil and is certainly best planted when still in leaf. It is splendid in clumps under trees among aconites or as an edging for a damp and leafy bed. These two forms, the spring and summer, are distinguished by their hollow flower stems, a point which strikes you when you pick a bunch and bring it to your desk for observation. They should both be planted at least three inches deep and as much apart in soils which are never too dry.

Whoever saw a pointed or a green-tipped snowflake? The name, however, comes to life if you hunt down the rarer autumn Leucojum called autumnale which is best, for most of us, when grown in a pot. It flowers in September before the thin leaves have

developed and its delicate white flowers on six-inch stems look like
a scattering of passing snow. You should pack its bulbs closely
together and plant them only an inch or two deep. Hence they fit
well into a five inch pot in a sunny plunge bed. Unlike the other
snowflakes, it prefers a warm and gritty home. In nature, it lives in
the south-west Mediterranean from Portugal down to west Africa.
It has a lovely pink cousin which is strictly for plunge beds or
unheated greenhouses only but is worth every penny and effort. If
you wish to size up a shower of these snowflakes in September
before risking them at home, you should look at the border just
inside the main gate of Wisley gardens where the drift of autumn
snowflakes below the wall would win round any hesitating gardener.
I prefer their shape in spring and autumn to the style of a
conventional snowdrop, so I hope you will give them all a chance.

When I come to the topic of the tulip, I turn back a few years to
my last autumn journey into Asia. Watching the rain in Istanbul. I
was brought back from thoughts of a life as a Sultan's gardener by
a very sad sight. On the outer edges of the old Spice Market, men
were selling plants for Turkish gardens, elongated trees of our
standard hybrid roses, pots of Basil, Zinnias and seed of the
unwearying cucumber. There was also a stall of flower-bulbs. The
tulips were topped by their photographs: Clara Butt and Queen of
the Bartigons, Marshall Haig and Captain Fryatt stood stiffly before
the crowds, direct from their Dutch suppliers. The yellow Caliph of
Baghdad was 'especially suitable for forcing'.

Before the days of Darwin and Mendel, when there were no
Cottage favourites and mid-season Triumphs, there were tulips
among the Turks which were worth ten civil servants' salaries,
flowers so prized that their 'onion roots they then so high did hold
That one was for a meadow sold'. Tulips are bright flowers, but
their habits are uniform. They can be crossed and bred, the flower
most obedient to man's will. Perhaps their brightness and their
obedience were causes of their favour at the Ottoman Sultan's
Court, that extravagant fantasy of eunuchs and high colouring. For
there were nearly half a million Tulips in the gardens of the
eighteenth-century Sultan's Palace. Their patterns were worked into
turbans and tiling and reflected the compliments paid to the
prettiest girls and boys in the capital. Ruby of Paradise, Restorer of
the Heart, Pearl of the Morning: these set the courtiers' hearts on
fire. It is possible to buy 'old-fashioned' Tulips from catalogues
which price them for collectors, but these are the old Dutch

17. Gypsophila paniculata Bristol Fairy in A. Holmes's garden at Sudborough

18. Rosa Rose d'Amour above Artemisia in the Scotts' garden at Boughton House

20. Erythronium revolutum, or Trout Lily, flowering at Boughton five years after seed was scattered in rough grass, very slightly shaded

19. Tulipa praestans in paving

21. Alstroemerias, or Peruvian Lilies, massed at Sissinghurst below Rose Albertine and Paul's Lemon Pillar

22. Ramonda myconi

23. Viola Jackanapes

24. Pulsatilla vulgaris Rubra

varieties, in so far as they are old at all, the sort of flecked and broken colour which you can enjoy as well from the cheap and charming Rembrandt mixture. I know of no source for the truly old Turkish varieties, which seem to have been bought and bred from Persia as well as from European stock.

Once a year, the Vizier would invite the Sultan to inspect the Imperial Tulips. 'Beside every fourth flower', wrote a French ambassador, who witnessed it, 'is stood a candle, level with the bloom and along the alleys are hung cages filled with all kinds of birds'. Where tulips had grown up blind, the gaps were filled with cut flowers placed in bottles. Lamps lit the trellises and dangled on green shrubs which had been lifted from the nearby woods. Mirrors reflected the lights; musicians bowed and blew their way through the Turkish songs of the moment; Sultan, harem, eunuchs and courtiers were guests at the Vizier's expense until the tulips dropped their petals at their feet. One way, you may feel, of making free with public spending which not even the patrons of your Council's park bedding schemes have yet been able to imagine. The harem, of course, would be loosed among the tulip-beds on high days and holidays: the girls 'rushed out on all sides, like bees settling on the flowers and stopping continually at their honey'. At the drop of his handkerchief, the Sultan would signify his choice for the evening: the others would return, having failed to catch the eye on their annual bid for bedding-out.

If you find such formalities excessive, remember that the tulip burst unforgettably onto the shapes and colours of the Turkish tiles which were made for the mosques by Persians, Christians and Armenians. Suddenly the tiles of Iznik, the finest of all varieties, break out from their former blues, greens and whites to a red of exceptional richness. Tulips and carnations swirl across their surface; the kiosks of the court come alive with a new red rhythm. It is thought, perhaps rightly, that the red was inspired by the red of the wild tulip. I would like to believe this, for the Turks who favoured it had spanned the whole range of Asia's tulips. No people who have lived in their landscape could ever be blind to the wild tulip's charms. On the steppes and pale brown uplands of Central Asia and Turkestan, the tulip in spring strikes the one bright note of unforgettable colour. Its varieties have hardly yet been listed, and few have been brought into western gardens. As the Turks moved west through Iran into their present home, they were seldom out of sight of the tulip. No doubt it was grown already in Persian gardens, while the wild tulips of western Asia do not fall far short of the yellows, reds and striped varieties recorded in the Turks' own Turkestan. The formal hybrids among which the harem sported are probably lost to cultivation: Clara Butt is more reliable, but somehow I doubt if she ever began an orgy. It is still possible to grow a few of the wild Asian varieties, and I have come to think them as fine as any Darwin hybrids.

The commonest variety may persuade you that the tulip is indeed the origin of the red on Turkish tiling. Fosteriana, from Samarkand, is the biggest and brightest red of any tulip, improved into a form called Red Emperor or Madame Lefebre whose huge red flowers are not, however, resistant to wind and rain. About a foot tall in its ordinary form, this spectacular plant will teach you vividly the nature of spring in a Central Asian landscape. There is also a tulip called linifolia which grows wild round Bukhara. You can buy it for a mere £1.50 a dozen, but its brilliant red flowers and red and green twisted leaves are so dramatic that it can light up a dull spring flower-bed, just as its clumps brighten the open grazing round its home valleys, until summer shrivels them, or the goats go in among their leaves. It is not a difficult plant and it only grows a few inches high. The leaves radiate out along the ground so you need only space them in threes or fours to fill a pocket in a raised bed. The variety called Maximowiczii is similar, but earlier. I can think of no better tulips with which to begin a collection, and unlike many collectors' items they are extremely bright.

Once started, you should not ignore the golden-flowered tulip of north-west Persia. I enjoyed this variety called Urumiensis for six years until it finally died out, perhaps because of the wet summer of 1972. At £1.50 a dozen it is not expensive to replace and if the drainage in your new plunge-bed is sharp, I doubt if you will lose many of the bulbs you buy. Its flowers open widely and their brilliant golden-yellow petals are marked with bronze on the outside. A few bulbs go a long way, especially as each bears several stems of flower. These tulips, of course, are very lowly, suited to the open hills on which they make the brightest of Oriental carpets. Urumiensis's flowers are born just above a flat rosette of leaves, so they are well suited to a bed on top of a wall or bank. The yellow and white flowers of Tulipa tarda are more often seen and offered, but I think they are less dramatic. So far as I know, urumiensis is the only small wild tulip to have been awarded the high honour of a First Class Certificate by the RHS. It deserved it, although it is not the easiest to grow outside a pot. Greigii, the parent of modern hybrids, is equally magnificent and more reliable. It is conspicuous, too, for its mottled leaves. I have lifted my six bulbs in May over the past three years and replaced them in autumn. They are still with me, and I prefer them to the Peacock hybrids which have been bred from them. Mass two-dozen in a flower-bed, ask the secretaries to view them, and perhaps you too may enjoy the success of a sultan as the girls go wild among your burst of vibrant colour.

The most vibrant of all only came my way two years ago and if I have been unable to keep it out of my April thoughts and writings, that is a tribute to its great merit. For years, Tulip praestans Fusilier scared me off by its description in catalogues. A pure, hard scarlet, said the lists, which will give you a riot of colour, as bright as a guardsman's tunic. It all sounded too much and whenever I saw its bulbs for sale, they looked big enough to send up long stems of flopping, red flowers. These would be too startling for most small gardens and I did not relish the thought of scarlet tunics running riot in the bedding-out. 'See how the flowers, as at parade, Under their colours stand displayed . . .'. The poet Marvell had the pleasant fancy of describing tulips as if they were riflemen-at-arms in the garden of his Yorkshire patron, a retired military officer. Fusilier seemed like a tulip which would make his ordered vision come true.

In fact, Fusilier is small, elegant and in no way top-heavy. The flowers have pointed petals and appear on stems about six inches high among fresh pale-green leaves. They still look like a wild tulip, ready to career across the drab steppes of Central Asia, their natural home. The colour is scarlet with a touch, I think, of orange, but the effect is pure, vibrant and all the best things which you can say about strong red. Better still, one bulb produces several flowers and persists from one year to the next. It likes to be buried quite deeply because of its relative size and it prefers the sharp drainage which all wild tulips enjoy. It is an excellent choice for a window box where the bigger Darwin tulips topple over or look too tall. There is another named form of this splendid bulb for which I am scanning the market. Called Zwanenburg, it is said to be a dark crimson and would be a welcome present if you know its whereabouts. Wild tulips tend to vanish after a few years, but praestans seems the amateur's answer. Fusilier does not fizzle out.

I first appreciated it when it appeared among some rough periwinkle and old tree roots on the central mound of my Oxford college garden. In April the periwinkles' young green leaves run

123

round a platoon of Fusiliers and look as if they are throwing up brilliant red flowers of their own. Like most good ideas, this was not mine, but it has brought a dull corner to life. Perhaps it will do the same for the College, so that tourists can be persuaded that yearly, behind closed doors, the Fellows initiate their newly-admitted females into the last surviving ceremony of Turkish tulip-worship, dancing round their drifts of Tulip Fusilier with their Warden as Sultan and their Bursar as Vizier. If this book goes into a second edition, I might name a Chief Eunuch too.

So far, I have written about bulbs with particular problems. Most of them have had to be ordered when in leaf or rewarded with sharp drainage. They may die out and waste your time or they may not turn up in the usual catalogues. You will notice that I never even mentioned that bright acid-yellow iris for early spring, the one called danfordiae which was found by a Mrs Danford in the Caucasus and has refused to persist at a flowering size for more than a year in most British gardens ever since. If this is the nature of better gardening, you are probably congratulating yourself on your daffodils. Do not rest easy. I have views on them too, for even here, some are better than others and not all of the best are obscure or difficult.

First, how and when should you plant them? In September, say the books, and they probably mean late October by the time you have a free weekend. Most daffodils will put up with that, but I must put in a plea for an earlier start. While digging out my endless bindweed in late August, I sometimes hit a clump of double-nosed narcissi and cannot help noticing that they are already thick with white roots. Daffodils dislike to be cut down too soon after flowering and these new roots suggest that in nature, they are only dormant for a very short while. Plant them, therefore, as early as you can, for your efforts will show in fewer blind bulbs in the following seasons. Plant, too, at the proper depth. When you are advised to plant 'six inches deep', the six inches begin from the nose of the bulb, not from the base. There is no skill in planting them, but you must be certain that the base, showing those dried little roots, rests flat at the bottom of the hole which you have dug. Do not wedge it into a V-shaped split, so that there is an air pocket underneath it.

Personally, I like the narcissi best, granted that the paler trumpet daffodils are now so expensive. Sempre Avanti (white with a bright orange cup), Carbineer (deep yellow with a bright red-orange cup) and Ice Follies (creamy white) make a vigorous and varied mixture. I am fond of ice-white daffodils, but will pass on the advice of a daffodil-fancier who wrote to me to point out that the lovely pure white Mount Hood, still the cheapest of white daffodils, lasts for a few years only and is not suitable, in his view, for a big planting in long grass. For some while I had a hundred bulbs in a spring flower bed, but since his letter of complaint they faded away in sympathy. I mention this in case you are considering buying a 25 kilogram pack of a single colour. Mount Hood should not, perhaps, be your only choice. The other whites, Beersheba and Mrs E.H. Krelage, would give a better run for slightly more money. Remember, of course, that all daffodil leaves are poisonous to cattle, so keep them away from the milking sub-division of your smallholding. The bulbs are large and have to be planted six inches deep with a spade, so if you are short of time, build up to a big plantation year by year. Away from the cows, we take them for granted as the natural covering for rough grass, parks and all those areas which we attack with a rotary mower. But they were hardly part of the great landscape parks of Capability Brown nor even the shrubberies of the Victorians. Our daffodils are modern discoveries, the best of which have been bred since the 1920s. What were they like before that?

Narcissi set a very old fashion among flowers. Wild varieties have been found in funeral wreaths in ancient Egyptian tombs: it was a narcissus, probably, which diverted Persephone with her playmates as they gathered flowers so fatefully in Sicily. There are double narcissi in Chinese paintings some 600 years old and a few varieties are wild in China, Japan and Kashmir. If you want to see wild narcissi, there are no richer countries than Spain or Portugal. Their daffodils also spread across the straits into North Africa and spill over into France and Italy. But there is nothing quite like the narcissus meadows of the Iberian Peninsula. There, the king of the wild varieties is the group now known as the Tazetta. These are the scented varieties with bunches of small flowers. The power of their scent has been traced back into their name, connecting 'narcissus' with the 'narc' part of narcotics, as a flower with a scent which causes numb lethargy. If you ever feel dizzy in the orchard during April, you might try blaming the narcissi blooming in its rough grass.

The true Tazettas are not thought to be hardy, but by one of those strange reversals which turn up in gardens' history, they seem to have been highly prized in the past. In the eighteenth century they were massed at Blenheim and Hampton Court. Many varieties were bred in Holland or shipped west from the Turkish markets. The largest was known as the Sacred Lily of China and used to be grown in bowls of pure gravel. Nowadays, the scented Tazettas are grown only in the south-west, in Cornwall or the Scillies where the flowers are forced for cutting. Elsewhere, the leaves start into growth too early and the only garden members of this old Mediterranean group are hybrids bred with greater stamina. The best of these are very good. You may know those two large-flowered Narcissi with bright orange-red cups, Cragford and Geranium. Like the long-lost 'Sacred Lily', they too will thrive in a bowl of nothing but pure gravel, watered freely to bring them to flower. If you do not want the mess and expense of compost in your flat, these modern Tazetta hybrids will grow without any earth at all.

Outdoors, the best of the group are surely the white and yellow forms of Cheerfulness. My neighbour grows them splendidly in a sunless raised bed, a hint which I have taken up. They are late flowering, a useful sequel to other hybrids. The flowers are those small double buttons, like a prolific jonquil's and the stems are only a foot high. The yellow one is just as good. If I could buy only one small daffodil for flower-beds in a small town garden, Cheerfulness would be reliable and easily maintained from year to year. It does not insist on sun. For grass, however, I would stand by my beloved Lent Lily. This flowers on a stem only six inches high, so it is a bulb for mown grass where it will match your pale blue anemones in the late March sunshine. Further west, it opens earlier. There are spectacular wild meadows of it in Dorset and above all, near Dymock in Gloucestershire. It is a Lent lily not because it is abstemious; it is simply the earliest wild variety, flowering as soon as February Gold in West Country gardens. Do not be put off by its modest height. In February it stands out quite clearly. If you live on the heavy soil which it likes, you will delight in its pale yellow and cream white trumpet flowers. The bulbs persist and multiply if you do not mow down their leaves before mid-June. I use them in groups of ten along the edge of my lawn and flowerbeds and consider them the perfect small daffodil for a small garden. Their names are a muddle, but lists tend to call them Pseudo-Narcissus. If you order in bulk, the most reasonable price is quoted yearly by Peter Nyssen, Railway Road, Urmston, Manchester. Specialists like Broadleigh Gardens sell other, pricier variations of which moschatus is a good pure white and Van Sion the 'original double yellow daffodil with an iron constitution'. My royalties on this book will go towards stock of them both.

The business of breeding big trumpet-varieties never bothered British growers until the mid-nineteenth century. Amateurs started the industry, of whom the first, as often, was a clergyman. Not until the 1850s did Dean Herbert 'cross a trumpet with a poet', or poeticus variety, in order to prove that wild narcissi might be hybrids. Others followed him, but when Wordsworth had wandered earlier, 'lonely as a cloud', he could not have been tracking anything as showy as the modern golden-yellow King Alfred. Probably, he too was picturing a field of small Lent Lilies.

Since the birth of the big modern trumpet, there have been other good finds in the wild, of which the most charming is the small milk-white Angels Tears, or Triandrus albus. Although its flowers hang like drops from the Milky Way, its name and origin are not celestial. A group of collectors once set out into the hills beyond Oporto, two elderly men and a young Portuguese boy called Angelo. Half way up a steep hill the party tired and here the stories diverge. The prettier version says that Angelo was sent on ahead by his older masters and told to dig up any yellow daffodils between their rest-place and the summit. He missed the daffodils and brought back the small, pale Triandrus albus instead. When they ticked him off, he burst into tears and by the time he calmed down, they realised that he had found a new variety for cultivation. So Triandrus albus became Angel's Tears, a small narcissus for walls, raised beds and rock gardens where it will flower and persist more reliably than any other small form from Spain or Portugal. Tazettas and the Triandrus forms have been married frequently and among their varieties, I recommend two beautiful forms with pale lemon and creamy white flowers. Their Tazetta blood makes them slightly tender, so they are best in the plunge bed or cold frame with which I began. On 15-inch stems, they bear several trumpet-shaped flowers in these ghostly colours. Silver Chimes will show up to ten separate flowers on one stem, while Thalia's flowers are rather larger. If you are bored with daffodils which have to be staked in bowls indoors, these pale hybrids are smaller and possibly even prettier. In their blood runs two good stories, the past of the old Tazetta which once caught Persephone and the Triandrus form which disappointed a Portuguese small boy. Among the other narcissi, large and small, I leave you to wander at will, warning you that the wild Hooped Petticoat is nowhere so good as at Wisley and that it lets you down at home unless you can give it as damp and rich a meadow as the RHS.

Just to show that I like straightforward plants as much as these specialist daffodils, I will put in a word here for the heavenly lily of the valley. A truly angelic plant, it was known to mediaeval gardeners by the name of ladder-to-heaven. Probably, this name derived from the white flowers which are set like a step-ladder up the stem. However, I also like to think that it refers to the direct route of scent, the spring bulb's most heavenly asset. In catalogues, the lily-of-the-valley appears as Convallaria. It likes semi-shade, a light leafy soil, no disturbances and a dedicated day of planting. Do not be carried away, as I have been, by the cheapness of bundles of corms, the so-called pips which are sold by the hundred in early spring as if fit to flower at once. To plant them is a slow business, as the long roots are matted and each one must be untangled and set at a full length of six inches so that its nose is at ground level. Unless you have a long and narrow shaded bed which is full of a light soil, you will find the job of planting them as far as possible from any ladder to heaven. Begin with a few corms instead and give them two years to settle in while watering freely in early summer and dressing them with a loose covering of leaf mould and powdered fertiliser in early April. The birds may remove some of this for their spring nests, but the lily-of-the-valley only thrives if it is fed early with this mixture, the one way in which to bring out the best in it. It is never happier than in narrow beds in a shaded town garden where it will tolerate dry shade if the soil is rich and light. There must be countless such sites, yet few gardeners now think of this gloriously scented flower for them. If you can give them a wet spring you will have them at their scented best.

At this point, better gardening rears its head again, involving you in trouble and expense. For the finest form is called Fortin's Giant and although the corms cost £3 for 10, they are worth the expense. They are stronger and bigger in flower. I only mention the rare pink form, for which bidding starts at £2 a corm, and a superb double called prolificans at £3.50 each. As a treat, they live up to expectations. So many scented flowers are twice as sweet in a double form because the petals are thicker. Prolificans ranks with the best. If you wonder how good its best can be, you should think back to their esteem in north German gardens where landlords would even demand bunches of lily-of-the-valley as rent. Like primroses in English woods, they attracted crowds of pickers from the towns, until Whit Monday became the Day of Action for all lovers of lily-of-the-valley. 'On that occasion', wrote a witness of the scene near Hanover, 'cottages are erected for the sale of coffee and while the gentlemen go out to pick, neither the pleasure of tobacco nor the twirling of the waltz is omitted'. Newmarket seems vulgar by comparison, so you should stock up with Fortin's Giant and waltz your way into the garden's high season of early June.

When you reach that point in the year your better gardening comes up against one of my worst mistakes. Two years ago, I fell into the trap of yet another British bargain and capped my cut-price 'pips' of lily-of-the-valley with a load of something even more useless. For a few pounds, I bought Alstroemerias in bulk, twenty-eight pounds in weight of a flower which is quite unlike any other and which puts better gardening on the map. Undoing the string, I began to suspect that I had bought a huge bulk of the wrong variety.

The right one is so good that I may jolt you into finding space for it. You will need a jolt because it is not the flower for a quick return nor is it the easiest of plants to handle. The popular name of the Alstroemeria is Peruvian Lily, which I shall now adopt. The best variety, indeed the only one which is neither too rare nor too predictable, is the strain called Ligtu Hybrid. I know nothing else with the colours to be found in this, except perhaps the Ghent Azaleas which will not grow in my soil. The Peruvian Lilies shoot up to a height of two and a half feet by mid June, but will stand well at the front of a border if you give them a frame of peasticks for support early in their life. Their flowers are prolific, held like hundreds of small funnels at the top of each stem. They seem to whisper of warmth, light soil, sunny walls and a happy life against Hampshire's old rectories where, indeed, they flourish famously along that garden-visitor's road to Mecca, the central stretch of the A272. The Peruvian Lily's mixed colours span peach pink, flame and apricot, colours which you would want from paints and fabrics but never expect to find in a garden. They are flowers for lime-ridden gardens which open to a knowing public. My favourite mass of Peruvian Lilies stands in a small square enclosure of Kiftsgate Court's fine garden, near Chipping Camden, Gloucestershire. In early July, it matches perfectly the shower of similar milk-blue flowers on Campanula lactiflora, an inspired choice as its companion. Beside them, a white Philadelphus spreads the scent whose absence is the only weak point of these wonderful flowers.

My bagful of tubers came to nothing. After two years a few flower stems of the common orange aurantiaca appeared for my troubles, but ungraciously I cut them down. In fact, this orange form has good black markings and is another fine match for milk-blue Campanulas. When I manured its bed, it disappeared for good. Meanwhile, the tubers had been a planter's nightmare. They remind me of the Shakespearean 'dead man's fingers' and an hour or two spent in trying to choose the right side to plant uppermost would soon lead you to call them by grosser names. They are also very brittle and as they will not show up for their first year or two, you can never be certain that they have survived your handling. Once they have settled, they spread with that determined vigour which seems to be reserved for plants which begin by sulking quietly. But first, you should try to plant the bare tubers deeply, at least six inches from the tops of the matted tubers to the level of the soil. This advice, not disproved by my own experience, derives from the elderly heir to a long-dead Edwardian gardener, whose borders of Alstroemeria were said to have been exceptional. So I trust him, even beyond the grave. If you have your doubts and wish to avoid this labour, I cannot blame you. Instead, you can order a lovely Ligtu mixture in a more convenient form from Broadwell Nurseries, Moreton-in-Marsh, Gloucestershire, who have made them a speciality for over 20 years and have views on how best to establish them. Caught by my cut-price substitutes, I am sure that it pays to buy these from a specialist's stock. Broadwell will only sell their stock in pots, already growing, for the Peruvian Lily is like the snowdrop: it changes homes most readily when it is not transplanted as a dry mat of tubers. Broadwell advise that they should be moved when they have died down, in late July or so. From this, you will see that the owner of the Peruvian Lily is much concerned with the problems of gaps. By late summer their three foot high stems are dead and gone. So you must plan to cover them over with creeping plants which make their growth late in the year. As the Peruvian Lily likes to lie deeply below ground it is not upset by to-ing and fro-ing above its head in August. I have enjoyed the almost hardy slate blue Convolvulus called mauretanicus, an excellent late-season plant, the invaluable trailing white Viola cornuta alba, and also the fine cloud of the pinkish-white flowers on Gypsophila Rosy Veil, that spectacular plant which makes its best growth from July onwards. Annuals are another obvious replacement, not least the convenient Nasturtium. These plants will give your group of

Peruvian Lilies an autumn season. Forethought is advisable here. The Peruvian Lily must have a light, warm soil facing south or west and it appreciates lime or chalk. Of all companions the Gypsophila, then, is particularly good, as it likes the same conditions and spreads in a rush from a few grey green tussocks in early June to a billowing cloud of flower stems nearly two feet wide in late July. It is not a tall plant, so you must cut down the Alstroemeria's dying stems to give it the run it deserves.

With Peruvian Lilies, I pass from the plunge bed to the warm summer border, a home for three types of bulb, in particular, which I would always want to risk in my summer garden. If the frost catches them, they are not too expensive to replace. They are bulbs of differing tastes, one less hardy, another for damp waterbeds as well as dry walls and a third as dependable as any flower for a light soil and southerly aspect.

I freely admit that the green-flowered Ixia, or Corn Lily, is on the border of hardiness, but when I saw it exhibited by Orpington Nurseries at the Chelsea Flower Show in 1976, I thought it the finest flower in the main marquee. Admittedly it comes from South Africa but this form of Corn Lily, a foot or so high, bears flowers of a bold electric green. When settled in a warm soil, it is as beautiful as any bulb I know. To settle it is not always easy, and for fear of frost it is often grown in pots in a cold greenhouse. But I am sure that we should be more adventurous, especially at the foot of south walls where the soil can be made light and sandy. The Ixia does not like to be damp in summer, yet it should also be buried three or four inches deep to protect it from sharp spring frost. Its leaves are slender, and it is important that they are not exposed too early in the year. They must stand in the sunshine, as the Ixia's flowers do not open on dull days. I do not see why the bulbs should be planted before March outdoors, though the books suggest October and a thick covering of ashes or bracken against frost. Otherwise, you can call on the plunge bed and start off your bulbs in late autumn in the shelter of that hospitable sand-pit. I would not mention this bulb if it was not quite out of the ordinary. Five of the small bulbs fit into a pot and the brilliant flash of electric colour from the flowers will remain with you all your gardening days. If only the green Corn Lily would do the same, but it is better to have known it than to dismiss it without experience.

A similar moral was once attached to another family which I want to smuggle in here as an extra in case the green Ixia is too elusive.

Known as the Tiger Flower, it was found in Mexico and should be planted in April in a light sunny soil. When the contributor to Curtis's Botanical Magazine had to write an accompaniment to its gorgeous picture, he berated the transience of all beauty. The Tiger Flower, he said, 'appears to us to surpass every competitor: we lament that this too affords our fair countrywomen another lesson, how extremely fugacious is the loveliness of form: born to display its glory but for a few hours, it literally melts away'. Why do not more of us bother with these so-called peacock flowers, or Tigridias? True, each flower only lasts a day but a bulb produces many of them during high summer and they are so extraordinarily exotic that in July and August you can hardly believe how these tropical flowers are growing in your garden. Again, I think they are a useful answer to a frequent request at the top end of the market: what can be grown to liven up a seaside house here or abroad in the holiday months or what can be grown round the edge of a British swimming pool with enough of a tropical look to match the bright blue of the water on our summer's two sunny days? They could always remind any girls in bikinis that all good things soon come to an end.

Top prices for Tigridia are around £1.50 for 10, but 20 make a dazzling impact at a height of a foot or so. Their three-petalled flowers are like some gorgeous butterfly, while their shades of butter-yellow or rose pink around blotched purple and white centres, are as spectacular as any orchid. You must lift their bulbs like dahlias each autumn and store them in a dry place away from all rodents. I have just lost last year's supply to mice, so be warned of the danger.

I now return to my original threesome and find myself back with a South African wild flower as the Tigridia's petals fall away. Here, I have a correction to much received wisdom. I remember the days when I was taught that the lovely Cape Lily would only grow in a warm, south-facing bed. True, these Crinum bulbs were often at ease there. But they had their competitors for this precious space, and many gardeners felt that their great clumps of strapping leaves and late heads of trumpet-shaped pink and white flowers were not worth the best room in the garden. 'They produce ample foliage', I quote at random from an old authority, 'and are far too big for small gardens'. It took me years to learn to disagree.

Even for these authorities, there was a hint of the truth. As the buds formed, the Crinum seemed to like to be watered heavily. In fact, it will stand happily in very wet sites throughout the year. This is invaluable. In South Africa, the species forms are reported to grow by the edges of ponds and lakes. In Europe they will flourish in a similar site. Off one bulb, you can expect eight pink or white flowers on a thick stem, some three to four feet high. If you do not know them, imagine an indoor Amaryllis and reason from that to a pale pink variety outdoors. If you do not even know the Amaryllis, picture a flower like an open funnel or trumpet, set in twos and threes round the top of a thick stem. The leaves are a thick arching clump and the general effect is architectural. Put it beside a pond or in a sodden bed which still receives full sun. There, there are fewer competitors. I have long wished for something bolder than the vulgar Spiraea and less temperamental than the half-hardy blood-red Lobelia. The Crinum is not a plant for a cold or exposed site, but in a sunny bog, it is superb. I have never seen it better than along an Oxfordshire stream and below the walls of the nearby rectory which stood on a water-bed. You could smell damp fungus in the house but, in August, the damp was a home for thick beds of Crinum. Order your bulbs in spring at anything from 75p each upwards. They are as big as a croquet ball. You should plant them about two feet apart and it is important to dig out a deep hole with a spade, so that the bulb is buried up to the neck. In a water garden, this is easily done. Their top-knot of young leaves will poke out above the ground, but they will come to no harm if they are in a sunny site away from sharp spring frost. A damp place in a sunny corner is not within reach of every gardener, but if you have one, the Crinum is a spectacular occupant. The flowers intermarry, but the best variety in Britain is, for once, the common one. Sold as powellii, it has huge trumpet flowers of a pleasant pink. The white form is more expensive and, to my eye, more handsome. Two whites to three pinks make a fine mixture wherever the air is warm and the ground wet.

A brief experience of wet conditions is always said to have sufficed for the most dependable of my summer trio, the Nerine or Guernsey Lily. I began by career as a columnist with its famous story, how it travelled as cargo on a ship from the Cape to the English Channel which sank in a rough sea. The Nerines are said to have floated to take up their tax-free residence on the nearby coast of Guernsey. They are supposed to have floated ashore on Guernsey sand and startled the tax-haven's early emigrés by sprouting pink lilies in the following autumn. No doubt this is only a story, and the variety to which it refers is no longer of interest to

133

gardeners. But it does express the truth about Nerines in our gardens. They like a very sandy soil, plenty of sun and intelligent watering. I still do not think that enough owners of small gardens, especially town gardens, know how to plan and use the best garden varieties or indeed what the best hardy variety is. Nerines' bulbs should not be buried deeply. They like to stand with the tip of their neck just above soil level. The hotter the site and the sandier their soil, the more they thrive. In addition to a light soil and sun, they like plenty of water in dry weather from July onwards as they run up to flower. This last point is sometimes missed, as everybody writes about their preference for a thorough baking or a roasting in a sunny bed. But a free supply of water makes a serious difference to all the Nerines I know, raising their flowers by as many as a third. You can still plant them in late April but you cannot expect them to settle properly until their second year. I think they are completely hardy in one of those narrow beds below a south-facing wall on a London house, the perfect site for them. Private growers are bringing a mass of the older varieties back on to the market, including the deeper rose-reds and the less hardy breeds from Edwardian greenhouses. Until their stocks build up, I will direct you to the best that is freely available, the named Fenwick's variety.

This form was raised in the Gloucestershire gardens of Abbotsbury by a family whose most green-fingered member still lives in my Oxfordshire village. In a stony bed beside the cobbled courtyard of her former stables, the true Fenwick's variety still runs riot, allowing one to compare it with the plain forms. It is stronger, a clearer pink and decidedly larger in flower. As it multiplies quickly, it is the right one for better gardens, although its price is five times higher than the mainstream Nerine. The flowers appear on strong two-foot stems, their petals a brilliant pink in September and October, crinkled like ribbons with a permanent wave. If I had a garden on sheltered sandy soil, I would consider growing this Nerine as a commercial crop. Its bulbs multiply freely after three years and can be sold to any sensible gardener. At the same time, the old stock would be covered in cut-flowers for the local florist. I have had many requests for ideas for otiose patches of kitchen garden from readers who can no longer afford any help with them. On light soil, a small Nerine business seems to be an entrepreneurial possibility, at least to the cost of a part-time gardener's wages. Except for weeding, the cultivation is of the simplest.

In rivalry, Jersey also has her lily, the near-hardy form of the garden Amaryllis. Its big trumpet flowers will emerge in a warm summer beneath a south wall, but its big bulbs are not a risk to be lightly run. Guernsey has the edge for gardeners inland.

I can hardly sign off from better bulbs without a word for those justifiable favourites, the Gladioli. There are no difficulties in growing the florists' autumn varieties and suppliers' lists will tell you all you need to know. But my heart was won recently by an even smaller sort, the varieties of Mediterranean gladioli and those which are sometimes listed under the name Gladiolus nanus. These, I can assure you, are far too little known. They are not expensive. As often, a visit to another garden stirred me into action. White gardens are everywhere nowadays, and as I ran through the plants in a pretty public one last summer, it seemed too easy to predict them. Pink Mrs Sinkins, Iceberg roses, grey-leaved Artemisia and the lamb's ear which does not flower, white Delphinium Galahad, white Campanula, all of them excellent, especially the long flowering alliarifolia Ivory Bells and the white variety of the good tall lactiflora: all these, and the glorious white Musk Rose Pax, are the backbone for fashionable gardeners who want white borders to suggest a cool light round their weeping silver pear trees.

But who bothers with a small white Gladiolus called The Bride? Yet in early July, I saw it used as a carpet, hundreds of white spikes above thin and elegant leaves about two feet high in that wonderful white garden round the espaliered fruit trees at Manor House, Cranborne, Dorset. A nurseryman in Chelsea, Mr Colville, first came up with it, by crossing a basic red Gladiolus with a South African yellow, best seen in the wild in Natal. The results were not quite hardy in open ground, but all of them are pretty and noted for their early flowering. In most years, The Bride would be past its best by the end of June. There is nothing difficult about growing its corms. They are available from any of the bigger and cheaper suppliers, usually in their spring catalogues. When you plant them, you have a choice again. You can play safe with the plunge bed and put six corms two inches deep in a six-inch pot, in early October. The glass roof and the sand pit will blunt the frost and by April your small Gladioli will be shaping up for buds. Otherwise, you can take a gamble beneath a warm wall in light soil. I still have corms which survived the 1981/2 winter outside, though it decimated the stock. They were not in a promising bed, so I believe that this group is rather hardier than many suppose. After all, the corms could be lifted like dahlias and stored away safely in autumn. I do assure you that they are worth any effort. Outdoors, I would delay their first planting until early April.

No variety is ugly, although The Bride, a pure white, is particularly pretty. Nymph and Blushing Bride are good companions, basically white, but with a reddish marking in their throats. Prince Claus is better still, a white with red blotches on its lower petals. If you can still find Amanda Mahy, it is an unusually deep pink with a pretty violet-purple blotch in the centre. Grown in a pot, it is admirably strong. As none of these plants exceeds two feet in height, they will not topple forwards if you leave them indoors. They can be increased by division and if you grow your own freesias, these gladioli will pose no problems, needing similar care. Outdoors, I put much trust in the shelter of neighbours as a good guard against frost. The mounds of a Cistus and the winter leaves of an Acanthus must help, I feel, to shelter whatever goes beside them.

Perhaps you already grow the rose-purple wild Corn Lily, Gladiolus byzantinus, that distinction of wild gardens, orchards or shrub rose beds in early summer. It is certainly a flower I would add into a sunny wilderness of moderately tough grass as it prolongs the season into July and is hardy in all but the fiercest winters. We have all made too little of it, but if you are nervous of the nanus forms, although my two nearest lists call them 'completely hardy', you might like to watch out for corms of byzantinus's unusual white form. It is not cheap, but is a safer compromise on most soils if you want elegant small gladioli in midsummer.

As the gladioli fade, they join my final summer bulb before the Autumn Snowflakes start the season again. Lilies are not the best bulbs for my own lime soil, so I contain them in large pots where I can give them their leafy, acid soil and yearly top-dressing. As their enemy is wet in winter, the past year's frost and snowdrifts hit them very hard because the ice melted through their soil, rotting the bulbs beneath. Another year, I will store all potted lilies in a garden shed for the winter. Of many good varieties, the best in a pot is the lime-hating speciosum and its many named forms, which bear reflexed flowers of blush-white, spotted heavily with pink. They respond to regular doses of Phostrogen in season and stand out for their quality in July and August, lining a brick path away from my back door. Obligingly, they prefer to stand in shade, four bulbs deep down in a large nine-inch clay pot. Plastic pots are not a good home as they blow over in the wind when the lilies are in full flower. Plant them as early in the year as you can and never keep the bulbs dry or waiting, as they are not dormant.

Outside a pot, mercifully, I grow this chapter's grand finale, the wonderful Regale Lily. It flourishes on lime and a dry sunny soil and in July, it breathes a scent of exceptional coolness from those white trumpets of flower marked with lines of maroon purple on their exteriors. I like it best in a small square bed to itself with an underplanting of trailing silver leaves and Geranium Buxton's Blue for continuity. Anyone can grow this easy and persistent miracle, in towns or cottage gardens, in pots on a terrace or clumps among old roses. It prefers to grow on without manure and looks best in a big clump. As prices now reach 50p a bulb, that sounds like lavish advice, but this book's most economical tip is the raising of Regale lilies by the hundred from their own seed. They can be sown in the spring after flowering from seed saved the previous autumn. Store it in envelopes when it turns brown and dry and the old pods split. After one year in a seed-bed, the young regales are ready to move to a permanent home, flowering freely in their second and third years. Better gardens should never miss them, the cheapest source of a powerful scent which lifts you beyond all worldly distractions on a cool, clear evening in July.

Chapter Six

Better Alpines

I have now reached the level where my own heart lies. The small plants from mountains, alpine meadows and distant woodlands first turned my interest in gardening into a passion. I expect to end my days with them, because so many need just the degree of attention which I imagine will suit my retirement. Several hundred will fit into the small garden which I picture for myself, when freed from the hateful chore of mowing a lawn. I was trained in a great botanic garden which arranged its alpines in separate, geographical sections. Perhaps that has left me with a more romantic view of them than of any other plants which I romanticise. I feel I can sense a common Chinese and Japanese quality to the fleeting Dawn Poppies, or Eomecon, and blue Meconopsis of spring, while a tougher, more abundant style marks out the yellow Onosmas, pink and white Erodiums and pale yellow alpine Hypericums from the Balkan mountains in high summer. Persuading myself that their natural home betrays them, I have never thought of such alpines as tame, garden plants.

On their merits and fascination, I run the risk of coming to resemble what I hate. 'Lo, the curtain rises', begins one of my old gardening books, 'the scene is set with heather in full bloom: a royal purple mantle has stretched away up the hills and is meeting the golden sunset as old Sol retires to rest behind the valley . . .'. A mass of heather is not unromantic in the wild, but I detest it in the confinement of gardens. Those leaves are so miserable after flowering and the flowers themselves are so scrawny and so obviously pining for a wild hillside. As plants, of course, they are useful against weeds and bare spaces. My soil disqualifies most of them and my taste rules out the rest. I save my purple patches for truer alpines of a more distinctive shape.

Second only to heather, rocks have given rock plants a bad name.

138

There is no need whatsoever to bother with outcrops of incongruous rock if you want to grow alpines well. At most, a boulder gives the plants a cooler root-run. But you can contrive this on the flat without going to the expense of a load of limestone. At last, preservation orders guard the natural pavements of Westmoreland limestone which were once plundered for urban rockeries. Yet in its infancy, the Alpine Garden Society faced a critical choice of options. One group argued powerfully that alpine gardeners should merely study alpine rocks and leave the plants in second place. The others, fortunately, won, allowing the AGS to develop into the most rewarding plant society in the country. If you ignore rocks, you can please most alpines by planting them between blocks of paving. Leave gaps about an inch wide between slabs laid flat on a mixture of good loam, grit and sand. Fill up the gaps with the same gritty soil and plant according to the paving's aspect. The late E.B.Anderson was a master of such 'alpine' pavements and crammed short lengths with exceptional plants. He claimed that the smallest space sufficed for a fascinating paved garden, proving the point by growing over 125 different plants in a stretch only fourteen feet long and three and a half feet wide. Watering was only necessary in very dry weather. Otherwise, plants revelled in a cool root run. He taught me that paved beds were a marvellous site for the lovely pale blue Hepaticas of March and early April, relations of the wood anemone with those pure, single flowers. This tip, he said, went back to William Robinson himself, that king of the wild and woodland garden, whose best Hepaticas flourished in a stretch of Sussex paving. Paved gardens should not be wasted only on thyme and yet more aubrieta.

Hepaticas thrive, too, in gardens built on the opposite principle. These beds are raised up above ground level for the sake of sharper drainage, free circulation of air, and controlled compost. They ease inspection and photography and suit an aching back. The best raised beds I know have been built and tended by Valerie Scott and her husband, David, round the Dower House, Boughton House, Kettering, Northants. They began this adventure a dozen years ago, after their marriage, and now look after the most interesting private collection of alpines in England. The beds were supported by railway sleepers to a height of two or three feet. Various soils fill them, ranging from acid peat compost for their contented pink and white forms of Sanguinaria, or the Canadian Bloodroot which all alpinists envy, to a mixture of grit and loam which pleases the violas, specal dianthus and many rare primulas and pulsatillas. My own fancy has been for raised beds which are surfaced with fine grit for sharp drainage round the plants' necks. I like their appearance and their ease and aptness for all the plants I will now discuss. If you have an unsatisfactory bed, I urge you to build it up, if only by nine inches, and edge it with wooden planks toned down by dark brown creosote. In full sun, refuting the usual wisdom, the Scotts grow magnificent Hepaticas, recommending their own Ada Scott form as the finest, now, in the family. If I add that David Scott is ninety-five and responsible with his wife for the maintenance of this lovely two acre garden and the propagation of many thousand alpines in frames every year for sale to visitors, I am only partly paying a tribute to the grip which a raised bed allows you to take on your garden. I am also saluting one of Britain's most remarkable gardeners.

Between paving stones or in raised beds, you can now plan a landscape of alpines without any lumps of stone. The same rules of contrast and colour apply to alpines too, so you will improve the effect if you plan them as if they were permanent shrubs. Most of them survive harsh winters, because they relish snow at home. Their enemy is a wet winter, not a snowy one. They tend to be evergreen, so they are pleasant companions in winter. For flowers, form and interest, they are the charmed group for any better garden. Once again, I will begin by naming ten good varieties for any gardener, however expert. I omit the families which I discuss later and again, I assume the soil is alkaline. The choice is unusually hard, so I should warn that in places, I try to be different.

In spring, I would begin with some good Pulsatillas. These are lavender-blue or rose-red flowers in the general family of the anemone. The flowers open like deep cups from the soft and silky buds in April before the leaves appear. Afterwards, the fluffy seed heads last for weeks over foliage like a wild carrot's. There are many good forms, of which the rarest was slavica Budapest, a pale lavender flower from golden buds. The true parent vanished, so deeper lavender blues now come from forms of Europe's native vulgaris. I suggest that you pick your plant when it flowers in April. There is a lovely red, rubra, a white and some uncommon yellows before you stray into other, more awkward alpine forms.

I would follow up with a fine form of common old Campanula carpatica called Blue Moonlight. This was developed from a true alpine parent and although it has been bred to its unique shade of silvery milk-blue the purists would forgive it anywhere. It is four inches high and makes a small mat of leaves from which the little stems bear wide cup-shaped flowers. It flowers with incredible freedom and in June, dominates its corner of the garden. Bressingham Nurseries of Diss, Norfolk, developed it and now sell it.

I could not omit a phlox and in order to be slightly different, I will choose Phlox divaricata laphamii. In the wild, this grows in woodlands from the Mississippi to the south-east coast of America and I find it the easiest form of its type. It thrives on my lime, but might prefer neutral leaf mould. I keep it in half shade where it spreads by its rooting layers and sends up thin stems about nine inches high in April. Each bears an open sky-blue flower whose petals are rounded and known for their lack of a revealing notch. Its enemy, I find, is the slug which cannot resist it in high summer. A named form called Chattahoochee turned up in Florida, but I preferred my plain laphamii when this polysyllabic wonder proved quick to die out on open ground. It belongs in a special sink. Meanwhile Ingwersens of Gravetye, East Grinstead, Sussex, sell laphamii and one plant soon gives you a dozen rooted stems.

Pale blues seem to attract me, so I will round them off with two more. In autumn, I could not omit the trailing Geranium Buxton's Blue, a garden form of an alpine from central Europe. For months, this shows open flowers whose zone of pale blue runs round a white centre. Its stems trail at ground level and put on a sudden spurt of growth during late summer. It will grow anywhere and fills in conveniently for my other blue, the rarer Codonopsis, or Himalayan Bell Flower. Any beginner could grow this easy plant, whose pale lavender bells have inner markings of orange and black matched only in a passion flower. All the varieties are good, but clematidea is the commonest, a trailing plant which shoots up to a foot in midsummer and then dies back below ground later in the year. So long as you do not dig into it while it is dormant, it will last for years. Buxton's Blue covers up for it in the closed season.

It is time now for a strong yellow. None is stronger than the American forms of small Evening Primrose, or Oenothera. On a dry and well-drained soil, the form called Missouriensis is spectacular. Big cups of flower open off the creeping stems and are the boldest primrose-yellow. Wet soil or a wet winter upset its long tap root, but otherwise it grows with abandon. It needs a quieter companion and for sound value I would include one from the family called Erodium. They are all grossly neglected, although they flower for weeks and develop pretty clumps of finely cut leaves. My favourite is a spotted one called guttatum whose white flowers are marked with a central blotch of chocolate-brown. It multiplies from cuttings and flowers for weeks, a quiet and curious plant for a dry and sunny soil. It is a close cousin to the wild Geraniums, so you can rely on it. Ingwersens list it still at 75p and one plant spreads into stock for cuttings in late July which root with alacrity.

In eighth place, I think we need a dramatic shrub. On any soil, my favourite is the pale lemon-yellow broom called Cytisus kewensis. The flowers have a poor scent, but the plant has the other virtues of a good broom without either of the vices. It is not harshly coloured and it is not too upright or leggy. It will spill forwards over a low wall or the top of a bank set with alpine plants. In time, it reaches two feet and a width of a yard or so, but your front garden's wall can still house it.

A similar site would suit a South African shrub which used to be thought half-hardy. Euryops has survived the recent winter without dropping a leaf and its silver foliage is so handsome that I could not possibly omit it. It will not grow more than nine inches high or wide in its usual sunny site, but I learnt by chance that Euryops is possibly better in light shade on a far from gritty soil. My biggest plant of it grows there and I know reports of others a yard wide in shade. It prefers a moist home in its native New Zealand and loses none of the silver in its leaves. If neighbours overhang it, it dies back and on any view, it lasts at its peak for only five years. Summer cuttings root like weeds if set in any flower bed, so it is not easily lost. I do not care for the yellow discs of flower, but they do the plant no harm.

I will end with an old friend to reassure you. No Top Ten on a dry and sunny site could omit the family of sun roses. Catalogues sell them under Helianthemum and the many named varieties are the best value for money. I like those with flame coloured single flowers or with the word Wisley in their titles. These shrubs love their namesake, the sun, and will only fail on wet or poorly drained soil. After three or four years their wide mats begin to go brown in their ageing centres and are best replaced from easily rooted cuttings. White fly can sometimes be a problem in summer, but otherwise these are the great carpet-plants for a bed in June. The various shades of green or grey now bred into their leaves are a pleasure for the rest of the year.

These plants are intriguing but easy and ought to grow for anyone who wards off slugs. I now turn in more detail to some of my favourite families and in order to put my top ten in their place. I will begin with a mountain plant which is the best thing in my garden and probably the best tip in this book. It flowers continuously, grows anywhere and splits into a hundred children. Viola cornuta is at home in Spain's Pyrenees but in catalogues is never made to sound exciting. It is surrounded by rich descriptions of ruby red pansies, blues with black markings and apricots stained with orange. Who would bother with a single white flower or worse, a lavender mauve? When Ruskin had the absurd idea of renaming all garden flowers with English names, he had to call these violas Horned Pansies. The very idea would put most people off. There are two forms, one white, the other lavender, and I think you should use the next month to find a plant of them both.

I would encourage you in the search. Three years ago, I bought one plant of the white-flowered form. It flowers at a height of six inches, but is covered with so many flowers that its mat of fresh green leaves is invisible from late May until July. It then draws breath and starts to flower again in August. All the while, its stems are spreading about a foot wide so that you can dig up small pieces and multiply your stock by cuttings which are already rooted. From my one plant, I already have 150 or more and can split them as many times again. Their stems block out all weeds and sit prettily between almost any planting – old roses, campanulas, irises and so forth. They like the dampness of my garden more than I do, so perhaps they have been unusually vigorous. But I can count on an edging which will flower throughout the summer, a match for any laborious bedding plants. The white form is such a fresh white, at its best in early evening when it stands out clearly beneath the dim shapes of old rose bushes and Day lilies. The mauve variety is more vigorous and will train itself up into a mound which you can usefully pull over blank spaces or the gaps left by early poppies and anchusas in the border. Lavender mauve sounds a dreary colour, but in this viola it is soft and clear and will match almost anything. The flowers are larger than a violet's but not so large as a pansy's. They are known as horned because of the shape of their many seed pods after flowering. Find a plant from a friend, or order the seed and sow it in July. It is small, firm and a bright red brown. It comes up like cress.

It is customary nowadays to mourn the passing of the old-fashioned violet, and my laments have joined in the chorus. I doubt very much if any of the aristocratic violets were ever so good in the garden as this white Horned Pansy. It has none of their scent, but has the vigour and long season which they lacked. Pansy-fanciers can now turn to a remarkable list which has brought the violas and violettas back into fashion. Down in New Eltham, Richard Cawthorne first turned his gardens into a nursery of these brightly-coloured plants. In his spare time, he took over several allotments and made his London nursery a place for lovers of flowers to visit in June and July. He first caught the public eye with his prize exhibits at Chelsea and has kept up a personal crusade for the violettas, old and new. He has recently moved to 28 Elm Road, Sidcup, Kent, from where he lists the old-fashioned pansies and his many new crosses, violettas and a range of violas species. Stock is limited and he only despatches his plants in April for orders taken in the preceding year. His list adds two desirable colours to the range of the Horned Pansy. Belmont Blue is a soft sky-blue which I failed to establish on my first attempt. In his view, it ranks as ground-cover, so I am trying new plants in the cool, semi-shade which they obviously prefer. Among the rampant whites, they would look lovely. Gustave Wermig has settled itself more readily and throws up deeper mauve-purple flowers on longer stems. Lilacina is a silvery-lilac Horned Pansy, and I am trying it this year for the first time.

The blood of Viola cornuta runs in the family of the violettas, the small-flowered miniature violas which Mr Cawthorne has revived. I am not sure how to distinguish them from certain small-flowered violas and as it happens, my favourites in his list all fall in the viola section. Visitors to the superb gardens at Manor House, Cranborne, Dorset, can inspect a collection of many well-mixed violettas in box-edged beds, a neat idea for any front garden, however small. With me, they dislike a poorly-drained soil in winter but prefer a cool, semi-shaded place in summer. Like pinks, they can exhaust themselves by flowering too freely, so they should be dead-headed thoroughly in order to stop them setting seed. The slug, sliming quietly in cool and half-shaded places, is very partial to their flavour. Mr Cawthorne stresses the importance of spraying against greenfly, a primary pest on these small flowers.

My own favourite falls in the pansy class, where Mr Cawthorne lists some long-lost varieties. He has added several fine forms, raised by himself, of which one of the best promises to be the robust

Fiona, long-stemmed, sweetly-scented and the bearer of white flowers suffused with a pale lavender-mauve. Like Mr Cawthorne himself, I prefer the small-flowered varieties, closer to good old cornuta than to the garden pansies. The bigger, pansy-flowered varieties are less likely to survive the winter. Either group will root from late summer cuttings set in damp, sandy soil but they take up to two months to establish themselves. Though slow, they are not difficult.

My own taste is for the very dark colours or the very pale, meeting in a compromise with the pale lavender mauves and rose-lilacs. Iantha, one of the violettas, has a depth of violet-blue and a clearly marked outline whch stands out in the Cawthorne show-tables. Among the pale rose-lilacs, Vita derives from its namesake's garden at Sissinghurst and bears good flowers of this unusual colour, so well suited to a viola's simple shape. It is more showy than the smaller-flowered viola Nellie Britten which commemorates a great lady gardener. Her name has dropped out of general currency, but this perfect mauve-flowered viola is marked by darker lines which meet, on my plants, in a small yellow centre. The mauve is the true tone, not the half-way colour which has brought the name into disrepute, and in a well-drained soil, the plant will bear its small flowers, shaped like an open violet's, from May until October. Nellie Britten's name has given way to Haslemere, her former garden in Dorset, but Mr Cawthorne's list has corrected the error, I notice, although alpine nurseries still use Haslemere, if they stock the plant at all. It is an easy plant whose colour is like no other and all my friends want cuttings when they see it.

Jackanapes has no alternative name, unfortunately, but it boasts a very special pedigree. It was noticed by the great Miss Jekyll herself while she walked one day in her garden with her pet monkey on her shoulder. Noticing this new seedling, she named it after her pet. Its double colouring is fresh and clear on any bank or raised bed. The upper two petals are a deep mahogany brown, while the lower three are a pure butter-yellow. It flowers and grows very freely in a sharply drained bed and I would hate to miss it. I am less keen on the smaller-flowered forms with contrasting shades of yellow and purple or lilac. They soon look messy if you mass too many in one bed. But I give high marks to two clear pale yellows which are hardly distinguishable side by side. Moonlight is perhaps the stronger, while Jeannie Bellew has similar long stems and was first named at Broadwell nurseries. Mr Cawthorne's new and

145

vigorous Aspasia matches two tones of yellow on its upper and lower petals, while Velleda is a winning white violetta and Alcea a pale addition to the list. Mrs Lancaster is a shapely cream-white of vigour and hardiness. Its name honours the great lady gardener, now in her seventies, whom Mr Cawthorne used to assist in his earlier life when she took lessons to improve her shooting.

Mr Cawthorne complains of the 'poor habit' of old apricot yellow Chantreyland, but I value it as a flower whose colour is unique in the family and whose shape suggests a pansy more than a violetta. If you never allow the seed-box to dry out, this plant grows easily from seed, available through Thompson and Morgan, London Road, Ipswich. Chantreyland grows into a fine edging under white roses or the pale blue Campanulas of early July. Thompson and Morgan's seeds will give you some other good varieties, not least their aptly named King of the Blacks. I have designs on a black and white corner for my garden and when this pansy's seeds have germinated more freely than usual, I plan to try one. Otherwise, I can use the new Black Beauty, a form with wide flowers which Mr Cawthorne has raised himself.

Three last violas will round off this sample. Maggie Mott was common in Edwardian gardens, but her flowers of pale silver-mauve, marked with a pale cream centre, had slipped from the lists until Mr Cawthorne brought her back. I like to see her in isolation, for these violas and violettas can soon become a confusion if you mix too many colours in the same bed. Inverurie Beauty is distinctive and exceptionally good value. A Scottish variety, it spreads very freely and flowers with unusual generosity. The colour is pure violet purple, but the stems are especially long, making this a splendid flower for cutting. My other favourite is a large-flowered form of the lavender cornuta which is usually listed as the Huntercombe variety, either purple or violet. Its colour is deeper and its capacity for flower is unsurpassed. Some fifty years ago, this vigorous viola was a common suggestion for bedding schemes and rosebeds where its clear-cut colour and long season were appreciated. Now, we seldom see it outside gardens of the National Trust, one of the good things we have forgotten in the interests of new and brighter sorts of marigold. Viola Huntercombe is at its best in a rich and damp soil as an edging or underplanting, especially under the pink and purple of old-fashioned roses. It makes a mat a foot wide and nine inches high and shares the family's ease of propagation. There are other forms of similar habit in paler shades of blue – Irish Blue, Blue Maiden and so forth – but I have never found them so robust and persistent. Like the other good violas, the Huntercombe form falls between the pansy and the violet, but it flowers more freely than either. June and July are the months for sowing next year's crop, and a few plants, bought or begged, will start off many hundreds more, one of the best things in an easy summer garden. If you mistrust me, I will conjure with the magic name of Sissinghurst where this heavenly viola is bedded in big drifts under those huge pink Bourbon roses when you turn hard right from the forecourt and keep going straight to the rose garden's edge. This is not an alpine plant, but it ought still to be a better garden's friend.

After my preliminary tangle with violas, I will return to the alpinist's own terrain and begin with good words for the Saxifrage. This vast family has something for everyone, on lime or peat, sun or shade, in cool or unheated greenhouses, in sites for leaves or for transient flowers. I would like to retire and sort out its branches and their history. Meanwhile, I can only skim a few of the best in my experience. I want to centre on two of its branch lines, one called kabschia, the other aizoon. They sound like a mischievous sister and brother in some Saki short story of a weekend party. The longest list of kabschias is put out by Waterperry Horticultural School, Waterperry, Oxford. Aizoons can be bought from Ingwersens of East Grinstead, a supplier whom I take for granted in the names which follow.

Most of the kabschias flower earlier and prefer half-shade on rich and very gritty soil. I grew them best in a bed of ashes mixed with only a quarter, by bulk, of heavily manured loam. They dislike strong sunlight in summer and they flower on small, rock-hard cushions of grey or green rosettes, at a height of about three inches. If you drain them and shade them, you will admire them every spring. All the Kabschias are man-made hybrids and there are masses of varieties, two of which flower abundantly out of doors and two of which are too pretty to miss. The free-flowerers are Cranbourne and the amazing jenkinsae. Cranbourne has deep pink flowers on firm clumps of tiny green leaves and will resist the wildest March weather. Jenkinsae beats all competition in the family for its prolific flowers and willing growth. A five-year-old plant makes a mat of fifty flower buds or more, opening to a sweet blush pink. A pinkish memorial for a Mr Jenkins: this is a saxifrage of great vigour and eventually, it may well spill out into a grey-green mat a foot or so wide. The weather never spoils its mass of spring blossom.

For subtlety, however, I recommend the hybrid Burseriana major. It grows more modestly, but its flowers of pearl-white are rather larger and stand on deep red stems. The contrast is unforgettable on a well-contented plant. Among the yellows, the recent Valerie Finnis deserves its prizes, a saxifrage with spiky leaves of a green-grey whose stems are a charming shade of pink. There are hundreds of others, but I would begin with these four in a shaded bed, full of grit and a thin, but rich, dressing of loam. In shallow pans, they are possibly better still, as the flowers escape the spring rains while the sun and shade can be controlled to suit them. You can bring the pans indoors from that trusted friend, the plunge bed, and marvel at the mass of jenkinsae's flowers and the style of the lovely Burseriana without leaving your arm chair. They are totally hardy, but object to heavy central heating.

Aizoon saxifrages are tougher and come later into flower. Their season is April and May and they belong on slopes and walls, on harsh, dry sites where plants seem to cling for dear life. Their rosettes of leaf are larger, in the best forms, and their encrusting silver coat helps them to retain water and avoid scorching in a hot place. Again there are many worth growing, but they may not flower every year, for reasons I never fathom, so I like to choose the most spectacular silver rosettes of leaf for the blank seasons. Beyond a doubt, these leaves occur on the legendary Tumbling Waters form which grows happily out of a wall or at 90° angles off a bank. Eventually, a huge foaming stem of white flower shoots off its silver strap-like leaves to a length of a foot and a half. This effort tends to kill the plant off. I once saw a wall with a dozen such Waters all Tumbling at once, perhaps the most dramatic sight in any alpine garden. Even without the flowers, the leaves are magnificent. You can compromise, however, with a smaller choice called Southside Seedling. Its plume of flowers is about nine inches long and each tiny flower on it is beautifully marked with red. The rosettes of leaves are silver, too, and the plant survives the business of flowering. Set where they face you from a wall, these saxifrages are spectacular. Better gardeners will value them in May and explore the rest of their varied family. One mention never does justice to the saxifrage, so I will suspend my pen against the hope of a monologue in my old age. Remember, only, that this is the family to explore for yourselves, beyond the two branches whose star-turns I have singled out.

Even a classic rock garden of Saxifrages needs a taller shrub or two, a well-branched evergreen which will fit in with the boulders and lead the eye away from the stone. I detest dwarf conifers almost without exception and see nothing but coyness and a quaint, misshapen interest in their sombre shapes of green, gold or blue. Better gardeners would gladly burn them all. Instead, they might like to risk a Daphne, the most desirable shrub from the company of small alpines and one whose family caters for all skills and tastes.

Daphnes scare off amateurs by a reputation which only a few varieties deserve. Even the most notorious can prove amenable for a few years. I have a stony bed near the house, facing north on a cold, wet soil. Once, when digging there, I found the top half of a pair of false teeth, set in metal, suggesting that somebody before me had lost patience with its heavy soil. On impulse, I planted the awkward Daphne called blagayana in this unpromising site. For six years, this spreading Daphne grew apace, creeping over the soil with those stems which like to be pinned down with stones or brick wherever they touch the ground. In mid-career, it flowers to the full, an unforgettable carpet of white tubular flowers at the tips of each bare stem. Stained with yellow at their centres, they smelt powerfully of white Regale lilies, open already in April. A Hungarian Count Blagay came across the plant in a Hungarian woodland. It will seldom survive for ten years, but if you like a challenge and can give it a square yard or more over which to hug the ground, this sweetly-scented shrub will become a part of your life. The longer it grows, the more stones you must heap on to its stems. They will root when forced on to the ground and will keep the shrub going when the centre, inevitably, begins to rot. Eventually, the stems decide to turn brown and succumb to disease or weariness, perhaps to a variety of wilt. But the experiment is worth the effort, not least for the scent of the flowers in the matt dark green axils of the leaves.

Blagayana is not the most difficult Daphne, but before going up the scale of awkwardness, I must insist on five shrubs of great garden value. The first is remarkably easy and for that alone, I admire it. It is sold either as Daphne burkwoodii or as Daphne Somerset, the latter being the form offered by John Scott, the Royal Nurseries, Merriott, Somerset, who first selected it. It will grow into a bush three or four feet high, maybe more, and will spread quite widely in a few years. It is not evergreen. It is said to prefer sunshine and a rich gritty soil, neither of which I have given it. It still grows freely, and although it is not an exquisite plant, I welcome its masses of pinkish white flowers buried in the tips of the shoots in late spring. Anyone can grow this vigorous variety, a shrub which would fill in prettily between bigger specimens. It fans out into a broad head and if it has a fault, it is the bareness at its base which increases with the years. I would never dare to cut a Daphne back.

Next comes my favourite, one of the essential garden shrubs. The golden-leaved form of the scented Daphne, odora, is always said to be hardier, and I like the brightness of its gold and green leaves even if this belief is unproven. It is a shrub for the foot of a south or west wall where it proves totally hardy, never better than after the long, hard winter of 1981/2. It is also an excellent pot plant for a cold greenhouse. The flowers open to a rose-white from deep ruby red buds in a collar of leaves, but the scent is the magic, heavy, sweet-centred, a dream come true. The bush grows about three feet high and wide without much trouble. I give it the prize for the best scent in a spring garden, so you have to find room for it somehow. Mercifully, it roots freely from summer cuttings taken back to the point where new and old wood meet. Between April and July, I find they root on average within two months. It is in the highest class, a shrub worth risking as cover over a sheltered rock garden which needs more body and form.

Two slower and smaller ones are hardly more difficult, though few people know them. The smaller and slower is a Chinese evergreen called retusa. I have been horrible to this plant, but it grows steadily and covers itself in pale rose-white flowers against dark glossy evergreen leaves in early May. I bought it in the year of the great drought and almost forgot to water it in its whalehide pot. I planted it in the teeth of a north wind which gathers force across twelve miles of open countryside. In the ferocious 1981/2 winter, its small, sturdy branches dropped most of their leaves, but new ones soon came along with the usual flower buds. After six years the bushes are scarcely a foot tall, though thick-stemmed and densely-branched. In a sink or on top of a wall, they would be far more exciting than a dwarf conifer. Their slow growth continues over thirty years to a height of three feet. The scent, again, is miraculous. Whoever found a miniature Fir which smelt of rose-powder? Retusa thrives on a lime or acid soil and although I feed it fortnightly on Phostrogen in summer, I cannot call it any more difficult than a bush of Cistus.

From Naples comes a similar shrub, the dependable Daphne

collina. This does not like to be dry or waterlogged, but in any damp and sunny soil it will push steadily on to an eventual height of two feet or so. Its leaves are dark and glossy, but the flowers are a deeper rose-purple in late April. If you like, you can grow it in a pot and cart it annually indoors. But it is completely hardy and thrives on lime or acid soil, perhaps showing its best form in a lime garden. It has been grown in England for two centuries and I am sad that we have all been scared into forgetting it because Daphnes grow so slowly. Maybe they do, but they also flower abundantly from an early age and Daphne collina will cover itself in buds when only nine inches high in its second year.

I save the best and the rarest for the end. The best, with me, has a reputation for unpredictability, like some of the spring Gentians. Daphne cneorum commemorates an old and low-growing shrub, formerly imported from Europe into seventeenth-century English gardens. On a modest rockery in the grounds of the Waterperry Horticultural School, near Oxford, I saw the queen of all varieties, the ruby-red form called eximia which was flowering like a weed in April across two square feet. Half the battle with this plant is to find a vigorous parent for your piece and in the days when the School still sold rare alpines to the pestering enthusiasts who scoured its cold frames, I came home with a well-rooted cutting off this very plant. It had been grown as an alpine should be, not in a pathetic peat mixture for rapid re-sale but hard and long, in a potful of gritty, local loam. I turned it out near my two retusas on the top of a sloping bank and it has never looked back. In May it glows with fifty scented ruby-red flowers at the tip of each radiating stem. After this frightful winter, it looks to have set more buds than ever. I feed it with Phostrogen and pray to the pagan gods for its survival. The soil is limey and leafy, and I doubt if there are any bigger five-year-old mats of it in cultivation. It is my most special plant, so I hope you will hunt for a similar cneorum eximia and share the scent and the brilliant colour.

All this sounds immodest, so I will cut short my love of this wonderful family with the story of a rarity of which, at most, I dream. In 1877 the great collector Charles Maries returned to work again in the Far East for the West Country nursery of the Veitch family. He crossed to Ning-po solely to find a new Lilac, said to be exquisite and readily found in a known private garden. The garden, however, had none of it, nor did the Snowy Mountains upriver nor did a valley where the residents proved far from friendly. So back went Maries, down to Ning-po to buy a ticket home. As he entered the ticket office he saw in the street a Chinaman who was carrying a bunch of pale mauve flowers. These were the very Lilac, he assumed, for whose sake he had left London. Down behind the wooden huts, surrounded by rice-fields, the owner had a garden filled with bushes of it. Their leaves were purplish and the flower shoots were about two feet long. They were wrapped from base to tip with flowers 'like a stick bound round with Lilac'. It flowered from March to May and is said to thrive 'only in yellow loam and leaf mould'. That makes its rarity hard to bear. Down in the bed where I later found the metal set of teeth, I have a beastly yellow loam. Leaf mould is no problem, but where is this lilac Daphne?

We ought to agitate the nurserymen. Some say it is difficult; among others, I know one who had it, loved it and never bothered it until he tried to move it nearer his house. It promptly died. It is popular in America where we ought to find new stock. Its discoverer remarked that it ought to be useful for forcing in Britain and in the New York Botanic Garden, rumour has it that the bush is already ten feet wide. When I told its story in the newspaper, company directors obliged their secretaries to ring me up and tell me all about their unsuspected Genkwa. A few queries proved they were mistaking it for our common wild Daphne mezereum, wreathed in rose-purple flower. There was a great will to own it, but Genkwa remains a fabulous rarity. I am sure we are all too scared of the Daphnes, a family too big to be nothing but temperamental. They have given me the high spots of my gardening life and if only the nurserymen could bring these forms back, even Genkwa, 'wreathed in Lilac', might get its teeth into my soil.

Meanwhile, if I could be granted the art of growing only one alpine to perfection, I think I would choose the Ramonda and its relations. Whenever I look at this family I am left with the feeling that the Ice Age was a greater disaster than anything man could ever do to nature. You know by now what primeval flowers do for my prose. In the flowers of a Ramonda you see a last trace of pre-glacial Europe, days, I presume, when turf looked like the foreground of Botticelli's Primavera and tropical flowers grew all over Germany. The weather, then, was warm and damp. Flowers opened to the richest colours. African violets and the lovely Streptocarpus are echoes from the modern tropics of the sort of flower we should picture everywhere before the ice arrived. Ramondas and their family survived the shock of the age of frost. I always thought their

25. Raised beds in the Scotts' garden, Boughton, with Pink Constance Finnis and Norah Lindsay and Helianthemum Jubilee in sun, Meconopsis and Orchis latifolia in shade and peat behind

26. Daphne retusa

27. Androsace lanuginosa: Rock Jasmine

28. Iris Katherine Hodgkin

29. The Cottage Garden of reds and yellows at Sissinghurst with Aquilegias in the foreground

30. A corner of the author's garden showing orange red Lily Enchantment, among a mixed planting of whites, lilac and pink

31. The purple border at Sissinghurst with pale blue Campanula lactiflora, magenta Geranium psilostemon, purple Salvia, blue Clematis Perle d'Azur

32. Rose La Ville De Bruxelles with the big heads of Allium christophii (albo-pilosum) at Sissinghurst

flowers were unusually simple, pristine if you like, before I discovered that they were so old. They join the ginkgo tree, the magnolia, the White Gean and the Dawn Redwoods as echoes of this long-lost era and make me wish once again that I had been a dinosaur to see them all together. Nowadays the Ramonda hangs out in the Pyrenees and in the Balkans. The Balkan mountains also house most of its best relations, plants which are well able to survive long droughts in summer, a habit which helps them in post-glacial living. I need hardly say that none should ever be collected in the wild.

Of the best-known relations, I shall begin with a good one and move on to the best. The Ramonda's cousins, the Haberleas, are beautiful if not my first choice. They are a Balkan group and turn up in Macedonia and central Bulgaria, where they are a memorable sight between large cliffs of limestone. In summer they look shrivelled and all but dead to the innocent eye. In autumn, however, they revive in those heavy Balkan mists and are ready to flower their heads off in late spring. No other European plant recovers so spectacularly, a clue to the Haberlea's easy tastes in the garden. If you give it a well-drained place, you can water it sparsely in summer and revive it in autumn, relying on the return of its rosettes of grassy pointed leaves. They send up short stems, bearing as many as five lavender-violet flowers. These are not unlike an open cowslip in their usual form. Their charm is their yellow throat and an exceptional freedom of flower at a height of six inches or so when you please them. There is a form known as ferdinandi-coburgi which is the more conspicuous as it holds its flower in a full-fronted way. Otherwise, Haberleas hang away from you and make less of an impact. As they are natives of limestone, they will grow happily in a lime soil. They prefer the shade. They will take root from leaf-cuttings and live almost for ever when happy. In a pot they would be charming, especially if you kept them damp but not too wet at the neck and avoided too sunny a window-sill. Hilliers of Winchester, Hants, list two varieties at around £1.50 a plant. If you like the greenhouse streptocarpus, these similar small alpines are well worth a try.

They are not a match for their cousins, however, to whom I have led up through these better beauties. The Ramonda's flower is as exquisite as Chinese porcelain. The Pyrenean variety, called myconi, is the only one on the general market, but it happens to be the best. It has a famous home among the boulders of Spain's

Ordesa National Park. Its flowers are usually a translucent lavender-blue, but they have a yellow centre like an exquisite African violet. Its five petals face you full-on and are held on a six-inch stem. Outdoors the Ramonda is best planted so that its rosette faces out at you horizontally from a bed which has been surfaced with stones so that its neck cannot rot in winter. In most gardens, this is not too difficult to contrive. You could usefully fill a shaded dry wall with Ramondas poked on their sides between the layers of stone. They would revel in this. When I worked in the great man-made 'alpinum' in the Munich Botanic Gardens, I remember how we would huddle behind the huge rocks of the central, highest mound for shelter from the late April winds. Between the cracks of its massive boulders, Ramondas had seeded by the dozen, waving their flowers at us as if to say that some creatures were more accustomed to a hint of glacial living than the men who were supposed to look after them. Beside steps, on walls or wedged at an angle on a bank, the Ramonda would come into its own. It insists on a shaded place and a cool root-run and it will abandon its fondness for life on the slant if you wedge it into a pocket between slabs of paving.

These Ramondas are very hardy and not at all difficult. They flower quite freely if the balance of water suits them. Outdoors they are happy on lime or acid soil, but must have a damp and lightly shaded place. If you want to try a trick on one indoors, I will pass on an ingenious method. Plant your Ramonda in a narrow but deep pot, filled with grit, loam and leaf-mould. Set this pot inside a wider one which is filled with peat as an insulation. This keeps the dampness at a steady level. Cooks will know the uses of a bain marie and the Ramonda likes something similar, a pot within a pot to help it over its two dislikes, poor drainage and dry soil. In this double pot, the Ramonda needs only an occasional watering and a position away from direct sunlight. In our chilly British homes of the late-twentieth century, it will flower with the freedom of a young Streptocarpus. In May, its crop of flowers is simple and truly primeval, a crystalline shade of lavender from earth's prehistory.

To please the alpinists, I want to dwell on one more plant which can be challenging if you choose its forms from the highest altitudes. If you have no head for such heights, it has more lowly varieties which make good garden plants for very little trouble. Outside the charmed circle of specialists, they are little known. Yet if somebody told you to grow rock jasmine, you would no doubt clamour for it. You would imagine some small creeping plant which would hang

154

down a dry wall, mould itself to boulders, mix with your best purple phloxes and prolong the season when you were pulling out handfuls of growth from old aubrieta like hair from a moulting terrier. It would be scented, you would presume, and it would be hardy; white, perhaps, Chinese, no doubt. Why had you not heard of it before?

Because, among other things, the best of its family are very difficult. There is a Mr Watson, I now discover, in Newcastle-upon-Tyne who grows his rock jasmine in pots in a shaded greenhouse, placing them on a bench well surfaced with gravel. Every day, he inspects the chippings. If they are dry, he waters them so that the water soaks into the pot. If they are wet, he leaves them alone. Water is given through a fine rose; the chippings, too, are fine. 'This method', as reported, 'ensures constant humidity with no excess of wetness or dryness. It requires great dedication'.

. The rock jasmine is sold in catalogues as Androsace. This too may deter you. The name should rhyme with gassy or passé. By German authorities, it is agreed to include the small, yellow-flowered cushion plants called Dionysia. These are even more awkward, so you can ignore them. The rock jasmine is closely related to the primula and shares its home in the Himalayas. It is a challenging garden plant because it prefers not to be wet round the neck or to be sodden in winter. It is the dream, not of casual jasmine fanciers, but of gardeners who wish to pit themselves against a challenge. You will see it at shows, in unheated greenhouses or in clay pots surfaced with chippings. You will understand why the plants hate to be damp at the neck if you see a good photograph of rock jasmine growing wild in the Pyrenees. There are some marvellous glimpses of this in a recent guide to the entire family, written by Duncan Lowe, a chartered engineer, and George Smith, a chemistry lecturer. It was published economically by the Alpine Garden Society and now costs around £5 by post from D.K. Haselgrove, 278/80 Hoe Street, London E17 9PL. In the wild, the highest alpine varieties grow into cracks in the face of granite rock, spreading out over the surface of hard stone and reaching a height of about two inches. The cushions are covered in flowers until, from a distance, you could mistake their footwide drifts of white for traces of snow on the folds of a dark cliff. Keen gardeners will do anything for them because they know them to be one of the plant world's miracles.

Where can you buy them and risk your luck? Fill a pot half and

155

half with chippings and John Innes number 2 compost. Then write to an alpine nursery, like Ingwersens of Gravetye, East Grinstead, and ask for the pink-flowered carnea (quite easy), the white-flowered cylindrica (very small and compact) and the notorious imbricata, whose cushions are silver. This variety wins prizes at shows. It has defied me twice, but the others will oblige if you follow precise rules, now set out clearly in the AGS's guidebook. On the day they flower for you, all else seems earthly distraction. None of the flowers is so vulgar as to have a stem.

There are easier ones, of course. There is a charmingly dark green variety with rounded rosettes called sempervivoides because it resembles a small house-leek. Its buds are borne on long three-inch stalks which begin by spreading horizontally. The flowers are a bright mauve-pink. I have grown this without trouble on a dry bank, though the rosettes eventually turn brown. It does not object to a wet winter. A better buy would be the one which Ingwersens sell as strigillosa, a remarkably bright variety whose heads of pinkish-white flowers are prettily marked with purple and red. Do try this if you can find it: it hates to feel wet on its hairy central star of leaves in winter, but it seeds itself and is most noticeable. Despite its hatred of damp, it is quite unjustly ignored. So, universally, are the rock jasmines of the high Arctic where they grow, to my amazement, on the tundra round Bering Strait and flower delightfully during the few short weeks of summer. Any unpronounceable name is likely to conceal one in a seed list, but the general title ochotensis covers the only stock I have ever seen for sale. Perhaps an oil-man will reintroduce it for us before he digs up the permafrost in which it thrives.

More accessibly, I would suggest you look for a woolly-leaved one called lanuginosa which seems surprisingly reliable in my garden when wedged between stones in a half-shaded place. Its silvered stems trail outwards and bear charming pink flowers. I think it is more reliable than its commoner neighbour from the Himalayas called primuloides. The latter, I found, needed protection against wet in winter, the point at which I cease to consider an alpine to be a tolerable garden plant. If you try the high alpine forms, you would have to call yet again on the services of the plunge bed. For safer watering, their pots should be made of clay, not plastic, and their cushions should be kept from contact with the soil by slipping some stone chippings beneath their lower surface. They are not plants for the open garden, unlike the other forms I have suggested. But they are plants for a personal triumph.

To win you round to them, I would like to add a touch of romance. On the subject of rock jasmine, Reginald Farrer, the master of all writers on alpine plants, went further than usual over the top. He described the alpine forms in his manual on rock gardening as 'the royal rose-pink splendour of the highest shingles'. That sounds like a painful attack of chicken-pox. But there is a scene elsewhere in Farrer's travel-books which appeals to me. As he is probably the last gardener to have seen this setting for rock jasmine, you might like to look at your garden varieties as I do, through the verbal sketch which, once, he drew of them.

In late May 1915, Farrer was up on the trail of the Tibetan Rock Jasmine, beneath the Halls of Heaven, as he translated the Chinese name for these mountains, an 'amphitheatre of sun-flogged cliffs'. High and far across the River Da Tung's bed stretched the finest bridge of wood to be found in Tibetan Asia. Monks had built it long ago and now worked a closed-shop agreement with the traffic which had to pass their way. At either end of the bridge stood a hut where the holy men took orders for that vital commodity, paper. Saints would suspend their sainthood to barter for butter and to tax all the caravans in transit. There were stern faces of rock on either bank of their bridge and the cliffs ran far up into the distance, cushioned throughout with pink rock jasmine. On this lawn of 'scented velvet', Farrer sat for the evening and watched the caravans as they wound their way east to China through downs of dry brown grass and scented iris. The lawn was pure rock jasmine. Yet Androsace tibetica is now sold nowhere, and I doubt if it will be seen again by Englishmen this century. But its relations can still be bought for our suburbs. A gardener does not need to know the length of this family's pedicels if he is to understand why, of all alpine plants, they attract men's time and ingenuity.

Rock jasmine apart, the best thing in my garden last year was a plant which I had forgotten. Gentians, I grant, are not easily missed. There is no blue so intense, unless you grow Corydalis cashmiriana, which, I bet, you do not. There is no flower which is so satisfying when you have captured it and brought it to its best in a garden. Gentians are flowers of alpine meadows, Chinese marshes and oriental woodlands. They are quite remarkably varied; there is even a tall straw-yellow one called lutea, which likes open meadows and which I recommend, not least for its bold leaves and deep roots. In the 3 to 6 inch class, there is nothing to compare with the sky-blue farreri, whose trumpets are striped with olive-green and dark navy, or with plain acaulis, whose wider trumpets are a gloriously deep blue. How, then, could I have forgotten one?

Plain old Gentian acaulis has annoyed me for longer, even, than I have been writing gardening columns. Every year, I think I will defeat its obstinacy by some new trick. It will grow, throw out more of its pale green rosettes of leaves, but it refuses to show any buds in the months when it is all over any self-respecting European's office calendar. I have been told to stamp on it, walk on it in rubber shoes throughout the season, feed it on fresh pig manure hot from the animal, water it with warm water, douse it with salt water, allow it to struggle among leaves, place it at the highest point in the garden, leave it to be sodden in the lowest, cover it with a glass pane, plant it on a molehill and, of course, to buy only from reputable nurseries, such as yours truly's, which happens to have an expensive stock of it available at the time of asking. Last year, I found the answer, for I had at least one bud on one three-year-old plant. The trick is to buy it and never look at it, until it has set a flower.

Here and there, in almost every bed, I have a Gentian from the past. Then, in a pot which I had quite forgotten for two years, one was showing a long, pointed ink-blue flower bud which, in a week, became a trumpet. It was worth the ten false starts, the pig manure, the cow manure, the bucket of chicken-droppings, and the treading which led nowhere. There never was quite such a blue. Nobody can photograph it truly, nor paint it. Europeans take it for granted, and sometimes claim to prefer that dull, flannelly old Edelweiss. One acaulis does not make a spring garden, but I felt that, by accident, I had won the battle at last.

Why bother you with it? Because, maddeningly, it will often grow freely. There are garages, I am told, which have edged their petrol pumps with it, and a railway station, even, which had two borders of it in flower throughout April. You must try it, at least once. Perhaps, as so many experts claim, it does prefer a heavy soil, with or without lime. Perhaps it likes to be in country air, not in a town. But there are no rules, except that it would be foolish not to try, say, three plants, one in a low wet place, one in a high sunny place, and one, like mine, where you can forget it. If all three flower, I would be glad to visit you and swap memories.

If acaulis is too stubborn for you, there are other choices. They are just as attractive and never too easy or common to be taken for granted. If Edwardian gardening journlism was more of a reflection of Edwardian gardens than ours is, the smaller Star Gentian, called verna, was the one which particularly troubled our grandfathers. They were quite smug about acaulis, but this verna drove them to extreme remedies. They piped water to its roots; they sheltered it and never dreamed of kicking or crowding it. They used to keep a diary in red of the dates when it flowered. I do not find it difficult. It liked lime, a rich, open soil, and reasonable drainage. The starry flowers are an intense blue, unforgettable if you mass them in a stone sink, low trough, or similarly raised container. In their second year, they may flower so freely that they die back. Be warned, and pick off a few buds if your plants seem to be too generous. This prolongs their lives. If they set seed, it should be left on a saucer in the fridge overnight, then sown at once. It will usually germinate freely if you are patient. Broadwell Nurseries keep a stone sink full of Star Gentians in their limestone corner of the Cotswolds and prove to any visitor in late April that their stock will live up to its reputation.

If this Gentian scares you, there are two easy ones which certainly belong in all better gardens. In August, anyone can enjoy the obliging septemfida variety in an open, sunny place. It divides easily and a few plants soon build up into a handsome edging for a border or raised bed. It is no more troublesome than Batchelor's Buttons if you keep the slugs at bay in spring. The year's growth begins from a fragile core of green shoots which you must not spike with a fork or pull apart by mistake. Otherwise, there are no problems and this Asian Gentian will give you a bold show of deep blue trumpets which would impress outsiders. Perhaps they are duskier and not so radiant as the great alpine forms, but they are a fine sight none the less. If a good nursery lists the cordifolia variation, buy it, as it is stronger and brighter.

A Willow Gentian sounds too charming, and indeed, it makes a fine plant for the front of a half-shaded border or the lower reaches of a steep bank in July and August. Sold as asclepiadea, it is a good gentian to buy, as it will grow almost anywhere in a deep soil and will split into many more useful pieces. But it is not a tidy plant. Unless you support its thin stems, they fall outwards to a length of two feet from their central crown and look as if a cat had sat in their middle. The Willow Gentian must be propped up on pea-sticks, whereupon it becomes an upright plant with the quiet prettiness of dark ink-blue trumpets in the axils of its pairs of leaves. It is easy and generous but not spectacular and in its dark blue form, it impresses me as much as a late summer Monkshood.

However, it also comes in a rare but ravishing white form. This is the plant for better gardens, no more awkward but far less familiar. Gentiana asclepiadea alba will grow in half-shade or in a north-facing bed, but nobody seems to acknowledge it. The stems are no stronger, but the leaves run in the same pretty pairs up their length. I recommend this plant very strongly for your August border.

For those on lime-free soil, who can grow Azaleas, there is an even better buy. The Chinese Gentians, mostly, flower in autumn when their upright trumpets are a lovely drift of deep blue. This easy planting is often missed by those with the right soil for it. The most vigorous is called sino-ornata and can be bought most cheaply in the unusual shape of a thong. A thong is a small division, usually with two roots, like the prongs on a tooth. If planted in spring in a damp, acid soil, these thongs will send up a tuft of grassy leaves, and may even flower in their first autumn. They are easy, so long as they have no lime, and their colour is as good a navy blue as any. At a height of six inches, the plants make a ribbon of flower which will edge your front path too beautifully. Ordinary plants can be bought, too, but 50 thongs are better value. They multiply quickly and soon give you the most exquisite carpet. The acid soil of Scotland suits these varieties perfectly, so Scottish nurseries will sell them in bulk. Jack Drake, at Inschriach, Aviemore, lists the plain Chinese form and the many excellent hybrids which have now been bred with the help of its close relatives. They are all excellent, but as my soil has lime, I leave the choice to you.

'Not every man has Gentians in his house in soft September', began D. H. Lawrence, but he went on with a poet's botanical ignorance to write of Bavarian gentians, all of which have flowered by early summer. 'Reach me a gentian, give me a torch, let me guide myself with the blue, forked torch of this flower . . .'. Some torch, some fork, but I would grant him that there is a 'smoking blueness' in many of the sorts which I have sent in their time to death and those gloomy halls of Pluto. There is no other blue in nature like theirs, so a better garden has to give it a chance.

Among easier plants, alpine gardeners have their own alpine irises and devote much care to them. Better gardeners, I think, should offend the purists and excel them by buying the new man-made hybrids instead. None of the small wild forms has the colour or style of the breeders' miniature varieties. I began with the one which I still like best, the easy Iris Green Spot. This fits into any pure alpine garden and is a wonder on the top of dry walls. Its masses of flower are a pale greenish white and are marked in their centres with indigo and deeper shades. Their effect suggests pale wax, a quality found in no other variety. They would look plausible on a mountain or a raised bed. The plant is about six inches high and allows you to split it into dozens after a few years. By late summer, it looks miserable and all the tiny leaves die back to a mat of old rhizomes. Yet each spring, they revive again and throw up their lovely flowers in late May. This is the best small iris in the book, usually over-priced but willing to multiply quickly from a single root.

Green Spot, however, is only one among many more. At each year's Chelsea Flower Show, one lone table exhibits a carpet of the new and proven miniature irises. None of the bigger nurseries has picked up the idea and their exhibitor remains the sole inspiration for the general public. The world of the miniature iris, however, is not without its prickles. When I described this exhibitor, V.H. Humphreys, as the king of small iris growers in Britain, I received letters by return from other amateurs, complaining that their own trophies were bigger than his and that it was too much to crown a man as king when he had not won an All American Pan select Bronze engraved Medal. Still, he sells his stock, which they do not. Put out the flags, then, for V.H. Humphreys and his imported irises at 8, Howbeck Road, Arnold, Nottingham. He has convinced me that better 'alpine' gardens cannot ignore the breeders' new advances. Novelty and a small demand keeps the newest varieties to £5 a plant, but there are older ones from 40p upwards and a new one can soon be split into many flowering clumps.

They are very easy to grow. They like a sunny, dry place, lime and a position which allows their mat of rhizomes to rest on the surface of the soil. Do not bury them, but anchor them, rather, by their roots so that they are exposed to the sun. Otherwise their flowers will be fewer. If you are planting irises for the first time, inspect a clump in a good public garden and check how you should rest the rhizome on a flat saddle of earth down either side of which the roots can extend deeper into the soil. If you do not know a good public garden, you have my sympathy, but you should swallow your pride and ask a friend to help.

The small bearded and lilliput classes of iris grow six inches and a foot high respectively. Anybody has room for them but few gardeners have yet woken up to the colours which have been developed here in the past twelve years. At Chelsea, I was impressed by the new Blue Pools, a variety which was bred in the UK to the most elegant shape and combination of white with a blue spot. I am not surprised to find Mr Humphrey's list remarking that 'a clump of this variety is a mass of laughing eyes'. At £2.50 each, it has to be good. Among older blues, I thought the early-flowering Arnold Velvet, the clear Blue Denim and the ruffled flowers of Tinkerbell were all worth a place. You can mass these as edging plants or place them in the paving of a terrace or front garden. So long as you do not squash them with a deck chair, they look particularly apt in such a paved walk, filling a whole pocket between the stones with their tufts of tiny iris-leaves. Good reds, as yet, are harder to come by, but Cherry Garden is at least as good as more recent attempts. It has large flowers but there is no mistaking the depth of the red. These smaller forms are matched by the neglected group of table varieties which stop conveniently at a height of two feet. Mr Humphreys describes Day Star as 'a cute little runt' in the cream-coloured range, and fear of misreading him or misquoting should not deter you from it. Other splendid varieties are Lodestar which combines scarlet and yellow or Parakeet which pairs buff and orchid-pink. In the front of a border these varieties make a strong impact in the weeks before the roses. Afterwards, you can train violas and some late lobelia around their clumps and hardly notice the gap. If you think, then, that irises are too large and too short-lived to be worth while, you are still living in the 1930s. These small ones will fill dry walls and paving and make up for my ban on golden alyssum in late April. The taller table varieties are plants for borders or emphatic points, but their merits seem to be missed. All of them increase rapidly, so I have one final tip. Tests have persuaded the experts that the best time to lift and split up the younger growths on an old iris's mat is not immediately after flowering, as many books say, but two or three weeks later when the strain of flowering is over and the plant has settled down. Practical for once, I leave these modern winners to your prompt attention.

Like the iris, the pink, or Dianthus, comes in wild alpine forms which alpine gardeners tend with pride and spread between their cliffs and screes, moraines and tufa walls. Again, I find the wild forms far less interesting than the ones which gardeners have bred. In the wild, the pink of a pink's flower is sour or rosy, while there are some beastly deviations into lilac and mauve. The flowers are tattered at the edges or the petals are far too small. One yellow does the rounds, called knappii, but it is a straggly sort of plant, not worth space in a garden. Breeders have done so much for the family that I cannot recommend these natural forms to anyone.

For the last decade, I have admired the frequent shows of pinks among grey leaves which are staged by Ramparts Nursery, Colchester, Essex, at the Royal Horticultural Shows. I am aware that the long-stemmed border pink grew too tall for a wall or an edging, but its days are now over. A new group, semi-double and very free-flowering, has come to the fore with coy female names which range from Samantha to Tracey and back again. For seven years I have grown them myself and although I have chosen the most obvious I cannot recommend them too highly. For £1 in April 1976 I bought 25 rooted cuttings of the salmon-pink Doris, the mother of most of these newer show pinks. It only rained once during the summer when I planted them out on a dry bank, but Doris was quite unperturbed and flowered from June till late August. She is the strongest in her group, an honour which she justifies when you take her cuttings. Doris's cuttings root and grow away quickly, whereas many of the other varieties drag their feet. In my garden's first year, Doris was the only plant which distinguished itself. In those miserable days of drought in 1976, the dandelions grew roots more than two feet long, I kept all but one gardening expert out of the house and she announced firmly over the sherry that she thought Doris a repulsive colour. I never took her outside and am not sure whether she had a sixth sense or had somehow seen my pinks from her seat on the sofa.

The prettiest, if not the strongest, are surely the laced pinks. Ramparts sell one called Gran's Favourite which can be forgiven its fearful name. I find that it flowers and persists if you follow their advice and limit the number of its buds in its first year. Ingwersen's offer an excellent white and red-brown variety called London Brocade which I also recommend. Laced varieties have a dark tracing on the white ground of their flower, like a smart suit of race colours. Everybody loves them when they see them well grown, and there are others not yet on the general market which I rate as highly as any plant for a wall, path or border's front row. They are a heavenly match for roses. Much praise is sometimes given to an old single white called Charles Musgrave because its flower is ringed with a central zone of green. I have too much of it and cannot rate it very highly.

Good pinks flower profusely and span all colours from white-and-brown to dark crimson. They also smell of that heavy powdered scent, so strong in their first cousins, the carnation. The newer hybrids are best grown from cuttings which you should take in June, applying a very sharp blade below the bulging joints of an unflowered stem. Do not pick the cuttings off by hand, as you will pull off your piece with a hopeless tube of soft stem. When set in a sandy pot or a small propagator with a plastic cover (priced at £1.89), they will root within a month. Every three years, the old parents should be replaced before they exhaust themselves. Pinks, I need hardly say, prefer a sharply drained soil in a sunny place. You are beginning to see why this book should indeed have been entitled Better Drains. On a clay or cold soil, pinks rot at once in winter. At the same time they respond strongly to feeding with Phostrogen while they are growing and setting buds. They prefer lime in their soil and also like more than a modest dash of sand. When fed, drained and given a free run, these named modern varieties are marvellous plants. Make straight for the laced varieties and then to the shades of raspberry, scarlet, white with red and lavender-violet. Through these, clever breeders now appeal to our love of colour and scent.

Among the other plants for walls and edgings, thymes are the great soft sell. Everybody believes that they are powerfully scented and delicious in the cooking. Novels beguile their readers with scented gardens, heavy with banks or lawns of thyme, although the scent would never hit you if you merely stood on the margin of their imaginary world. The leaves must be bruised before they give off a scent, so you have to tread on a thyme to catch the best of it.

If you fail to squash it, its charms are the flowers and the colours of the leaves. During the past decade, some good thymes have crept onto the market and have not yet received their due. They would be superb in the warmer garden of any reader who lives on a light soil sheltered by walls. I will begin with two mystery hybrids, whose leaf and colour of flower are a match for any variety. Nobody seems sure of their parentage. They were born, it seems, on the wrong side of the beehive. Nurserymen should force them on to the chain stores' lists.

Doone Valley is a small thyme but has leaves of the most brilliant colour all the year round. They are more of a golden yellow than a green, and the bushes are speckled so brightly that they stand out on any slope. Each bush is about six inches high but spreads widely.

They are first class foliage plants, but the flowers also open to a pretty lavender from dark reddish buds and do not quarrel with the golden leaf. I have lost it in one site, while growing it happily in another for five years. Before explaining why, I will alert you to a partner of similar ease. Thyme Porlock is an equally uncertain hybrid and cannot boast such a brilliant leaf. It is taller, some nine inches high, and is a pleasant deep green when not in flower. The leaf is an excellent spice for cooking without any false trace of lemon. The flowers are profuse, a mass of clear pink which will open in July and last fairly well. This is the easiest of the thymes which combine a serious show of flower and a cook's dream of a leaf. Too few gardeners know it.

The case of these thymes was understood long ago by the herbalists who thought that the family cured anything from whooping cough to gamblers' fever. Sicknesses all took thyme, they used to say, and they also believed the plant was a sympathetic pair to common lavender, thriving best when near to it. The sympathy, of course, amounted only to the two plants' common taste for a very sharply drained soil where they would never suffer from heavy ground in a wet winter. Neither thyme nor lavender likes a rich soil. Thyme is at its best beside a path or between paving-stones where the soil is poor. As soon as I put the Doone variety down in a valley or on a heavy patch of soil, I lose it in the winter. The bogs and quicksands, the lush pasture and ponds of its fictional namesake would never have suited it.

Higher up, on more gravel than earth, the same plant thrives with the Porlock variety beside it. Winter wet is lethal to it, so I try to dig in some gravel when I plant it as an edging. You can multiply it endlessly from cuttings taken in July off shoots which have not yet flowered. They root so quickly that you should never buy more than one plant of any variety. Usually, you can pull some rooted pieces straight off their parent. Other thymes are a challenge to the ambitious, especially to those with a dry European garden. The most spectacular is a Spanish one called membranaceus, which makes a low and rounded bush. It is covered in pink flowers which are backed by marvellous bracts of a paper-white. I write with regret of this superb plant as I lost mine in a recent wet winter. Keep it for a south-facing dry wall and regard it as a gamble. Otherwise, plant it all over your bolt-hole abroad. In a dry climate all the Spanish and Portuguese forms of thyme are splendid, but this one is the best. British exhibitors are so proud of it that they grow it specially in pots in a cold greenhouse or unheated frame.

Far less bothersome is a fine Greek one, the 'white-haired' thyme called leucotrichus. The heads of flower are a purple pink and are borne in thick clusters above the white hair on the edges of the thin leaves and twiggy stems. The plant is not much higher than a mat, but as yet it seems quite hardy and is reliable in a dry English corner. It is not yet a common plant, but you should snap it up wherever you see it. It has a future with us.

The many forms of lemon-scented thyme are more familiar. Most gardeners, indeed, go straight for Silver Queen on name alone. This is the best thyme for edging a dry bed where it will spread into a mat of grey-green and silver-cream leaves at a height of six inches or so. I have seen it used on the grand scale down the central path of a cottage garden which combined it with the bright magenta forms of the small hardy Cranesbill, or Geranium. This made a very sensible match for its pale colour. It is best, I think, in a block several feet or so across. Clip it quite firmly after flowering, using any of the bits as cuttings for the next year. Otherwise, it may sprout a bare patch in its middle. Be warned that shops sell Silver Queen forms of the common thyme and lemon thyme quite indiscriminately. The former is the better for cooking.

For scent alone, the strongest of all are to be found on Corsica. These varieties are sold as Thyme herba-baroni, a low growing and wiry form which is easy in any dry garden. Beth Chatto of Elmstead Market, Colchester, Essex, will sell you a selected lemon-scented and carraway-scented form, each of which is exceptionally sweet. The common forms of Europe's ordinary thymes are usually sold to cooks under the blanket heading of herbs. This Corsican brand has the better of them. As front line plants among roses or day lilies, these various thymes are not often given their heads. They combine leaf, scent and flower while remaining evergreen. The best forms, as usual, are far better than those which everyone knows, and I prefer them to the rich pink and rose-red mats of the prostrate creeping varieties. These are the thymes which are proposed for small lawns of thyme or for herb-seats, on the model of the famous thyme-cushion which was set in a stone seat at Sissnghurst Castle. A thyme 'lawn' is only manageable on a small scale in ground which has been totally cleared of rooted weeds. The thymes take two summers to make a carpet and meanwhile, you cannot use weedkillers between them. In a wet winter, they turn brown in the centre of their mats, letting the weeds begin again. After three years they need trimming,

splitting and replanting. As for the seat, it is horribly prone to
bumble-bees. I prefer the thyme as a lasting shrub which is hardy
enough to scramble through the wet or frost of most English winters
and easily backed up with pot-grown cuttings in case of disaster.
The one gamble which it never cures is the gamble taken on its own
life.

What, then, happens on your dry walls, paving, banks and raised
beds when the best of the pinks and thymes are over? From late
August and on and off before then, I have come to rely on the
Penstemon. Its family is not easily sorted out and its naming can be
fluid. To find the best, you may have to go to an alpine plant
specialist. The Penstemons are mostly American, not true alpines
but plants from homes in the dry shale of Wyoming and Colorado.
It is worth remembering this home. Books still worry over the
ability of the Penstemon to resist frost. They say less on their
capacity for rapid death in the damp. As in nature, they should be
given very sharp drainage by digging gravel thoroughly round their
ball of roots. On clay soils, the best are a gamble.

The family divides roughly into two. There are the border
varieties whose flowers are in full flow in later summer. They will
root easily from cuttings taken between July and October: these will
often put out roots if kept only in a glass of water which is
sweetened by a piece of charcoal. The parents are not too hardy, so
you should winter these cuttings in a shed or frame in case your
stock dies outside. There are several ways of starting a collection.
The cheapest is to order the seed of those Penstemons which
seedsmen list as annuals. Like snapdragons, they are in fact near-
hardy perennials, some of which will endure a mild winter outside.
Their open tubular flowers are usually white inside and a shade of
pink, red or lavender as a contrast. These plants are about two feet
high and will flower from August onwards, a fine match for a sheet
of pale blue clematis or the other blues of early autumn. For a total
cost of £1 and as much bother as a marigold, you can lay the
beginnings of a lovely grouping. Every autumn, you must take
cuttings and keep them for safety indoors. These are not hardy
plants.

If you ignore the seed, you can begin by buying a plant or two of
the named hardy forms. The names waver on the borders of several
old families, but one usual parent is the tall form with ruby-purple
flowers which used to survive almost anything the Edwardians could
throw at it. Garnet is the nearest child nowadays, a subdued plant

with deep ruby flowers and dark leaves. I much prefer one called Firebird, a near-scarlet red which is almost completely hardy and lasts for a long season. As a first buy, this is the pick of autumn reds. Others are not quite so hardy, but there is a superb scarlet called Southgate Gem and a red and white called Middleton Gem. May I warn you, however, against an oddity called Sour Grapes? Its latest champion writes of its flowers as 'like opals, soft green, amethyst and blue'. My clump has flowers of a muddy blue purple which I find very dull for the price.

Alpinists will be shaking their heads, protesting that these border plants are two feet tall and have nothing in common with their mountain flowers. Firebird, at least, seems excusable in any large rock garden where the colour is fading by August. As for the others, I agree that they are also border plants but I cannot see that they are out of place on walls, raised beds or the other general homes for alpines without any rocks. After all, they have some exciting first cousins from the wild who fill up the other branch of the family. These flower earlier in the season with a small show later, in many of their forms. They are fit for any alpinist and among the many American forms there are a host of good varieties which gardeners are slow to recognise. Who grows one called scouleri? You can order it with confidence from Broadwell Nurseries, Moreton-in-Marsh, Glos., and if you put it in a dry wall I think it would please anyone. It flowers for weeks and carries lavender-pink flowers, baggy like a snapdragon's at their mouth. It is a foot or so high, and is second only to its rare white form which is worth buying from Hilliers of Winchester, Hants, with a bank loan. From the same sources you can order the charming new Pink Dragon, a smaller plant which pleases me very much by its long season and handsome pink bells.

The blues, however, are the star turn. The best is the one called Blue Gem, a plant of exceptionally bright and clear blue trumpet flowers. Farrer's bible for alpine plantsmen, his book on Rock Plants, goes to town on 'the dainty trumpets of opalescent loveliness which sound their music in August and September'. You could hardly put it worse than that. A 'serene dawn-blue' comes nearer the mark, a colour which asks to be massed in the front of borders or on dry slopes. Blue Gem is not a long-lived plant, but cuttings root very quickly. It can be seen to good effect in several National Trust gardens and I think it is one of the purest colours, a rare beauty which adventurous gardeners have been reluctant to try. It is not the most reliable form nor will it always last beyond two or three years. One of its expert growers suggests that it is best on a soil with no lime. If you plan cuttings as replacements, you could mass Blue Gem on a front wall or in a container and expect at least two summers' spectacular show. I cannot promise anything of this desirable plant, but at its best, it is memorable.

The same, perhaps, could be said of the most common Penstemon in the marketplace, the one with small needle-leaves which earn it the name of pinifolius. I have always found this a wretched disappointment. At least while Blue Gem survives, it flowers like a dream. Pinifolius spreads into a mat, but it does not show more than a stem or two of red-orange tubular flowers. These are tantalising but too sparse, so I have demoted it to the bottom of the list. I have also demoted the sombre rose-ruby Penstemon which passes as roezlii in most nurseries' catalogues. The true plant ought to have dark violet-blue flowers, but perhaps it is pedantic to protest at a false name. The plant behind it is also a poor selection, though its rounded leaves and craggy branches suggest a small shrub. The flowers are a bilious colour and are not too keen to appear. Others are so much better, the self-explanatory Amethyst whose haze of pale blue tubular flowers goes well with white scouleri, the lavender-purple flowers on the bushes of the old Six Hills Hybrid and its pretty grey-green leaves, the mass of blue-purple bells on the fresh green mats of menziesii, a plant with a variable name. The best, in my view, is my own, grown from a cutting off an old plant in a local clergyman's garden. Perhaps it is menziesii in one or other disguise, but I give it away in batches and hear nothing but good of it in May and September. It may seem pointless to praise a plant in my keeping, but I use it to point one moral of this family. Beware of the names. Nobody yet knows exactly which variety is which, so you should stay with the suppliers and varieties I mention in order to be safe. Most of these wild ones flower in early summer, and then the border varieties will carry on the good work. They respond to any dead-heading with a new burst of buds. America has its Penstemon societies and I presume their gardens are full of them before the fall. If you take pot luck in a specialist American seed-list you will soon hit on a worthwhile variety. Never forget their taste for a home like the Rockies. Only if you expose them to heavy soil and bad drainage will you fail to see their point. Otherwise, they are the prelude to summer and an epilogue for early autumn which takes the edge off the sadness in the turn of the year.

Chapter Seven

My Best Garden

You have noted the Cut-leaved Beech and perversely opted for another double pink Cherry. You have sprung to the defence of dwarf Conifers and wondered if heathers would fill the front garden more easily than any weird Viburnum or unproven Strobilanthes. You liked the sound of Horned Pansies and approved the choice of so much Mock Orange Blossom. Your Ramonda is safely in a double pot and you are willing to arm the kitchen window-box with Tulip Fusilier. But can such plants, you still wonder, make a better garden than the annual riot of petunias and Iceberg roses? You still have to be convinced that a garden, as a living whole, can ever be better than one which is properly tended and loved. It was all very well, you may be muttering, to burst on that poor Kashmiri's lunchtime and tell him that pansies and Cosmos daisies now came in separate colours. He was merely cut off from modern catalogues, and anyone could have bettered his garden by giving his name to a mail-order firm.

There are gardens, however, which have quite changed my taste, proving to me that gardening can be conducted on a higher and better-considered plane. I will only discuss one, because I am in the happy position of being sure which is the best garden in the world. Naturally, I have not seen them all, but you expect strong prejudice from a man who has already damned your decorative Dahlias. My choice is not unusual, for the best of its class seldom is. Between April and October, you can test my judgment by visiting Sissinghurst Castle's gardens, near Cranbrook, Kent, now in the keeping of the National Trust.

Sissinghurst's barrel continues to roll. Ten years ago, the garden drew some 8,000 annual visitors. Now, there are well over 100,000 a year paying an entrance fee which has outpaced inflation. Some, I dare say, have been intrigued by the portrait of its makers' marriage, the minuets and trios lived out by Harold Nicolson and Vita Sackville-West. Others may be bitten by all things Bloomsbury and go to relish this oasis, on the margin of an in-grown group who turn up in the letters of Vita to her beloved Virginia Woolf. Every year there are more Americans who wish to add a footnote to their thesis on Virginia Woolf or the Bloomsbury period. But they cannot account for the entire rise in Sissinghurst's visitors. Its main cause must be horticultural, because most people go to admire the plants and their relationships, grown in a classic English setting. They leave with an interest in colour and old roses, not in the romances of Vita and Virginia. However, readers of Orlando, modelled round Vita, may return to it wondering whether the thorny problems of book and garden do not throw a certain light on one another.

I need only say here that the world-famous garden was made from a derelict confusion of brambles by the Nicolsons in the 1930s. The site had once housed a glorious Tudor castle built round successive courtyards until the Georgians, those arch-vandals, pulled it down. Round the tower and outbuildings, the Nicolsons made their pattern of interlocking gardens and vistas. Harold drew the firm lines and saw to the perspectives. I would rate him with Repton and above Brown and Lutyens in the ranks of English garden designers. Eighteenth-century gardeners assumed that moral and aesthetic attitudes belonged together. The plan of the Sissinghurst garden reflects the outlook of a man who appreciated taste as a mark of character in men and letters. Sissinghurst's design was only possible for a man who brought a love of literature to bear on the way he saw things, who prized views or objects for the Horatian quality of apt propriety. His plan brings together so many different observations, the shape of the old Kentish threshing-floors, the elegance of a pleached French alley, the emphasis on Italian sculpture, odd fragments of journeys in Persia and Morocco and above all, the strong lines of classic English yew, aligned with steps and well-groomed water or left to run across a plan which might otherwise fall into too many small rooms. It is an eclectic taste, throwing many different features into the same plan. But they are carefully underplayed and supported by a use of line which the eye seems to sense without ever being forced to notice. There are precise points of perspective where the views and apparent right-angles seem to meet in harmony, but they are seldom picked up by visitors to the broad Long Walk or the vistas beyond the famous White Garden. They are there deliberately, but they work their effect without needing to be tested and sized up pedantically. The various features were matched at Sissinghurst to the natural genius of the place and were held together by one man's point of view. They are a lesson in firm, coherent planning which does not confuse mere decoration with design.

They were also, of course, lit up by Vita's sense of colour and romantic fancy. Its sources are worth pondering. She combined a passion for Tudor style, perhaps to the point where she could see no others clearly. I do not know her views on primeval flora, but she certainly drew on a recurrent strain of Orientalism, fed by her own journeys through Asia. She also knew her Edwardian borders, the colour-principles of Miss Jekyll and her style, the whites, silvers and informal groupings of the Surrey school of the early 1900s. But, rarest of all, she combined acute botanical knowledge with a love of the old and proven cottage flowers. The reading and writing of poetry strengthened her, surely, in this plain taste. It is the point at which Sissinghurst excels its forerunner and contemporary, the great garden at Hidcote Manor in Gloucestershire. Here, the brilliant eye and taste of that 'quiet American', Lawrence Johnston, designed the first of his marvellous gardens. It rivalled Harold's own architectural taste and his use of a living green backbone to the plan. A remarkable man, who adopted England as his country, Lawrence Johnston perhaps gave less weight to Vita's plainer love of ordinary flowers. Unfortunately for his fame, he also had none of her gifts as a writer and less of her literary knowledge. Vita's writings on plants were born from pure genius. Her newspaper articles on gardening were reprinted for hundreds of thousands of readers in books whose titles range round the words In Your Garden. They are still far the best books which I know on the subject. A selection is published by Michael Joseph with the title 'V. Sackville-West's Garden Book', but it is still worth looking for the originals which contain so much more. When I made the early discovery that I liked gardening, I would bicycle miles to the one public library which stocked her books and would return after school lights-out to a world of Clematis on wire netting, white gardens and barn owls, roses called Nuits de Young, the unknown Indigofera and the ability to see the tracery of great cathedrals in avenues of winter elms. Her ascetic hatred of gadgets and her exotic love of garden scent were truly monastic.

These two gifts, a literary art and an eye for cottage-flowers, raised Sissinghurst's gardens above their contemporaries. Earlier, the large Edwardian volumes in the old Country Life series, written by Weaver, Jekyll and Elgood, give an insight into the south-of-England style among which Vita had grown up. Many of her touches were already common currency, the colour planning, the masses of climbing roses and the use of enclosed gardens within a larger whole. But there was a blunt rusticity about the pergolas, a Georgian dullness to the tapering lily-ponds, a strident note to the Dorothy Perkins roses up poles and posts. Vita explored the older, better-shaped roses and the beauty of less obvious flowers and contrasting leaves. Her books and plantings shared an exuberance and an eye for detail, and admired the plain simplicity in plantings of Clematis or carpets of Violas, massed polyanthuses and purple Cherry Pie. The same qualities light up Virginia Woolf's own essays on English literature. These appreciated books, without criticising them blatantly, but their taste told its own principled story. It brought them to life by small, human touches and by drawing a context round her chosen authors. The essays proved how it was possible to be eclectic and despise nothing as too lowly without losing a coherent point of view. They were never dull, nor written for dull books. Sissinghurst's gardens, made by her closest friend, were like Virginia's Essays, expressed in plants.

Their style is directly relevant to any better garden. These plantings, sceptics say, were all very well for the Nicolsons and their three gardeners when £10 a week bought a man's time. On the contrary, Sissinghurst is the single most fertile source for owners of small gardens who want them to be beautiful and do not have to worry about the needs of small children. The styles of each small compartment could make up a whole garden. The small garden of reds and yellows, oranges and flame-coloured flowers is a brilliant example. It was conceived against a background of old silver and red brick but it covers less than a quarter of an acre. Any cottage-garden could develop the idea and learn from its ground plan. I know none which does. By matching the fiery scarlet of the brilliant Lychnis chalcedonica to the clear yellows of Day lilies and evening primrose, Vita turned a strong colour into a pure one. The yellows were so well chosen, the easy Potentilla called recta warrenii which you should also try, the yellow Sun Roses and Black Eyed Susan which are simple, cottage flowers. Brick-red Snapdragons and the rare, tender musk called Mimulus glutinosus kept company in the same bed. The rarities and the old favourites rubbed shoulders together in the interests of a common colour-plan. Behind, the scarlet Flame Creeper, or Tropaeolum, was draped across the setting of an evergreen hedge. Beneath ran scarlet Sweet Williams and aquilegias chosen only in reds and yellows. This is brilliant gardening, but we all have room for its principles at home. It occupies no more than a small front garden. The controlled colours and bold groups of her best-loved plants suggest so many combinations. The White Garden is famous, a limited planting of greys and whites which uses a silver pear tree and silver thistles among rambling white roses, Campanulas, 'pinks' and wild geraniums. Towering groups of the huge Cardiocrinums show their rare long trumpets of scented flowers in the background. But the white garden shades into touches of grey-blue in its hostas, bellflowers and glaucous leaves. This tone lifts it out of the conventional limits set by earlier fashion.

Nearby, in July, stands one of my favourite matches between simple, woodland plants. In a semi-shaded corner, there has been a fashion since the 1960s for turning to the family of Astrantias. Flower arrangers began it when they saw those faded rose-pink and green-white flowers, not unlike a scabious, with which gardeners had never previously bothered. I had continued not to bother with them, thinking them dull, except for a cream-white variegated form called Sunningdale with pretty leaves. There are forms with brighter petals, of which the best pair are called carniolica rosea, a sound shade of pink, and one called involucrata which has cream-white flowers. They both reach as height of about two feet and will last in flower for most of the summer. The flowers pick well and the plants are happy in any semi-shaded site. They flourish in a damp bed but will hang on anywhere, even in the shade of trees where they look no more dull than anything else. So far, so boring. The Astrantia, you might feel, would have done better to stay in its alpine meadows where it went very well in the hay. At Sissinghurst, however, it was matched by a mass of pale purple and white martagon lilies. Normally, I would not think the martagons worth a small garden's while. Their flowers are small, though prettily reflexed, and their shape, scent and colouring have been left behind by modern hybrids. However, the keepers of Sissinghurst had noticed that these two unlikely flowers coincided in height, season and colour. The clear shades of the martagon lily brought out the best in the Astrantia's subtle colouring. The tall stems of these lilies rose neatly above their lower companion and stood out in a harmony of white, purple-pink and the yellow of the lily's stamens. By a well-judged marriage, two old bores had become quite charming. You could repeat the effect in any shaded corner, but you ought to use several plants, at least five of each. They grow very easily and would be invaluable in shade, beside a water garden or on the edge of a wild or wooded patch. The richer their soil, the better these simple plants will flourish.

More generally, Sissinghurst shows how it pays to choose the best-coloured variety of quite common flowers and concentrate on it alone. We grow too many mixed annuals without thinking. The detailed bedding-schemes suggested by old Edwardian gardeners reveal how our standards have altered. They planned for every sort of harmony, pale pink and silver, deep purple and white, pink, blue and white in a trio and so forth. The best of them omitted yellow, a taste with which I agree. Admittedly, they also centred their interests on bedding geraniums and thought stiffly in terms of dot plants, the odd silver leaf to set off a level sea of red begonias. But if you contain the colours more cleverly, the effect can also be bold. At Sissinghurst, only one petunia features in the front courtyard, a superb shade of deep ink-purple called Purple Defiance. It is matched only with the yellow in the yellow-leafed form of Helichrysum petiolatum. Anybody could manage a similar pair, perhaps using the darkest purple Cherry Pie instead of the petunia which many seedsmen have dropped in favour of their horribly frilled and ruffled forms. Limit yourself, however, to these two colours.

These are ideas for any better garden, but they are repeated throughout Sissinghurst at all levels. In early July, the famous bushes of old Bourbon roses are thick with flower, but their companions are just as intriguing. With a masterly eye for small details, Vita matched the lilac-pink of her old roses to the dusky pink heads of flower on the bulbous forms of flowering onions, or Allium. The heads themselves come in bold shapes and sizes which would need the eye of a master artist for a proper portrait. Flowering onions bunch a mass of small individual flowers into a rounded or drooping head, like the lights in a large chandelier. Their colour is only a part of their interest. The best known and most impressive is the one called albo-pilosum. This onion has huge rounded heads on two-foot stems, each of which is a mass of star-shaped flowers of lilac pink. Their petals are so thin and finely spaced that the flower will glisten in direct sunlight. The bulbs are easily grown in any open soil and like all the flowering onions should

175

be planted at a depth which is twice their diameter. Five or six bulbs of this variety go a long way and could be placed at intervals near the front of a long border. This old favourite is only the beginning of the story. At Sissinghurst, I first fell for an exquisite relation called cernuum, whose heads of deeper rose-pink flowers droop downwards like small tubes at a height of only a foot. This is a marvellous plant once you have been taught to look at it seriously. The stems are green-grey, like a chive's, but the flowerhead is remarkably subtle in line and colour. Vita used it to edge the beds of old roses where its colour matched theirs and ran freely along the verbenas and violas. It was a perfect choice in colour, shape and season. I cannot understand the price which big nurseries charge for it – £1.50 for five – as it seeds itself in any well-drained soil and is easier to grow than any lobelia. If you begin with half a dozen and save their seed in August, you can build a long edging quite quickly. Its Latin name means the 'drooping onion', but I assure you that it is a bulb of the highest quality.

These plantings are only a few examples from a garden whose qualities changed my perception of gardening's colours and forms. Critics sometimes say that Sissinghurst is not what it was in the 1950s and that it has gone downhill. But the oppposite seems to me to be true. Since Vita's death in 1962, the garden has picked up after a slow start in public hands. It owes an enormous debt to its two brilliant gardeners, Pamela Schwerdt and Sibylle Kreutzberger, who understand her principles and pursue them with a discretion that eludes most other National Trust gardens. Ground cover has been kept firmly in its place. Vita herself saw value in rare and and ignored plants, but she never had the Trust's range of other gardens on which to draw. The 1970s have added new plants in keeping with the old colour schemes until the place is now a plantsman's paradise: the pairing of Martagon lilies and Astrantias was in fact first noticed by Pamela Schwerdt while in Bavaria and was patiently copied after the five years needed to raise the lilies from seed. At the level of its small plants and half hardy features for urns and bedding, Sissinghurst now commands the best from the Trust's other properties and from donors who recognise its lady gardeners' skills. Time, of course, has added new plants from nurserymen, forms which Vita herself would have welcomed.

Its art is an informal planting within a coherent, formal design. Better gardening should not lose sight of this English principle. But the result is also a personal expression, as every garden must be.

When I last visited it, two women visitors were making notes on a bell-shaped pink Clematis Etoile Rose which was spreading through an established shrub. 'You can see how she likes to train one thing over another', they remarked. Vita Sackville-West had been dead for nearly 20 years. But they were right. She had liked to train things, and the garden is still true to her vision. 'I think the secret of your gardening', her husband wrote to her in June, 1937, 'is simply that you have the courage to abolish ugly or unsuccessful flowers'. It is no coincidence that the secret is the moral of this book.

Acknowledgements

Among many better books, I recommend A.G.L. Hellyer's Amateur Gardening: a Pocket Guide (1971) and his Collingridge Encyclopaedia of Gardening (1976) and C.E. Lucas Phillip's The New Small Garden (1979) as general guides. P.M. Synge and Roy Hay, The Dictionary of Garden Plants in Colour (1976) has good photographs and very good descriptions. Artistic and practical advice are combined in Lanning Roper's fine Sunday Times Gardening Book (1967) and Christopher Lloyd's classic The Well Tempered Garden (1970), best in hardback. Anthony Huxley's Plant and Planet (1973) covers a wide canvas. John Raven, A Botanist's Garden (1971) is full of sharp and unusual observation. Alice Coats's Flowers and their Histories (1968) and Garden Shrubs and their Histories (1963) are excellent introductions to the subject she made her own. My quotation for Tichbourne on p. I is from Allen Paterson, The Gardens of Britain, vol. 2 (1978), p. 146, an exemplary guide-book. Seed of Tagetes minuta, when available, is offered to members of Henry Doubleday Research Association, Convent Lane, Bocking, Braintree, Essex. Their cheap pamphlets, The Tagetes Effect and The 1961 Tagetes Experiment, explain it.

Better Trees: W.J. Bean's Trees and Shrubs Hardy in the British Isles, vols 1–4 (1970–80) is indispensable. Christopher Lloyd, Foliage Plants (1973) has helped to form my taste. On cherries, G. Chadbund, Flowering Cherries (1972); on fruit, I still turn to G. Bunyard, O. Thomas, The Fruit Garden (1904). On Trelawny at p. 23, W. St Clair, Trelawney (1977) Ch. 25. On Christmas thorns, M.E. Burnett, Plantae Utiliores (1842–50), vol. 2, p. XLIX. On quinces, E. Schafer, The Golden Peaches of Samarkand (1963). On Metasequoia, Professor Merrill, J.R.H.S. 73 (1948) 211. For the trees I discuss, try Hilliers, Winchester, Hants; Notcutts,

178

Woodbridge, Suffolk; Jas. Smith, Tansley, Matlock, Derbyshire; John Scott, The Royal Nurseries, Merriott, Somerset.

Better Shrubs: A.G.L. Hellyer, Garden Shrubs in Colour (1971) is clear and illustrated to scale. W.J. Bean, Wall Shrubs and Hardy Climbers (1951) is full of good ideas. Neil Treseder, Magnolias (1978), a magnificent monograph; K. Jennings and V. Miller, Growing Fuchsias (1979) discusses most varieties. Graham Thomas, Shrub Roses of Today (1974) and Old Shrub Roses (1979) are indispensable. M. Haworth-Booth, Hydrangeas (1959) is valuable, esp. pp. 135–142 on blueing. Hilliers Manual of Trees and Shrubs (1973), the basic list. Roses from Peter Beale, Intwood Nurseries, Swardeston, Norwich and David Austin, Albrighton, Wolverhampton. Suppliers as for trees, with Sherrards Nurseries, Donnington, Newbury, Berks; Keith Steadman, W.W. Nurseries, Wickwar, Wootton-under-Edge, Glos.; Christopher Lloyd, Great Dixter Nurseries, Great Dixter, Northiam, Sussex. Fuchsias from Clapton Court Nurseries, Crewkerne, Somerset, among others.

Better Border Plants: join the Hardy Plant Society, Miss B. White, 10 Barnabas Rd., Emmer Green, Caversham, Reading, Berks. Graham Thomas, Plants for Ground Cover (1970, J.M. Dent) is stimulating. Lanning Roper, Hardy Herbaceous Plants (1965, Penguin) and Alan Bloom, Hardy Plants of Distinction (1965) are very helpful. Mrs Underwood, Grey and Silver Plants (1971), is an expert's record. Plants from Bressingham Nurseries, Diss, Norfolk; Beth Chatto, White Barn House, Elmstead Market, Colchester, Essex and Ramparts Nursery, Braiswick, Colchester, Essex. My naming of Hostas follows Jim Archibald, Buckshaw Gardens, Holwell, Sherborne, Dorset, whose 1981 newsletter lists those which I grow.

Better Bulbs: P.M. Synge, Collins' Guide to Bulbs (1971) is fundamental, with E.B. Anderson, Hardy Bulbs (1964, Penguin), F.C. Stern, Snowdrops and Snowflakes (1956), Lady Beatrix Stanley, New Flora and Silva 11 (1939) p. 226 on Crimean Snowdrops. Wilfrid Blunt's charming Tulipomania (1950) is my source on p. 121. Nurseries include Broadleigh Gardens, Barr House, Bishop's Hull, Taunton; Peter Nyssen, Railway Road, Urmston, Manchester for bulk orders only: for rarities, Potterton and Martin, The Cottage Nursery, Moortown Rd., Nettleton, Caistor, Lincs; Orpington Nurseries, Rocky Lane, Gatton Park, Reigate, Surrey; and P.J. and J.W. Christian, Pentre Cottages, Minera, Wrexham, Clwyd.

Better Alpines: join the Alpine Garden Society, Lye End Link, St John's, Woking, Surrey, not least for its world-famous seed list. Collectors' Alpines by Royton Heath is a classic (1978), but so are E.B. Anderson, Rock Gardens (1960), Alpine Gardening (1963) by Roy Elliott and The Propagation of Alpines by Lawrence D. Hills, the latter two reprinted by Theophrastus Publishers, 545 Madison Av., 16th Floor, New York, N.Y. 10022. On Ramondas, E.B. Ferns, Gesneriaceae, Alpine Garden Society, Bulletin, 47.2 (1979) 123. Daphnes by C.D. Brickell and B. Mathew (1978), pp. 98–9 is my source on p. 151–2. With Lowe and Smith's Androsaces, it is available from D.K. Haslegrove, 278/80 Hoe Street, Walthamstow, London E.17. Violets, by R.E. Coombs (1981) is a labour of love. David Wilkie, Gentians (1950) and H.C. Crook, Campanulas and Bellflowers in Cultivation (1959) are basic guides. Plants from Broadwell Nurseries, Moreton-in-Marsh, Glos.; P. & J. Christian, as above; Ingwersens, Gravetye, East Grinstead, Sussex; Jack Drake, Inschriach, Aviemore, Scotland; E. Strangman, Washfield Nursery, Hawkhurst, Kent; S.W. Bond, Thuya Alpine Nurseries, Glebelands, Hartpury, Glos. and J. & A. Watson, Mill Farmhouse, Mill Lane, Whatlington, Battle, E. Sussex.

On Sissinghurst, there is a book by Ann Scott-James (1974) and on Lawrence Johnston a short study by Alvilde Lees-Milne (in National Trust Year Book, 1977/8).

Index

Abutilon suntense 45
Acer capillipes 31; griseum 30, 31;
  palmatum Chitoseyama 30,
  heptalobum 30, Osakazuki 30, Senkaki
  30; pennsylvanicum 31; platanoides
  Crimson King 32, Goldsworth Purple
  32, Schwedleri 32; rufinerve 31,
  saccharinum 32
Agapanthus 88–90; campanulatus albus 89;
  Headbourne Hybrids 89; Isis 89;
  Profusion 89
Alchemilla mollis 74–5
Allium albo-pilosum 175; cernum 176
Alstroemeria Ligtu Hybrids 129–30
Amaryllis 135
Amelanchier canadensis 27
Androsace 155–7; carnea 156; cylindrica
  156; imbricata 156; lanuginosa 156;
  primuloides 156; sempervivoides 156;
  strigillata 156; tibetica 157
Anemone blanda 106; fulgens 27
Angel's Tears 127
Artemisia arborescens Faith Raven 99;
  borealis 99; Lambrook Silver 6, 98;
  Silver Queen 66; splendens 99; Valerie
  Finnis 99
Aster pappei 1
Astrantia carniolica rosea 174; involucrata
  174; Sunningdale Variegated 174
Azalea Palestrina 43

Baby's Breath 85, 90
Baret, 'Monsieur' 58
Beech, Cut Leaved 35; Dawyck 35
Blueing Hydrangeas 56
Blue 'Plumbago' 68
Bougainville, Monsieur 58
Bowles's Golden Grass 81–2
Buddleia alternifolia 44; Lochinch 44, 52,
  65, 96
Bupleurum fruticosum 50
Buplevers 50

Calamintha nepetoides 85
Camassia cusickii 107; esculenta 107
Camellia Donation 43
Campanula alliariifolia Ivory Bells 92;
  burghaltii 92; carpatica alba 92;
  carpatica Blue Moonlight 92; lactiflora
  93, 129; latiloba Highcliffe 92–3; Mist
  Maiden 92; persicifolia 91; persicifolia
  Telham Beauty 91; van houttei 92
Canterbury Bells 91
Cape Lily 132
Cardiocrinum 174
Carpenteria 48
Catalpa bignonioides aurea 9–10
Catmint 1, 73
Ceanothus 10, 51–2; burkwoodii 51;
  Cascade 51; Delight 51; Dignity 51;
  Gloire de Versailles 52; Marie Simon
  52; thyrsiflorus repens 52; Topaz 52;
  veitchianus 51
Ceratostigma plumbaginoides 69;
  willmottianum 68
Chaenomeles simonsii 46
Cherry, Winter 13–14
Choisya ternata 47–8
Cistus cyprius 46
Clematis texensis Etoile Rose 177
Codonopsis 141
Convallaria Fortin's Giant 128; prolificans
  128
Convolvulus cneorum 68; mauretanicus
  130
Cornus alba sibirica elegantissima 45
Coronilla glauca variegata 68
Cortaderia Gold Band 84; Sunningdale
  Silver 84
Cotoneaster Exburyensis 49; franchettii
  49; horizontalis variegatus 49;
  Rothschildianus 49
Crab Apples 15
Crambe cordifolia 77
Cranesbill 75
Crataegus crus-galli 21; monogyna praecox
  21; prunifolia 20
Crinum powelli 132–3
Crocosmia Emberglow 95; Lucifer 95;
  masonorum 95; Spitfire 95
Cut-leaved Beech 35
Cydonia Champion 19; Vranja 19–20
Cytisus kewensis 142

181

Photographs by courtesy of: Valerie Finnis: 6, 10–13, 16–20, 22–28, 30; Harry Smith Photographic Collection: 1–5, 7–9, 21, 29; Adrian Bloom, Bressingham Nurseries: 14, 15; Pamela Schwerdt: 31, 32.